# easy
# **Spanish**

HarperCollins Publishers
Westerhill Rd, Bishopbriggs, Glasgow, G64 2QT

www.harpercollins.co.uk

First published 2001
This edition published 2006

© HarperCollins Publishers 2006

Reprint 10 9 8 7 6 5 4 3 2 1 0

ISBN  0 00 720833 2

A catalogue reference for this book is available from
The British Library

Consultants: Carole Robinson & Barry Grossmith

Photography: Carole Robinson & Barry Grossmith
With additional photography/material from: Teresa Alvarez,
Robert Grossmith, The Printer's Devil
Spanish National Tourist Office (F Ontañón: pp 92[tr], 93[tr],
94[bl], 96[bl], 97[ml], 101[bl] & [mr], 103[br], 105[tr]; Juan
José Pascual: pp 93[bl], 95[tr], 100[tr]; Mario Brossa: p 96[tr];
Garrrido 102[tl]; De la Puente: [101[tl])
Artville (pp 91, 92, 94, 95, 96, 97, 98, 99, 100, 102, 103, 104,
105, 106)
Wine guide: Andrea Gillies
Food Map: Heather Moore
Layout & Origination: The Printer's Devil and
Davidson Pre-Press Graphics Ltd, Glasgow

Other titles in the Collins Easy Photo Phrase Book series:
French (0 00 720840 5)
German (0 00 720839 1)
Greek (0 00 720837 5)
Italian (0 00 720836 7)
Portuguese (0 00 720835 9)
These titles are also published in a CD pack containing
a 60-minute CD and Easy Photo Phrase book.

Printed in China by Imago

# Contents

# Useful Websites

**Currency converters**
www.oanda.com
www.x-rates.com

**UK Passport Office**
www.passport.gov.uk

**Foreign Office travel advice**
www.fco.gov.uk

**Health advice**
www.traveldoctor.co.uk
www.dh.gov.uk/PolicyAndGuidance/
 HealthAdviceForTravellers/fs/en

**Pet advice**
www.defra.gov.uk/animalh/
 quarantine/index.htm

**Facts and figures**
www.cia.gov/cia/publications/
 factbook

**Weather**
www.bbc.co.uk/weather

**Internet cafes**
www.cybercafes.com

**Hostels**
www.hostels.com/es.html

**Hotel bookings**
www.parador.es (Parador listings)

**Rail fares and tickets**
www.renfe.es
 (national rail network)

**Transport**
www.metromadrid.es
 (Madrid metro)

**Spanish airport websites**
www.iberia.es (national airline)

**Driving abroad**
www.drivingabroad.co.uk

**Spanish motorways**
www.aseta.es (Spanish motorways)

**Tourism**
www.spaintour.com
 (National Tourist Office site: links
 to national parks, what's on, etc.)
www.okspain.org
 (to Spain from the US)
www.goski.com (skiing information
 for Pyrenees & Andalucia)

**Culture**
www.surinenglish.com
 (Costa del Sol news in English)
www.gomadrid.com
 (what's on in Madrid)
www.cyberspain.com
www.webmadrid.com
 (information on the capital)

# Introduction

In the age of the euro, the internet and cash machines that offer a choice of languages, foreign travel might seem less of an adventure than it once was. But English is not the universal language yet, and there is much more to communication than knowing the right words for things. Once out of the airport you will not get far without some idea of the language, and also the way things are done in an unfamiliar culture. Things you might assume are the same everywhere, such as road signs and colour-coding, can turn out not to be. Red for trunk roads and skimmed milk, blue for motorways and full cream? Not everywhere! You may know the word for 'coffee' but what sort of coffee will you get? Will they understand what you mean when you say you're a vegetarian? What times do the shops open, and which ticket gives you the best deal? *Collins Easy Photo Phrase Books* keep you up to speed with handy tips for each topic, and a wealth of pictures of signs and everyday objects to help you understand what you see around you. Even if your knowledge of the language is excellent, you may still find yourself on the back foot when trying to understand what's on offer in a restaurant, so the food and drink section features a comprehensive menu reader to make sure eating out is a pleasure.

The unique combination of practical information, photos and phrases found in this book provides the key to hassle-free travel. The colour-coding below shows how information is presented and how to access it as quickly as possible.

 *General, practical information which will provide useful tips on getting the best out of your trip.*

**keywords**

| keywords | |
|---|---|
| **a la derecha** | |
| *a la de-**re**-cha* | |
| right | |
| **a la izquierda** | |
| *a la eeth-**kyer**-da* | |
| left | |

**< keywords**

these are words that are useful to know both when you see them written down or when you hear them spoken

**key talk >**

short, simple phrases that you can change and adapt to suit your own situation

| talking | |
|---|---|
| **excuse me!** | **can you help me?** |
| ¡oiga por favor! | ¿me puede ayudar? |
| **oy**-ga por fa-**bor** | me **pwe**-de a-yoo-**dar** |
| **do you know where ... is?** | |
| ¿sabe dónde está ... ? | |
| **sa**-be **don**-de es-**ta** ... | |

The **food and drink section** allows you to choose more easily from what is on offer, both for snacks and at restaurants.

The practical **Dictionary** means that you will never be stuck for words.

# Speaking Spanish

We've tried to make the pronunciation under the phrases as clear as possible. We've broken the words up to make them easy to read, but don't pause between syllables. The syllable to be stressed is shown in **heavy type**. Spanish isn't really hard to pronounce and once you learn a few basic rules, it shouldn't be too long before you can read straight from the Spanish.

Most letters are pronounced as in English: *b*, *ch*, *d*, *f*, *k*, *l*, *m*, *n*, *p*, *s*, *t*, *y* and (*usually*) *w* and *x*.

As for the vowels, *a* is always as in **tap** (never as in **tape**); **e** is always as in **pet** (never as in **Pete**); **i** is always '**ee**'; **o** is always as in **hop** (never as in **hope**); **u** is always '**oo**' rather than the English sound **hut**. They keep their sound even in combination with other letters, so '**au**' (eg **autobús** ow-to-**boos**) is like English '**ow**', not like English **automatic**.

The letter **h** is always silent, and **r** is always rolled (even more strongly when double **r**). Spanish **v** and **b** are pronounced exactly the same, something like English **b**, while **q** is like English **k**.

The letter **c** before **e** or **i** and the letter **z** are pronounced like the **th** in **thin**. The letter **g** before **e** or **i** and the letter **j** have the guttural sound you hear in the Scottish word **loch** and which we show as *kh*.

Basic rules to remember are:

| spanish | | sounds like | example | pronunciation |
|---|---|---|---|---|
| ll | | million | **calle** | **kal**-ye |
| ñ | | onion | **mañana** | man-**ya**-na |
| c | | cat | **comer** | ko-**mer** |
| c | (before **e/i**) | think | **hacer** | a-**ther** |
| g | | got | **gafas** | **ga**-fas |
| g | (before **e/i**) | loch | **hijo** | **ee**-kho |
| z | | think | **zapatos** | tha-**pa**-tos |
| j | | loch | **hijo** | **ee**-kho |
| q | | kick | **quiero** | **kyer**-o |

# Everyday Talk

> There are two forms of address in Spanish, formal (**Usted**, often written **Ud** or **Vd**) and informal (**tú**). You should always stick with the formal until you are on a first name basis. For the purposes of this book, we will use the formal.

**yes**
sí
*see*

**no**
no
*no*

**ok/that's fine**
¡vale!
*ba-le*

**please**
por favor
*por fa-bor*

**thank you**
gracias
*grath-yas*

**thanks very much**
muchas gracias
*moo-chas grath-yas*

**don't mention it**
de nada
*de na-da*

**that's very kind**
muy amable
*mwee am-ab-le*

**hello**
hola
*o-la*

**goodbye**
adiós
*ad-yos*

**good day/morning**
buenos días
*bwe-nos dee-as*

**good evening**
buenas tardes
*bwe-nas tar-des*

**good night**
buenas noches
*bwe-nas no-ches*

**see you later**
hasta luego
*as-ta lwe-go*

**excuse me!**
¡oiga por favor!
*oy-ga por fa-bor*

**sorry!**
¡perdón!
*per-don*

**I am sorry**
lo siento
*lo syen-to*

**I don't understand**
no entiendo
*no en-tyen-do*

**I don't know**
no sé
*no se*

## Addressing people

Friends and acquaintances often greet each other with a kiss on each cheek if one of the people is female. When being introduced, a handshake is a safe bet with either sex. In more formal situations or if there is uncertainty, wait and see how the other person addresses you. In shops and offices, it is usual to say *Buenos días* or *Buenas tardes* to the people around you, with no physical contact, and *adiós* when leaving.

**how are things?**
¿qué tal?
*ke tal*

**fine thanks**
muy bien gracias
*mwee byen grath-yas*

**and you?**
¿y usted?
*ee oo-sted*

**hi, Teresa!**
¡hola Teresa!
*o-la te-re-sa*

**bye, Pedro**
¡adiós Pedro!
*ad-yos ped-ro*

**see you on Saturday**
hasta el sábado
*as-ta el sa-ba-do*

*Asking for something in a shop or bar, you would ask for what you want, adding **por favor**.*

**keywords keywords keywords**

| | | |
|---|---|---|
| 1 | **uno** | *oo-no* |
| 2 | **dos** | *dos* |
| 3 | **tres** | *tres* |
| 4 | **cuatro** | *kwat-ro* |
| 5 | **cinco** | *theen-ko* |
| 6 | **seis** | *seyss* |
| 7 | **siete** | *syet-e* |
| 8 | **ocho** | *o-cho* |
| 9 | **nueve** | *nwe-be* |
| 10 | **diez** | *dyeth* |

**a ... please**
un/una ... por favor
*oon/oo-na ... por fa-bor*

**a white coffee**
un café con leche
*oon ka-fe kon le-che*

**a beer**
una cerveza
*oo-na ther-be-tha*

**a tea**
un té
*oon te*

**a phone card**
una tarjeta telefónica
*oo-na tar-khe-ta te-le-fo-nee-ka*

**the ... please**
el/la ... por favor
*el/la ... por fa-bor*

**the menu please**
la carta por favor
*la kar-ta por fa-bor*

**the bill please**
la cuenta por favor
*la kwen-ta por fa-bor*

**another...**
otro/otra...
*o-tro/o-tra...*

**that is everything**
nada más
*na-da mas*

**another beer**
otra cerveza
*o-tra ther-be-tha*

**another tea**
otro té
*o-tro te*

**2 more beers**
otras dos cervezas
*o-tras dos ther-be-thas*

**2 more coffees**
otros dos cafés
*o-tros dos ka-fes*

## To catch someone's attention

To catch someone's attention, say *oiga, por favor* (excuse me, please).
The informal version is *oye*. A lot of young people speak basic English,
particularly on the coast and in the big cities. Don't assume older people
will have the same ability. Apart from the *Costas* and international hotels,
airports and major tourist attractions, almost all signs will be in Spanish
only.

**excuse me!**
¡oiga!
*oy-ga*

**can you help me?**
¿puede ayudarme?
*pwe-de a-yoo-dar-me*

**do you know where ... is?**
¿sabe dónde está...?
*sa-be don-de es-ta...*

**how do I get to...?**
¿cómo voy a...?
*ko-mo boy a...*

*By combining key words and phrases you can build up your language and adapt the phrases to suit your own situation.*

| ¿tiene...?<br>**do you have...?** | **do you have a map?**<br>¿tiene un mapa?<br>*tyen-e oon ma-pa* | **do you have a room?**<br>¿tiene una habitación?<br>*tyen-e oo-na a-bee-tath-yon* |
| --- | --- | --- |
| ¿cuánto?<br>**how much?** | **how much is the cheese?**<br>¿cuánto cuesta el queso?<br>*kwan-to kwes-ta el ke-so* | **how much is the ticket?**<br>¿cuánto es el billete?<br>*kwan-to es el beel-ye-te* |
| quería...<br>**I'd like...** | **I'd like a red wine**<br>quería un vino tinto<br>*ke-ree-ya oon bee-no teen-to* | **I'd like an ice-cream**<br>quería un helado<br>*ke-ree-ya oon e-la-do* |
| necesito...<br>**I need...** | **I need a taxi**<br>necesito un taxi<br>*neth-e-see-to oon tak-see* | **I need a receipt**<br>necesito un recibo<br>*neth-e-see-to oon re-thee-bo* |
| ¿cuándo?<br>**when?** | **when does it open?**<br>¿cuándo abren?<br>*kwan-do a-bren* | **when does it close?**<br>¿cuándo cierran?<br>*kwan-do thyerr-an* |
| | **when does it leave?**<br>¿cuándo sale?<br>*kwan-do sa-le* | **when does it arrive?**<br>¿cuándo llega?<br>*kwan-do lyeg-a* |
| ¿dónde?<br>**where?** | **where is the bank?**<br>¿dónde está el banco?<br>*don-de es-ta el ban-ko* | **where is the hotel?**<br>¿dónde está el hotel?<br>*don-de es-ta el o-tel* |
| ¿hay...?<br>**is there...?** | **is there a market?**<br>¿hay mercado?<br>*aee mer-ka-do* | **where is there a market?**<br>¿dónde hay un mercado?<br>*don-de aee oon mer-ka-do* |
| no hay...<br>**there is no...** | **there is no bread**<br>no hay pan<br>*no aee pan* | **is there no train?**<br>¿no hay tren?<br>*no aee tren* |
| ¿puedo...?<br>**can I...?** | **can I smoke?**<br>¿puedo fumar?<br>*pwe-do foo-mar* | **can I go by train?**<br>¿puedo ir en tren?<br>*pwe-do eer en tren* |
| | **where can I buy milk?**<br>¿dónde puedo comprar leche?<br>*don-de pwe-do kom-prar le-che* | |
| ¿está...?<br>**is it...?** | **is it near?**<br>¿está cerca?<br>*es-ta ther-ka* | **is it far?**<br>¿está lejos?<br>*es-ta le-khos* |
| me gusta...<br>**I like...** | **I like red wine**<br>me gusta el vino tinto<br>*me goos-ta el bee-no teen-to* | **I don't like cheese**<br>no me gusta el queso<br>*no me goos-ta el ke-so* |

*These are a selection of small but very useful words.*

**keywords keywords keywords keywords keywords**

**grande**
*gran-de*
large

**pequeño**
*pe-ken-yo*
small

**un poco**
*un po-ko*
a little

**basta**
*bas-ta*
enough

**más cercano**
*mas ther-ka-no*
nearest

**lejos**
*le-khos*
far

**demasiado caro**
*de-mas-ya-do ka-ro*
too expensive

**y**
*ee*
and

**con/sin**
*kon/seen*
with/without

**para**
*pa-ra*
for

**mi**
*mee*
my

**esto/aquello**
*es-to/a-kel-yo*
this one/that one

**ahora enseguida**
*a-or-a en-se-gee-da*
straightaway

**más tarde**
*mas tar-de*
later

**a large car**
un coche grande
*oon ko-che gran-de*

**a small car**
un coche pequeño
*oon ko-che pe-ken-yo*

**a little please**
un poco por favor
*oon po-ko por fa-bor*

**that's enough thanks**
basta gracias
*bas-ta grath-yas*

**where is the nearest bank?**
¿dónde está el banco más cercano?
*don-de es-ta el ban-ko mas ther-ka-no*

**it is too expensive**
es demasiado caro
*es de-mas-ya-do ka-ro*

**it is too big**
es demasiado grande
*es de-mas-ya-do gran-de*

**is it full?**
¿está lleno?
*es-ta lyen-o*

**is it free?**
¿está libre?
*es-ta lee-bre*

**a tea and a coffee**
un té y un café
*oon te ee oon ka-fe*

**a beer and a dry sherry**
una cerveza y un fino
*oo-na ther-be-tha ee oon fee-no*

**with sugar**
con azúcar
*kon a-thoo-kar*

**with cream**
con nata
*kon na-ta*

**without sugar**
sin azúcar
*seen a-thoo-kar*

**without cream**
sin nata
*seen na-ta*

**for me**
para mí
*pa-ra mee*

**for her/him**
para ella/él
*pa-ra el-ya/el*

**my passport**
mi pasaporte
*mee pa-sa-por-te*

**my keys**
mis llaves
*mees lya-bes*

**I'd like this one**
quería esto
*ke-ree-ya es-to*

**I'd like that**
quería aquello
*ke-ree-ya a-kel-yo*

**I need a taxi straightaway**
necesito un taxi enseguida
*neth-es-ee-to oon tak-see en-se-gee-da*

**is it far?**
¿está lejos?
*es-ta le-khos*

**I'll call you later**
le llamo más tarde
*le lya-mo mas tar-de*

*It is always good to be able to say a few words about yourself to break the ice, even if you won't be able to tell your life story. Remember there are different endings for male and female.*

**my name is...**
me llamo...
*me lya-mo...*

**I am from...**
soy de...
*soy de...*

**I am on holiday**
estoy de vacaciones
*es-toy de ba-ka-thyo-nes*

**I am here on business**
estoy aquí por razones de trabajo
*es-toy a-kee por ra-tho-nes de tra-ba-kho*

**I am single**
estoy soltero/a
*es-toy sol-te-ro/a*

**I am married**
estoy casado/a
*es-toy ka-sa-do/a*

**I have a boyfriend**
tengo novio
*ten-go nob-yo*

**I have a girlfriend**
tengo novia
*ten-go nob-ya*

**I am a widow**
soy viuda
*soy byoo-da*

**I am a widower**
soy viudo
*soy byoo-do*

**I am divorced**
estoy divorciado/a
*es-toy dee-bor-thya-do/a*

**I am separated**
estoy separado/a
*es-toy se-pa-ra-do/a*

**I have a child**
tengo un hijo
*ten-go oon ee-kho*

**I have ... children**
tengo ... hijos
*ten-go ... ee-khos*

**I work**
trabajo
*tra-ba-kho*

**I am retired**
estoy jubilado/a
*es-toy khoo-bee-la-do/a*

**I am a student**
soy estudiante
*soy es-tood-yan-te*

**this is a beautiful place**
es un lugar precioso
*es oon loo-gar preth-yo-so*

**I love Spanish food**
me encanta la comida española
*me en-kan-ta la ko-mee-da es-pan-yo-la*

**people are very kind**
la gente es muy amable
*la khen-te es mwee am-ab-le*

**I hope to come back soon**
espero volver pronto
*es-per-o bol-ber pron-to*

**thank you very much for your kindness**
muchas gracias, muy amable
*moo-chas grath-yas mwee am-ab-le*

**I've enjoyed myself very much**
lo he pasado muy bien
*lo e pa-sa-do mwee byen*

**we will be back**
volveremos
*bol-ber-em-os*

**will you write?**
me escribirá ¿no?
*me es-kree-bee-ra no*

**can I have your address?**
¿me da su dirección?
*me da soo dee-rek-thyon*

*People on the street and in bars are generally helpful. Don't be afraid to ask for assistance should you need help with any problem. There can, however, be a difference between ordinary people and 'officialdom'. There is, on occasion, a lack of flexibility with regard to standard rules and regulations.*

**excuse me!**
¡oiga por favor!
*oy-ga por fa-bor*

**can you help me?**
¿puede ayudarme?
*pwe-de a-yoo-dar-me*

**I don't speak Spanish**
no hablo español
*no ab-lo es-pan-yol*

**I am sorry, I did not know**
lo siento, no lo sabía
*lo syen-to no lo sa-bee-a*

**I am lost**
me he perdido
*me e per-dee-do*

**we are lost**
nos hemos perdido
*nos e-mos per-dee-do*

**I have lost...** | **my money**
he perdido... | el dinero
*e per-dee-do...* | *el dee-ne-ro*

**my tickets** | **my passport**
los billetes | el pasaporte
*los beel-ye-tes* | *el pa-sa-por-te*

**I have left...** | **in the restaurant**
me he dejado... | en el restaurante
*me e de-kha-do...* | *en el rest-ow-ran-te*

**on the train**
en el tren
*en el tren*

**I have missed...** | **my flight**
he perdido... | el vuelo
*e per-dee-do...* | *el bwe-lo*

**the train** | **the coach**
el tren | el autocar
*el tren* | *el ow-to-kar*

**I need to get to...**
tengo que ir a...
*ten-go ke eer a...*

**how can I get there today?**
¿cómo puedo ir allí hoy?
*ko-mo pwe-do eer al-yee oy*

**my luggage hasn't arrived**
no ha llegado mi equipaje
*no a lyeg-a-do mee e-kee-pa-khe*

**my case has been damaged**
me han estropeado la maleta
*me an es-tro-pe-a-do la ma-le-ta*

**someone has stolen...**
me han robado...
*me an ro-ba-do...*

**this is my address**
esta es mi dirección
*es-ta es mee dee-rek-thyon*

**my bag** | **my purse**
la bolsa | el monedero
*la bol-sa* | *el mo-ne-de-ro*

**my wallet** | **I have no money**
la cartera | no tengo dinero
*la kar-te-ra* | *no ten-go dee-ne-ro*

**I need to go to hospital**
tengo que ir al hospital
*ten-go ke eer al os-pee-tal*

**my son/daughter is missing**
mi hijo/hija se ha perdido
*mee ee-kho/ee-kha se a per-dee-do*

**go away!** | **that man is following me**
¡váyase! | ese hombre me está siguiendo
*ba-ya-se* | *e-se om-bre me es-ta seeg-yen-do*

*The British might have a reputation for not complaining, but the Spanish complain even less. Complaining does sometimes work, but don't expect miracles as it is not a major part of Spanish culture. However, if you insist on your rights, you'll be more likely to be satisfied. This is obviously easier if you're in a part of the country where English is understood.*

**there is no...**
no hay...
*no aee...*

**there is no soap**
no hay jabón
*no aee kha-bon*

**it is dirty**
está sucio
*es-ta sooth-yo*

**they are dirty**
están sucios
*es-tan sooth-yos*

**it is broken**
está roto
*es-ta ro-to*

**they are broken**
están rotos
*es-tan ro-tos*

**the ... does not work**
el/la ... no funciona
*el/la ... no foonth-yo-na*

**the ... do not work**
los/las ... no funcionan
*los/las ... no foonth-yo-nan*

**it is very noisy**
hay mucho ruido
*aee moo-cho rwee-do*

**the room is too small**
la habitación es demasiado pequeña
*la a-bee-tath-yon es de-mas-ya-do pe-ken-ya*

**it is too hot**
hace demasiado calor
*a-the de-mas-ya-do ka-lor*

**it is too cold**
hace demasiado frío
*a-the de-mas-ya-do free-yo*

**it is too expensive**
es demasiado caro
*es de-mas-ya-do ka-ro*

**you are charging too much**
me está cobrando demasiado
*me es-ta kob-ran-do de-mas-ya-do*

**I want to complain**
quiero hacer una reclamación
*kyer-o a-ther oo-na rek-la-math-yon*

**where is the manager?**
¿dónde está el gerente?
*don-de es-ta el kher-en-te*

**we want to order**
queremos pedir
*ke-rem-os pe-deer*

**the service is very bad**
el servicio es muy malo
*el ser-beeth-yo es mwee ma-lo*

**it is cold** (food, drink)
está frío
*es-ta free-o*

**this coffee is cold**
el café está frío
*el ka-fe es-ta free-o*

**this isn't what I ordered**
esto no es lo que he pedido
*es-to no es lo ke e pe-dee-do*

**please take it off the bill**
quítelo de la cuenta por favor
*kee-te-lo de la kwen-ta por fa-bor*

**there is a mistake**
hay un error
*aee oon er-ror*

**please check the bill**
compruebe la cuenta por favor
*kom-prwe-be la kwen-ta por fa-bor*

# Everyday Spain

*The following four pages should give you an idea of the type of things you will come across in Spain.*

open

push

closed

pull

**HORARIO**

mañanas : DE 10 a 1.30

tardes : DE 5 a 8

sabado : DE 10 a 1.30

**opening hours**
Opening hours for smaller shops are generally 10am–1.30pm, reopening 5–8pm. Shops usually stay closed on Saturday afternoons.

**CAJA**

cash desk/pay here

Kiosks marked **ONCE** sell lottery tickets. Draws take place 3 or 4 times a week, with big prizes at the weekend. The lottery is organised by the national organisation for the blind.

information

| | | |
|---|---|---|
| **do you sell...?** | **stamps** | **phonecards** |
| ¿vende...? | sellos | tarjetas telefónicas |
| *ben-de...* | *sel-yos* | *tar-khe-tas te-le-fo-nee-kas* |
| **where can I buy...?** | **plasters** | **a map** |
| ¿dónde puedo comprar...? | tiritas | un mapa |
| *don-de pwe-do kom-prar...* | *tee-ree-tas* | *oon ma-pa* |

talking

Paying machines are becoming more and more widespread.

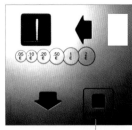

***importe exacto***
exact amount
***no devuelve cambio***
no change given

***cancelar*** to cancel

Postboxes are yellow. There are also red postboxes for priority mail and these take a different tariff.

for sale

for hire/rent

entrance

exit

Tobacconists are known as ***estancos***, state-licensed shops which sell tobacco products, stamps, bus tickets, postcards and basic stationery. Some offer a photocopy service. Look out for the maroon sign with the yellow script and the leaf logo. If you want stamps it is much easier to buy them here.

out of service

**excuse me!**
¡oiga por favor!
*oy-ga por fa-bor*

**what do I have to do?**
¿qué tengo que hacer?
*ke ten-go ke a-ther*

**how does this work?**
¿cómo funciona esto?
*ko-mo foonth-yo-na es-to*

**what does this mean?**
¿qué significa esto?
*ke seeg-nee-fee-ka es-to*

talking

**servicio no incluido**

**service not included**
Tipping in Spain is not all that common. Service is generally not included and a tip of between 5 and 10% is normal.

**AIRE ACONDICIONADO** air conditioned

Smoking is still popular in Spain and you will sometimes see people smoking on TV. However it is prohibited on public transport, in hospitals and government offices. Smokers in bars or restaurants are unlikely to give much thought to non-smokers.

**ZONA NO FUMADORES**

no smoking zone

PROHIBIDO FUMAR

no smoking

**ZONA FUMADORES**

smoking zone

**AVISO ESTA PROHIBIDO** — *warning – it is forbidden*

Sentarse sobre los pasamanos y escalones, introducir objetos entre los peldaños, correr sobre las escaleras, etc.

*La Compañía declina toda responsabilidad en los accidentes y daños que puedan ocurrir por el incumplimiento de este AVISO.*

The word **prohibido** means *forbidden*. Things which might seem quite innocent to us, may not be allowed in Spain.

**talking**

**can I smoke?**
¿puedo fumar?
*pwe-do foo-mar*

**do you mind if I smoke?**
¿le importa que fume?
*le eem-por-ta ke foo-me*

**I don't smoke**
no fumo
*no foo-mo*

**please don't smoke**
no fume por favor
*no foo-me por fa-bor*

**an ashtray please**
un cenicero por favor
*oon then-ee-ther-o por fa-bor*

**a non-smoking area please**
una zona de no fumadores por favor
*oo-na tho-na de no foo-ma-dor-es por fa-bor*

Toilets in Spain are free but vary considerably. The cleanest will be found in department stores and hotels, for which you rarely need to ask for a key. Disabled and baby-changing facilities here are generally good, but not so elsewhere. It is possible to use bar toilets, even if you are not a customer, but sometimes you need to ask the barman for a key. It is rare to have to pay to use a toilet, or leave a tip, although occasionally there are coin operated doors.

Automatic toilets are becoming more common.

not drinking water

red
*out of service*
yellow
*occupied*
green
*free*

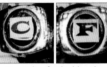

**Aseos** and **Servicios** are both toilets.

ladies

free

gents

occupied

Don't be fooled by the letters on the taps. **C** is for **caliente** which means *hot* and **F** is for **frío** which means *cold*.

**excuse me! where is the toilet?**
¡por favor! ¿dónde están los servicios?
*por fa-**bor** don-de es-**tan** los ser-**beeth**-yos*

**do you have a key for the toilet?**
¿tiene llave del servicio?
*tyen-e **lya**-be del ser-**beeth**-yo*

**is there a disabled toilet?**
¿hay servicio para minusválidos?
*aee ser-**beeth**-yo **pa**-ra mee-noos-**ba**-lee-dos*

**is there somewhere to change the baby?**
¿hay algún sitio para cambiar al niño?
*aee al-**goon seet**-yo **pa**-ra kamb-**yar** al **neen**-yo*

talking

# Asking the Way

*Most towns and cities provide local maps free of charge from the Tourist Information Office. Town plans are also prominently displayed, even in some of the smaller villages. Sectional street maps are particularly good in Madrid and can be found at street level outside every metro station (look for the red and blue metro sign). If you need directions, try to ask for help providing your own map. It's a lot easier! People on the street and the police are generally willing to assist.*

In Madrid street maps are displayed outside every metro station.

**Plaza** is the name for square.

**Calle** and **Paseo** both mean street.

Most towns and villages have maps on display.

**you are here**

**excuse me!**
¡oiga por favor!
*oy-ga por fa-bor*

**we're looking for...**
estamos buscando...
*es-ta-mos boos-kan-do...*

**do you know where... is?**
¿sabe dónde está...?
*sa-be don-de es-ta...*

**where are...?**
¿dónde están...?
*don-de es-tan...*

**how do I get to...?**
¿cómo se va a...?
*ko-mo se ba a...*

**is it far?**
¿está lejos?
*es-ta le-khos*

**is this the right way to...?**
¿se va por aquí a...?
*se ba por a-kee a...*

**do you have a map of the town?**
¿tiene un plano de la ciudad?
*tyen-e oon pla-no de la thyoo-dad*

**a street directory**
un callejero
*oon kal-ye-khe-ro*

**can you show me on the map?**
¿puede indicármelo en el mapa?
*pwe-de een-dee-kar-me-lo en el ma-pa*

*you are on the top floor* (VD. is short for **Usted**)

*toilets*  *phones*  *leisure and multi-*  *up to*  *information*
*cinema complex*  *parking*

city/town
centre

access to
beaches

Red roads are national roads, often dual carriageways (**autovía**).

Local streets are signposted in green (**glorieta** is a roundabout).

Places of interest to travellers (e.g. stations, hotels) are signposted in yellow.

Places of interest (e.g. museums) are signposted in maroon.

*el Lido* beach

**football ground**

Brown signs are places of geographic or ecological interest, while burnt orange (left) is for sport and recreational places.

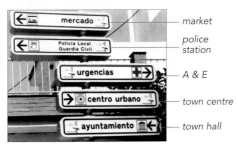

— *market*

— *police station*

— *A & E*

— *town centre*

— *town hall*

**a la derecha**
*a la de-re-cha*
to the right

**a la izquierda**
*a la eeth-kyer-da*
to the left

**recto**
*rek-to*
straight ahead

**vaya**
*ba-ya*
go

**gire**
*khee-re*
turn

**calle**
*kal-ye*
road

**plaza**
*pla-tha*
square

**semáforo**
*se-ma-fo-ro*
traffic lights

**iglesia**
*ee-gles-ya*
church

**primera**
*pree-me-ra*
first

**segunda**
*se-goon-da*
second

**lejos**
*le-khos*
far

**cerca de**
*ther-ka de*
near to

**al lado de**
*al la-do de*
next to

**enfrente de**
*en-fren-te de*
opposite

**hasta**
*as-ta*
until

# Banks & Money

*There is no shortage of banks, but check opening times as most close around 2pm. Many banks are open-plan and easy to enter, but some operate a double-door system, allowing one person in at a time. You usually have to press a green button to enter, the door slides open and you go in. There is usually a metal detector so it is advisable to leave keys, mobile phones, etc. in the lockers provided in the lobby area. If you don't, you may hear a recorded voice asking you to do so. The second sliding door will then open, allowing you to pass into the bank. Don't assume that bank staff will be fluent in English, although some have basic skills. There is not always a special counter for changing money, but if in doubt, ask the security guard who will normally be very helpful.*

**BANCO DE CASTILLA**

Most banks can be identified by the word **Banco** or **Caja**. The big banks in Spain include **BBVA**, **Banco de Santander**, **Caixa de Cataluña** and **Caja España**.

**business hours**

**HORARIO DE OFICINA**

| | | | |
|---|---|---|---|
| Lunes | 08.30 | a | 14.30 |
| Martes | 08.30 | a | 14.30 |
| Miércoles | 08.30 | a | 14.30 |
| Jueves | 08.30 | a | 14.30 |
| Viernes | 08.30 | a | 14.30 |
| Sábado | Cerrado | | |
| Domingo | Cerrado | | |

This bank opens 8.30am–2.30pm Mon–Fri. It is shut on Saturday and Sunday.

Cajero Automático
Electronic Money

There are cash dispensers everywhere.

**24 hour cash dispenser**

Cajero Automático
**24 HORAS**

Check that cash dispensers will accept your card. There will probably be a handling fee (**una carga**). If you use a non-Spanish card, they will automatically give you a choice of languages in which to carry out the transaction. You should be able to use a Switch card (check for the Cirrus sign).

Cirrus

Some cash dispensers are accessed by swiping your card in the door. Either the green light will flash for you to enter (*acceso libre*) or the red light will flash to indicate out of service (*fuera de servicio*).

Spain's currency is the euro, which breaks down into 100 euro cents (*céntimo*).
Notes: 5, 10, 20, 50, 100, 200 and 500 euro.
Coins: 2 euro, 1 euro, 50 cent, 20 cent, 10 cent, 5 cent, 2 cent, 1 cent.
Euro notes are the same throughout Europe. The backs of coins carry different designs from each of the member European countries.

**keywords keywords keywords**

**tarjeta de crédito**
*tar-khe-ta de kre-dee-to*
credit card

**cajero**
*ka-khe-ro*
cash dispenser

**número de identificación personal**
*noo-me-ro de ee-den-tee-fee-ka-thyon per-so-nal*
PIN number

**cambio**
*kamb-yo*
change

**introduzca**
*een-tro-dooth-ka*
insert

**billetes**
*beel-ye-tes*
notes

**efectivo**
*ef-ek-tee-bo*
cash

**moneda**
*mo-ne-da*
coin

**talking talking talking**

**where is there...?**    **a bank**    **a bureau de change**
¿dónde está...?    un banco    una oficina de cambio
*don-de es-ta...*    *oon ban-ko*    *oo-na o-fee-thee-na de kam-byo*

**where can I change money?**    **I would like small notes**
¿dónde se puede cambiar dinero?    quería billetes pequeños
*don-de se pwe-de kam-byar dee-ne-ro*    *ke-ree-a beel-ye-tes pe-ken-yos*

**where is the nearest cash dispenser?**
¿dónde está el cajero más cercano?
*don-de es-ta el ka-khe-ro mas ther-ka-no*

**I want to change these travellers' cheques**
quiero cambiar estos cheques de viaje
*kyer-o kam-byar es-tos che-kes de bya-khe*

**the cash-dispenser has swallowed my card**
el cajero se ha tragado la tarjeta
*el ka-khe-ro se a tra-ga-do la tar-khe-ta*

# When is...?

 The 24-hour clock is used in timetables and for train announcements in stations and for television programmes.

**mañana**
*man-ya-na*
morning

**tarde**
*tar-de*
afternoon

**esta tarde**
*es-ta tar-de*
this evening

**hoy**
*oy*
today

**mañana**
*man-ya-na*
tomorrow

**ayer**
*a-yer*
yesterday

**más tarde**
*mas tar-de*
later

**ahora enseguida**
*a-o-ra en-seg-ee-da*
straightaway

**ahora**
*a-o-ra*
now

| Time | at... |
|------|-------|
| 13:00 | **a las trece horas** — *a las threth-e o-ras* |
| 14:00 | **a las catorce horas** — *a las ka-torth-e o-ras* |
| 15:00 | **a las quince horas** — *a las keenth-e o-ras* |
| 16:00 | **a las dieciséis horas** — *a las dyeth-ee-seyss o-ras* |
| 17:00 | **a las diecisiete horas** — *a las dyeth-ee-syet-e o-ras* |
| 18:00 | **a las dieciocho horas** — *a las dyeth-ee-o-cho o-ras* |
| 19:00 | **a las diecinueve horas** — *a las dyeth-ee-nwe-be o-ras* |
| 20:00 | **a las veinte horas** — *a las beyn-te o-ras* |
| 21:00 | **a las veintiuna horas** — *a las beyn-tee-oo-na o-ras* |
| 22:00 | **a las veintidós horas** — *a las beyn-tee-dos o-ras* |
| 23:00 | **a las veintitrés horas** — *a las beyn-tee-tres o-ras* |
| 24:00 | **a las veinticuatro horas** — *a las beyn-tee-kwa-tro o-ras* |

| | train | bus | boat |
|---|---|---|---|
| **when is the next...?** ¿cuándo es el próximo...? *kwan-do es el prok-see-mo...* | tren *tren* | autobús *ow-to-boos* | barco *bar-ko* |

| | breakfast | lunch | dinner |
|---|---|---|---|
| **when is...?** ¿a qué hora es...? *a ke o-ra es...* | el desayuno *el de-sa-yoo-no* | la comida *la ko-mee-da* | la cena *la then-a* |

**when does it leave?**
¿cuándo sale?
*kwan-do sa-le*

**when does it arrive?**
¿cuándo llega?
*kwan-do lyeg-a*

**when does it open?**
¿cuándo abren?
*kwan-do a-bren*

**when does it close?**
¿cuándo cierran?
*kwan-do thyerr-an*

at...

**a las doce**
*a las doth-e*

**a las once**
*a las on-the*

**a la una**
*a la oo-na*

**a las diez**
*a las dyeth*

**a las dos**
*a las dos*

**a las nueve**
*a las nwe-be*

**a las tres**
*a las tres*

**a las ocho**
*a las o-cho*

**a las cuatro**
*a las kwat-ro*

**a las siete**
*a las syet-e*

**a las cinco**
*a las theen-ko*

**a las seis**
*a las seyss*

**a las dieciocho horas y cuarenta minutos**
*a las dyeth-ee-o-cho o-ras ee kwa-ren-ta mee-noo-tos*
at 18.40

**a las ... menos cuarto**
*a las ... me-nos kwar-to*
at a quarter to...

**a medianoche**
*a med-ya-no-che*
at midnight

**a las ... y cuarto**
*a las ... ee kwar-to*
at quarter past...

**a las ... menos veinte**
*a las ... me-nos byen-te*
at twenty to...

**a las ... y media**
*a las ... ee med-ya*
at half past ...

---

**have you the time please?**
¿tiene hora por favor?
*tyen-e o-ra por fa-bor*

**it's one o'clock**
la una
*la oo-na*

**it's five o'clock**
las cinco
*las theen-ko*

**what is the date?**
¿qué fecha es hoy?
*ke fe-cha es oy*

**it is the 8th of May**
(es) ocho de mayo
*(es) o-cho de ma-yo*

**it is the 16th of September 2006**
(es) dieciséis de septiembre de dos mil seis
*(es) dyeth-ee-seyss de set-yemb-re de dos meel seyss*

**which day?**
¿qué día?
*ke dee-a*

**which month?**
¿qué mes?
*ke mes*

talking

# Timetables

*Timetables all use the 24-hour clock. Bus and train timetables usually change once a year and boat and ferry timetables tend to follow peak Summer season schedules. You can pick up timetables for coaches, trains and ferries/boats at the relevant offices/departure halls.*

information  origin of train

train timetable

train

(1) No service on Sundays

(2) Lince train (type of train) runs on Fridays

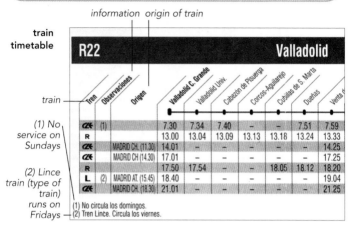

| | Tren | Observaciones | Origen | Valladolid C. Grande | Valladolid Univ. | Cabezón de Pisuerga | Corcos-Aguilarejo | Cubillas de S. Marta | Dueñas | Venta A. |
|---|---|---|---|---|---|---|---|---|---|---|
| | 𝗖𝗫𝗘 | (1) | | 7.30 | 7.34 | 7.40 | – | – | 7.51 | 7.59 |
| | R | | | 13.00 | 13.04 | 13.09 | 13.13 | 13.18 | 13.24 | 13.33 |
| | 𝗖𝗫𝗘 | | MADRID CH. (11.30) | 14.01 | – | – | – | – | – | 14.25 |
| | 𝗖𝗫𝗘 | | MADRID CH (14.30) | 17.01 | – | – | – | – | – | 17.25 |
| | R | | | 17.50 | 17.54 | – | – | 18.05 | 18.12 | 18.20 |
| | L | (2) | MADRID AT. (15.45) | 18.40 | – | – | – | – | – | 19.04 |
| | 𝗖𝗫𝗘 | | MADRID CH. (18.30) | 21.01 | – | – | – | – | – | 21.25 |

**R22**  **Valladolid**

(1) No circula los domingos.
(2) Tren Lince. Circula los viernes.

*CLE = Castile and León Express with free seat reservations and tickets can be purchased 15 days before the date of travel.*

**𝗖𝗫𝗘** = Tren Castilla y León Exprés con reserva de plazas gratuita y venta anticipada desde 15 días antes de la fecha del viaje.

**Hydrofoil timetable for Málaga to North Africa**

*Prices and times subject to change without warning.*

## BUQUEBUS
### HORARIOS
### MALAGA-CEUTA-MALAGA

| | LUNES | MARTES | MIÉRCOLES | JUEVES | VIERNES | SÁBADO | DOMINGO |
|---|---|---|---|---|---|---|---|
| SALIDAS DE CEUTA | 07.00 | 07.00 | 07.00 | 07.00 | 07.00 | 10.30 | 07.00 |
| | 19.00 | 19.00 | 19.00 | 12.00 | 15.30 | 19.00 | 19.00 |
| | - | - | - | 19.00 | 20.30 | - | - |
| SALIDAS DE MÁLAGA | 09.30 | 09.30 | 09.30 | 09.30 | 09.30 | 08.00 | 09.30 |
| | 21.30 | 21.30 | 21.30 | 16.30 | 18.00 | 13.00 | 21.30 |
| | - | - | - | 21.30 | - | 21.30 | - |

**INFORMACIÓN Y RESERVAS:**                                     O EN SU AGENCIA DE VIAJES
**Málaga:** Tels.: 952 227 905 · Fax: 952 212 836
**Ceuta:** Tels.: 956 505 353 · Fax: 956 501 505
Los precios y horarios están sujetos a cambios sin previo aviso.
Les recordamos su presentación al embarque 30 minutos antes de la salida.

*We remind you to present yourself for boarding half an hour before departure*

## LLEGADAS
arrivals

## SALIDAS
departures

## RETRASADO
delayed

| | |
|---|---|
| **enero** Jan | **julio** Jul |
| **febrero** Feb | **agosto** Aug |
| **marzo** Mar | **septiembre** Sep |
| **abril** Apr | **octubre** Oct |
| **mayo** May | **noviembre** Nov |
| **junio** Jun | **diciembre** Dec |

*departures  arrivals  frequency*

| Salidas Barcelona Nord | Llegadas Madrid | Frecuencias |
|---|---|---|
| 01:00 | 08:30 | Diario (*) |
| 07:00 | 14:30 | Diario (*) |
| **08:30** | **16:00** | Diario (**) |
| 09:00 | 16:30 | Diario (*) |
| **10:00** | **17:30** | Diario (**) |
| 10:30 | 18:30 | Diario (***) |
| 11:30 | 19:00 | Diario (*) |
| 12:30 | 20:00 | Diario (**) |
| 13:00 | 20:30 | Diario (*) |
| 14:00 | 21:30 | Diario (*) |
| 15:00 | 23:00 | Diario (***) |
| **15:30** | **23:00** | Diario (**) |
| 17:00 | 00:30 | Diario (*)(1) |
| 17:30 | 01:00 | Diario (*) |
| 21:30 | 05:00 | Diario (*) |
| **22:00** | **05:30** | Diario (**) |
| **23:00** | **06:30** | Diario (**) |
| **24:00** | **07:30** | Diario (**) |

*daily*

HORARIOS

MADRID
•
BARCELONA

*grupo* ENATCAR
ARATESA

bus timetable for
Madrid–Barcelona

**lunes**
*loo-nes*
Monday

**martes**
*mar-tes*
Tuesday

**miércoles**
*mee-yer-ko-les*
Wednesday

**jueves**
*khwev-es*
Thursday

**viernes**
*byer-nes*
Friday

**sábado**
*sa-ba-do*
Saturday

**domingo**
*do-meen-go*
Sunday

---

**(1) Para en Calatayud**   *stops at Calatayud*

**Aranjuez to Atocha timetable and key**

| Aranjuez | Ciempozuelos | Valdemoro | Pinto | Getafe Industrial | San Cristóbal Industrial | San Cristóbal de los Angeles | Villaverde Bajo | Atocha |
|---|---|---|---|---|---|---|---|---|
| x. **16.00** | 16.10 | 16.15 | 16.20 | 16.25 | 16.28 | 16.30 | **16.33** | **16.42** |
| **16.30** | 16.40 | 16.45 | 16.50 | 16.55 | 16.58 | 17.00 | **17.03** | **17.12** |
| **17.00** | 17.10 | 17.15 | 17.20 | 17.25 | 17.28 | 17.30 | **17.33** | **17.42** |
| **17.30** | 17.40 | 17.45 | 17.50 | 17.55 | 17.58 | 18.00 | **18.03** | **18.12** |
| a. **17.50** | 18.00 | 18.05 | 18.10 | 18.15 | 18.18 | 18.20 | **18.23** | **18.32** |
| d. **17.58** | 18.08 | 18.13 | 18.18 | 18.23 | 18.26 | 18.28 | **18.31** | **18.40** |

a.: Laborables excepto sábados.
d.: Sábados y festivos.
x.: Efectúa parada en Seseña 5 min. después de Aranjuez.
(1): No circula del 01/08/06 al 01/09/06 ambos inclusive.
(2): Circula diario del 01/08/06 al 01/09/06 ambos inclusive.

*a.: Weekdays except Saturdays*
*d.: Saturdays and holidays*
*x.: Stops at Seseña 5 minutes after Aranjuez*
*(1): No service from 01/08/06 to 01/09/06 inclusive*
*(2): Daily service from 01/08/06 to 01/09/06 inclusive*

**horario**
*o-rar-yo*
timetable

**salida**
*sa-lee-da*
departure

**llegada**
*lyeg-a-da*
arrival

**diario**
*dee-ar-yo*
daily

**circula**
*theer-koo-la*
operates

**no circula**
*no theer-koo-la*
no service

**para en**
*pa-ra en*
stops at

**hasta**
*as-ta*
until

**ambos**
*am-bos*
both

*keywords keywords keywords*

---

**do you have a timetable?**
¿tiene un horario?
*tyen-e oon o-rar-yo*

**what does this mean?**
¿qué quiere decir esto?
*ke kyer-e de-theer es-to*

talk

# Tickets

*Tickets for transport are **billetes**. Tickets for cinema, theatre and museums are **entradas**. The term **joven** (young) usually applies to people under 26.*

Automatic ticket machines are becoming increasingly common. This one is for train tickets.

If you don't have the correct amount, make sure the machine indicates that change is given (**devuelve cambio**).

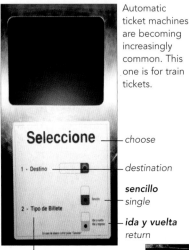

**Seleccione** — *choose*

1 - Destino — *destination*

**sencillo** *single*

2 - Tipo de Billete — **ida y vuelta** *return*

*type of ticket*

You can buy bus and metro tickets at the **estanco** where you see the **tabacos** sign.

**train ticket**

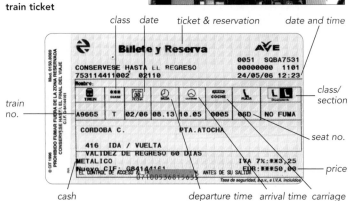

class · date · ticket & reservation · date and time

train no. · class/section · seat no. · departure time · arrival time · carriage · cash · price

Renfe local ticket:
one-journey bus ticket

10-journey bus ticket
known as a **bono-bus**.
It goes into the validating
machine in the direction
of the arrow.

**Renfe local
train ticket**

10-journey (**10 viajes**) metro and bus ticket (you must
validate it on the bus in the machine by the driver).

**cinema ticket**

screen

first floor

— War of the
Worlds

— date

— showing

A ticket to the cinema or theatre
is known as **una entrada**.

**billete**
*beel-ye-te*
ticket

**bono-bus**
*bo-no-boos*
10-journey ticket

**entrada**
*en-tra-da*
entry ticket
(*cinema, etc*)

**ida**
*ee-da*
single

**ida y vuelta**
*ee-da ee bwel-ta*
return

**adulto**
*a-dool-to*
adult

**niño**
*neen-yo*
child

**joven** (under 26)
*kho-ben*
young person

**jubilado**
*khoo-bee-la-do*
over 60

**tercera edad**
*ter-ther-a ed-ad*
over 60

**minusválido**
*mee-noos-ba-lee-do*
disabled

**suplemento**
*soo-ple-men-to*
supplement

**ventanilla**
*ven-ta-neel-ya*
window seat

**pasillo**
*pas-eel-yo*
aisle seat

keywords keywords keywords keywords keywords

# Public Transport

*i* *Bus services vary from town to town. Generally speaking, you can buy single-journey tickets on the bus from the driver. You can also get a 10-journey ticket (**bonobús**) from **tabacos** or **estancos** and some kiosks which works out a little cheaper. These have to be validated in the ticket machine on the bus by putting them arrow down into the machine next to the driver (see p. 27). Under-4s normally travel free. Senior citizens and students can get discounts on multi-journey tickets but not on single tickets.*

**bus station**

metro bus
tickets on
sale here

Bus stops indicating the number of service and the stops en route. It is advisable to flag down the buses at the bus stop as they don't always stop automatically.

Number and destination are normally shown on the front of the bus.

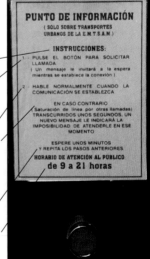

instructions

1. Press the button to get a line (a recorded message will ask you to wait while the connection is made)

2. Once you get through talk normally

If it doesn't work (there may be lots of calls) after a few seconds a new message will tell you that it is impossible to answer your query for the moment

Wait a few minutes and repeat the whole process

Business hours for the public from 9am to 9pm

**local bus information point**

There is a comprehensive long-distance coach network which is usually cheaper than travelling by train. All towns and cities have a central bus/coach station with information on routes, prices, times, etc. This is the best place to get information and buy tickets. Many coach companies run different routes and there is usually a board with a list of companies and destinations, showing the window number for specific routes. You need to go to the relevant window for information on prices and times. Advance booking is recommended especially at weekends and in high season. You can buy tickets up to 2 months in advance. Return tickets tend to be slightly more economical. Most coaches have toilets on board but few other facilities.

The bus station is usually quite central.

**Dársenas 1 a 60**

*coach stands 1–60*
Check which stand your bus leaves from.

DÁRSENA / PLATFORM 54

**coach stand**

SALIDAS / DEPARTURES

| Hora Time | Empresa Enterprise | Destino To | Dársena Platform | Observaciones Remarks |
|---|---|---|---|---|

Avisos Notices

Coach departure board. *Empresa* (in the second column) indicates the operator.

**where do I catch a bus to...?**
¿dónde se coge el autobús para...?
*don-de se ko-khe el ow-to-boos pa-ra...*

**which number goes to...?**
¿qué número va a...?
*ke noo-me-ro ba a...*

**is there a coach to...?**
¿hay algún autocar que vaya a...?
*aee al-goon ow-to-kar ke ba-ya a...*

**which bus goes to the centre?**
¿qué autobús va al centro?
*ke ow-to-boos ba al then-tro*

**does this coach go to...?**
¿este autocar va a...?
*es-te ow-to-kar ba a...*

**please tell me when to get off**
¡por favor! me dice cuándo tengo que bajarme
*por fa-bor me dee-the kwan-do ten-go ke ba-khar-me*

**excuse me! I'm getting off!**
¡perdone! me bajo aquí
*per-do-ne me ba-kho a-kee*

**this is my stop**
esta es mi parada
*es-ta es mee pa-ra-da*

talking talking

*Metro systems run in Madrid, Barcelona and Bilbao. Each operate their own ticket and travelcard system. In Madrid and Barcelona you can buy single tickets or tickets for 10 journeys which cover both the metro and bus system. These are valid for the central zone. It is possible to get a monthly pass (**abono mensual**) which covers the same system, but it is only worth getting one of these if you plan to spend 3 weeks of a calendar month in the city. For this option, you need to provide passport number and a photo. All types of tickets can be bought at metro station booths. Using the Metro is cheap and efficient. It is busy from 8.30 to 10am and the evening rush hour can start as early as 3.30pm and can go on till 8pm. Most journeys will be within the central zone, but trips to the suburbs, for example, may require a supplement.*

Madrid metro maps are available from metro station booths. The Madrid metro operates from 6am to 2am daily.

**metro sign**

Station name platform 2

The name of the station and the lines it serves; these are colour-coded (3, yellow and 5, green).

**ticket machines**
If you don't have the exact amount, check that the machine gives change (***devuelve cambio***).

end stops for line 2 (colour-coded red)

end stops for line 3 (colour-coded yellow)

When planning a journey, look for the final destination for your particular line and follow signs to it.

You must put your ticket through the barrier.

Access to metro (line 6) and suburban trains (**Cercanías**).

*Don't forget to take your ticket.*

**a single**
un billete
*oon beel-ye-te*

**a 10-journey ticket**
un billete de diez viajes
*oon beel-ye-te de dyeth bya-khes*

**a monthly ticket**
un abono mensual
*oon a-bo-no men-swal*

**have you a map of the metro?**
¿tiene un plano del metro?
*tyen-e oon pla-no del me-tro*

**where is the nearest metro station?**
¿dónde está la estación de metro más próxima?
*don-de es-ta la es-ta-thyon de me-tro mas prok-see-ma*

**I want to go to...**
quiero ir a...
*kyer-o eer a...*

**do I have to change?**
¿tengo que cambiar de línea?
*ten-go ke kamb-yar de lee-ne-ya*

**where?**
¿dónde?
*don-de*

**which line is it for...?**
¿qué línea es para...?
*ke lee-ne-ya es pa-ra...*

**in which direction?**
¿en qué dirección?
*en ke dee-rek-thyon*

**which station is it for...?**
¿cuál es la estación de metro para...?
*kwal es la es-ta-thyon de me-tro pa-ra...*

**please let me off**
me deja salir por favor
*me de-kha sa-leer por fa-bor*

talking talking talking talking talking

*The national rail network is called RENFE. Train tickets can be bought at: train stations at the **taquilla**, RENFE agencies in large cities, travel agencies displaying the RENFE sign, or over the internet on the RENFE website, www.renfe.es. You can then pick up your tickets at the station. Tickets can be bought up to 2 months in advance. A high-speed train service called AVE (**Alta Velocidad España**) exists linking Madrid with Seville (a good link with local trains for the Costa del Sol). AVE also offers high-speed train services called TALGO 200 which are as good as AVE but cheaper (the only difference is that it takes 15 minutes longer to reach your destination). The AVE network's base is at Atocha station in Madrid.*

road sign for the train station

exit — **Salida**
**Atención al**
customer — **Cliente**
service

**Taquillas**

ticket office

ticket machine for regional trains

| | | |
|---|---|---|
| a single to... | 2 singles to... | do I need a reservation? |
| uno a... | dos a... | ¿necesito una reserva? |
| *oo-no a...* | *dos a...* | *neth-es-ee-to oo-na re-ser-ba* |

a return to...
uno de ida y vuelta a...
*oo-na de ee-da ee bwel-ta a...*

2 returns to...
dos de ida y vuelta a...
*dos de ee-da ee bwel-ta a...*

| | | |
|---|---|---|
| a child's ticket | first class | second class |
| un billete de niño | de primera clase | de clase turista |
| *oon beel-ye-te de neen-yo* | *de pree-me-ra kla-se* | *de kla-se too-rees-ta* |

I booked my ticket on the internet
he reservado el billete por internet
*e re-ser-ba-do el beel-ye-te por een-ter-net*

where do I collect it?
¿dónde lo recojo?
*don-de lo re-ko-kho*

| | | |
|---|---|---|
| I want to book... | 2 seats | window/aisle |
| quiero reservar... | dos asientos | ventanilla/pasillo |
| *kyer-o re-ser-bar...* | *dos as-yen-tos* | *ven-ta-neel-ya/pa-seel-yo* |

a couchette
una litera
*oo-na lee-te-ra*

talking talking

board showing
different services

— name of station

— metro

— high-speed train

— ticket office

— regional trains

— information point

keywords keywords keywords

**sencillo**
*sen-theel-yo*
single

**ida y vuelta**
*ee-da ee bwel-ta*
return

**reserva**
*re-ser-ba*
reservation

**suplemento**
*soo-ple-men-to*
supplement

**taquillas**
*ta-keel-yas*
ticket office

**consigna**
*kon-seeg-na*
left luggage

**coche**
*ko-che*
carriage

**andén**
*an-den*
platform

**fumador**
*foo-ma-dor*
smoking

**no fumador**
*no foo-ma-dor*
non-smoking

— exit tickets
— check-in

*left luggage* (with attendant)

*left luggage*
(automatic
lockers)

Collection point for tickets
booked over the internet;
they have to be picked up
at least 45 minutes before
train departure.

**overhead board**

*train    destination    time  platform  remarks*

| Salidas DEPARTURES | | | | |
|---|---|---|---|---|
| Tren TRAIN | Destino DESTINATION | Hora TIME | Via PLATFORM | Observaciones REMARKS |
| 15 | VALENCIA | 14:00 | | |
| | TALAVERA | 14:30 | | |
| | Córdoba-Málaga | 14:40 | | |
| | C.Real-Badajoz | 14:40 | | |

**the train to...**
el tren para...
*el tren pa-ra...*

**is this the train for...?**
¿es éste el tren para...?
*es es-te el tren pa-ra...*

**which platform does it leave from?**
¿de qué andén sale?
*de ke an-den sa-le*

**this is my seat**
este es mi asiento
*es-te es mee as-yen-to*

talking

# Taxi

*i* *In most places taxis are plentiful, reliable and not particularly expensive. It is possible to order taxis in advance, or simply hail them in the street. Taxis can take a maximum of 4 passengers. Should you wish to make a complaint it's best to try to sort the matter out with the driver. Failing that, all taxis carry an identification number on the door which you can use to report the taxi to the town hall (**Ayuntamiento**). In each town there is usually a fleet of taxis specifically designed to take wheelchairs. These have to be ordered, either by hailing a normal taxi and getting the driver to radio for one or by telephoning the taxi company.*

Taxi stand with prices displayed.

Taxis to and from airports or stations often carry a supplement which considerably increases the fare. Tipping is not common but it is normal to round up the total cost.

Taxis are generally white. If a taxi is free it shows a green light and the word **libre**. If it has passengers it usually shows a red light with the word **ocupado**.

**where is the taxi stand?**
¿donde está la parada de taxis?
*don-de es-ta la pa-ra-da de tak-sees*

**to ... please**
a ... por favor
*a ... por fa-bor*

**how much is it to...?**
¿cuánto cuesta hasta...?
*kwan-to kwes-ta as-ta...*

**please order me a taxi**
por favor me pide un taxi
*por fa-bor me pee-de oon tak-see*

**for ... o'clock**
para las ...
*pa-ra las...*

**I need a receipt**
necesito un recibo
*neth-e-see-to oon re-theeb-o*

**keep the change**
quédese con la vuelta
*ke-de-se kon la bwel-ta*

**is there a special rate for the airport?**
¿hay una tarifa especial para el aeropuerto?
*aee oo-na ta-ree-fa es-peth-yal pa-ra el aee-ro-pwer-to*

# Car Hire

*Car hire is not difficult to find and isn't too expensive (except in the Balearics and Canaries). You must provide a full driving licence and identification (passport). You need to be 21 and have had a driving licence for at least a year. Check what is included in the price, particularly insurance. The better-known companies will be able to provide baby seats, etc. Most if not all companies will also provide you with instructions of what to do in case of an accident or breakdown (see also pp. 40 and 44). This information is often in English.*

vehicle hire

**I want to hire a car**
quiero alquilar un coche
*kyer-o al-kee-lar oon ko-che*

**for one day**
para un día
*pa-ra oon dee-ya*

**for ... days**
para ... días
*pa-ra ... dee-yas*

**I want...**
quiero...
*kyer-o...*

**a small car**
un coche pequeño
*un ko-che pe-ken-yo*

**a large car**
un coche grande
*un ko-che gran-de*

**an automatic**
uno automático
*oo-no ow-to-mat-ee-ko*

**a people carrier**
un monovolumen
*oon mo-no-vo-loo-men*

**how much is it?**
¿cuánto es?
*kwan-to es*

**is there a kilometre charge?**
¿hay que pagar kilometraje?
*aee ke pa-gar kee-lo-me-tra-khe*

**I am ... old**
tengo ... años
*ten-go ... an-yos*

**here is my driving licence**
aquí tiene mi carnet de conducir
*a-kee tyen-e mee kar-ne de kon-doo-theer*

**what does the insurance cover?**
¿qué cubre el seguro?
*ke koob-re el se-goo-ro*

**does it take unleaded petrol?**
¿usa gasolina sin plomo?
*oo-sa ga-so-lee-na seen plo-mo*

**how do the controls work?**
¿cómo funcionan los mandos?
*ko-mo foonth-yo-nan los man-dos*

**where are the documents?**
¿dónde está la documentación?
*don-de es-ta la do-koo-men-tath-yon*

**what do we do if we have a breakdown?**
¿qué hay que hacer si tenemos una avería?
*ke aee ke a-ther see te-ne-mos oo-na ab-er-ee-a*

**can we have a child's seat?**
¿nos deja un asiento de niño?
*nos de-kha oon as-yen-to de neen-yo*

**how is it fitted?**
¿cómo se pone?
*ko-mo se po-ne*

talking talking talking talking talking

# Driving

*The most noticeable aspect of Spanish driving is the overuse of the car horn. Although in general driving standards are quite good, drivers do tend to be impatient, particularly in traffic jams. The minimum age for driving in Spain is 18. There are strict laws on drink-driving. If bringing your car into Spain, you will need your vehicle registration document and driving licence. You may also need a Green Card, available from your insurer in the UK for a small fee. Within the EU your general UK car insurance covers you. You may want to take out extra breakdown cover (AA or RAC).*

**city centre**

north **Norte**

**Oeste** **Este**

*west* *east*

**Sur** *south*

Spanish numberplate **E** is for **España**.

### Speed restrictions

| | |
|---|---|
| built up area | 50 km/h |
| ordinary roads | 90 km/h |
| dual carriageway | 120 km/h |
| motorway | 120 km/h |

**radar speed check**

There are on-the-spot fines for traffic offences, notably speeding and drink-driving – and credit cards are accepted!

Colour-coding for Spanish road signs.

*Red with N- is a dual carriageway (**autovía**; these function also as motorways).*

*Blue with A- is a motorway, **autopista**.*

*Orange with a D- indicates a diversion; follow this to rejoin your original route.*

*Green and E- is a European route and a main road.*

*Orange with C- is a primary road.*

*Green with C- is a secondary road.*

*Yellow with C- is a third-class road.*

**pedestrian zone**

**end of pedestrian zone**

*forbidden to all vehicles pedestrian zone*

*Vía Preferente* indicates a bus and taxi lane.

**lorry exit**

Few drivers stop at zebra crossings. An oncoming driver flashing their lights does NOT mean 'after you'; it will probably mean '*I'm coming through*'.

**we are going to...**
vamos a...
*ba-mos a...*

**is the road good?**
¿está bien la carretera?
*es-ta byen la kar-re-te-ra*

**is the pass open?**
¿está abierto el puerto?
*es-ta a-byer-to el pwer-to*

**which is the best route?**
¿cuál es la mejor ruta?
*kwal es la me-khor roo-ta*

**can you show me on the map?**
¿puede indicármelo en el mapa?
*pwe-de een-dee-kar-me-lo en el ma-pa*

**do we need snow chains?**
¿hace falta usar cadenas?
*a-the fal-ta oo-sar ka-de-nas*

*Some motorways (**autopistas**) are free and some carry toll charges (which can be expensive). Look out for the sign **peaje** (toll). Payment is due on completion of each sector covered. You do not receive tickets. These toll motorways are similar to UK motorways but aren't usually as busy. Non-toll motorways, however, are more like dual carriageways with numerous exits. They offer a great number of possibilities for stopping, ranging from simple café/bars to restaurants, hotels and petrol stations. There are also big service stations with full facilities (cash dispensers, mini-markets, play areas, etc.), but they are few and far between.*

Spanish motorways are signposted in blue. The speed limit is 120kph. Motorway info website is www.aseta.es

*European route (E-15)*  *national road (N-340)*

*motorway exit 500m on the right; exit number 181*

*motorway (A-7)*

Services are available on taking the 162 exit. Service stations are known as **Areas de Servicio**.

Before you reach the toll booth there will be a sign showing which cards are accepted for payment.

At the toll stop you have a choice of payment: either cash (**manuales**) for all vehicles (**metálico** means cash), card (**tarjetas**) or prepaid (**telepeaje**).

card-only lane for payment

The amount is displayed at the booth. The front passenger will be closest in a right-hand drive car.

Roadside SOS phones have instructions in English, French and German as well as Spanish.

**motorway toll** PEAJE TOLL

It is compulsory to carry a fluorescent vest on all vehicles to put on when you breakdown on the motorway.

## If you break down on the motorway

There is a very small or no hard shoulder on Spanish motorways. If you have to stop or you break down, you must pull over as far as you can, put on your hazard lights and place your warning triangle 50 metres behind the vehicle. It should be visible for at least 100 metres. You must wear a fluorescent jacket (*un chaleco reflectante*), which can be bought in petrol stations and shops. Both *autopistas* and *autovías* have SOS emergency phones located at about 1500-metre intervals. You simply press the button and wait for assistance.

**my car has broken down**
se me ha averiado el coche
*se me a a-ber-ya-do el ko-che*

**what should I do?**
¿qué hago?
*ke a-go*

**I am on my own**
estoy solo/sola (male/female)
*es-toy so-lo/so-la*

**my children are in the car**
los niños están en el coche
*los neen-yos es-tan en el ko-che*

**the car is...**
el coche está...
*el ko-che es-ta...*

**before junction...**
antes de la salida...
*an-tes de la sa-lee-da...*

**after junction...**
después de la salida...
*des-pwes de la sa-lee-da...*

**registration number...**
matrícula...
*mat-ree-koo-la...*

**it is a blue fiat**
es un fiat azul
*es oon fee-yat a-thool*

Spanish drivers will often park wherever the fancy takes them. However, in general, parking can be a problem almost everywhere. The safest option is to find a multi-storey or pay-and-display area. There are restrictions regarding parking and these are clearly indicated. Cars may be towed away if parked in a restricted area. This is more common than clamping. If your car has been towed away you will have to pick it up from the local council compound, give details of the car and pay the fine. Police or traffic wardens will know where the local compound is. Semi-official parking attendants will often assist you in finding parking spaces on the street. A small tip of around 1 euro is expected. The Spanish for parking ticket machine is **el parquímetro** el par-**kee**-met-ro.

Signs for pay-and-display machines.

residents' parking only

**24-hour parking**

*per night*

No parking at all except disabled.

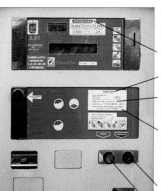

Pay and display machine (parquímetro).

coins (**monedas**)

tariffs (**tarifas**)

times when parking restrictions apply (**horarios**)

no change is given (**no devuelve cambio**)

to cancel (**cancelar**)

press for ticket

**parking charges**

*first half hour or part thereof*

*each further half hour or part thereof*

*maximum 24 hours*

| TARIFAS APARCAMIENTO | |
|---|---|
| PRIMERA HORA Ó FRACCIÓN | 1,00 € |
| CADA HORA RESTANTE Ó FRACCIÓN | 0,75 € |
| MÁXIMO 24 HORAS | 15,00 € |

IVA INCLUIDO
EN VIGOR A PARTIR DEL DÍA 1 DE ENERO DEL 2.002

*including VAT
in force from 1 January 2002*

Be careful:
**libre** means 'spaces'
not 'free of charge'.
**Completo** means full.

Laborables de 9 a 14 h.
y 16 a 20 h. excepto
carga y descarga

*no parking weekdays 9am–2pm
and 4pm–8pm except for loading
and unloading*

P CAJA CASH

**pay point**

**parking prohibited**
*you will be towed away*

PROHIBIDO APARCAR
LLAMAMOS GRUA

P SOLO TURISMO Y MOTOS
PROHIBIDO CARAVANAS Y AUTOCARES

*parking only
for cars and
motorbikes*

*caravans
and coaches
forbidden*

No parking
Thursdays from
8am–3pm for
a street market.

JUEVES DE
8 H. - 15 H.
MERCADILLO

**where is the best place to park?**
¿cuál es el mejor sitio para aparcar?
*kwal es el me-khor seet-yo pa-ra a-par-kar*

**where is there a car park?**
¿dónde hay un aparcamiento?
*don-de aee oon a-par-ka-myen-to*

**can I park here?**
¿se puede aparcar aquí?
*se pwe-de a-par-kar a-kee*

**how long for?**
¿cuánto tiempo?
*kwan-to tyem-po*

**the ticket machine doesn't work**
no funciona el parquímetro
*no foonth-yo-na el par-kee-met-ro*

Petrol stations are essentially the same as those in the UK. Although self-service (*autoservicio*) is common, many petrol stations still have pump attendants. Most accept credit cards. Be aware that leaded petrol still exists in Spain and you must ask for unleaded petrol (*sin plomo*) which is always coloured green. Many petrol stations offer a lot of services other than just providing petrol (car wash, air, water, etc.). Car washes are very similar in style and format all over Spain. Valet cleaning is generally not available. You will probably have to pay for air and sometimes water.

Colour-coded pumps: black for diesel (*gasóleo*), green for unleaded (*sin plomo*) and red for leaded (*super*).

LAVADO MANUAL Y CAMBIO DE ACEITE — hand wash & oil change
4ª PLANTA — 4th floor

**vacuum**

Aspirador

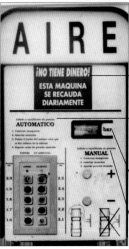

AIRE

**air**

*no money! This machine is emptied daily.*

*automatically balanced and inflated pressure (choose button for precise bar pressure measurement)*

*bar counter (to measure pressure manually)*

*manually balanced and inflated pressure (adjust using buttons)*

**where is there a petrol station?**
¿dónde hay una gasolinera?
*don-de aee oo-na ga-so-lee-ne-ra*

**...worth of unleaded petrol**
...de gasolina sin plomo
*...de ga-so-lee-na seen plo-mo*

**the card for the carwash**
la tarjeta para el autolavado
*la tar-khe-ta pa-ra el ow-to-la-ba-do*

**fill it up please**
lleno por favor
*lyen-o por fa-bor*

**pump number...**
surtidor número...
*soor-tee-dor noo-me-ro...*

**how much is that?**
¿cuánto es?
*kwan-to es*

talking

*i*  If you are a member of a motoring organisation, such as the AA or RAC, you will have access to the R.A.C. de E (Real Automóvil Club de España), Spain's national motoring organisation. This round-the-clock national emergency call-out service is based in Madrid. You can contact them on 91 593 33 33. You may need to contact your cover organisation in the UK to check if you have to pay a supplement for this or not. Kwik-Fit type fitters are few and far between in Spain but look out for 'Feu-Vert' signs (French-owned equivalent).

# TALLER MECANICO
## GRUA PERMANENTE 24 HORAS
### SERVICIO NEUMATICOS TURISMO
TLFNS: 926 33 91 15 - 926 33 93 40

**garage for repairs**
This one offers 24-hour pick-up truck and tyre service for cars.

**I have broken down**
tengo una avería
*ten-go oo-na a-be-ree-ya*

**the car won't start**
el coche no arranca
*el ko-che no ar-ran-ka*

**the battery is flat**
la batería está descargada
*la ba-te-ree-ya es-ta des-kar-ga-da*

**I have a flat tyre**
tengo una rueda pinchada
*ten-go oo-na rwe-da peen-cha-da*

**I need new tyres**
necesito neumáticos nuevos
*neth-es-ee-to ne-oo-ma-tee-kos nwe-bos*

**I have run out of petrol**
me he quedado sin gasolina
*me e ke-da-do seen ga-so-lee-na*

**where is there a garage?**
¿dónde hay un taller?
*don-de aee oon tal-yer*

**something is wrong with...**
algo le pasa a(l)...
*al-go le pa-sa a(l)...*

**the ... is not working**
el/la ... no funciona
*el/la ... no foonth-yo-na*

**the ... are not working**
los/las ... no funcionan
*los/las ... no foonth-yo-nan*

**can you repair it?**
¿puede arreglarlo?
*pwe-de ar-re-glar-lo*

**how long will it take?**
¿cuánto tardan en arreglarlo?
*kwan-to tar-dan en ar-re-glar-lo*

**when will it be ready?**
¿para cuándo estará?
*pa-ra kwan-do es-ta-ra*

**how much will it cost?**
¿cuánto me costará?
*kwan-to me kos-ta-ra*

**can you replace the windscreen?**
¿me puede cambiar el parabrisas?
*me pwe-de kamb-yar el pa-ra-bree-sas*

| **please change...** | **the oil** | **the tyres** |
|---|---|---|
| me cambia... | el aceite | los neumáticos |
| *me kamb-ya...* | *el a-they-te* | *los ne-oo-ma-tee-kos* |

talking talking talking talking talking

# Madrid District

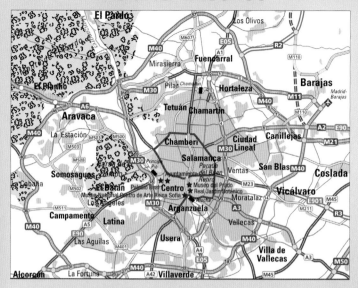

white: major route
signposted from a town

yellow: places of interest
to visitors – the port

green: street names

major route signposted
from a town; to the
*autovía* which are
prefixed N- (red signs)

a place of interest to
visitors; parking

In cities and towns, the
colour-coding on road
signs changes.

**town centre**
Notice the circular
pictogram for town
centre. This is
becoming more
common in Europe
to mean centre.

**city centre sign**
If you don't see your destination
signposted, follow the
*todas direcciones* (all routes).
To get to the town centre,
follow *centro ciudad*.

# Madrid City

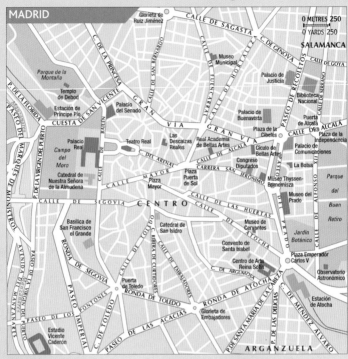

**paseo** and **calle** both mean street.

**plaza** (*pla-tha*) = square. **Plaza Mayor** means main square

abbreviation for **plaza** (*pza*) on bus

mercado — market

Policia Local Guardia Civil — police station

**sótano** basement

**aquí** here

urgencias — A & E

ayuntamiento — town hall

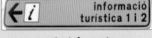

informació turística 1 i 2

**tourist information**
Notice the slightly different spelling in this Majorcan sign.

# Barcelona City

**BARCELONA**

Parc de l'Espanya Industrial · CR CREU COBERTA · CARRER DE NUMANCIA · AVINGUDA DE ROMA · COMTE D'URGELL · AVINGUDA DE ROMA · Museu d'Història de la Medicina · Casa Milá · AVINGUDA DIAGONAL · JOAN

CARRER D'ARAGO · EIXAMPLE · CARRER D'ARAGO

Parc Joan Miró · Plaça de Braus Les Arenes · Plaça d'Espanya · Universitat · PASSEIG DE GRACIA · Plaça de Tetuan

GRAN VIA DE LES CORTS CATALANES

SANTS-MONTJUÏC · SANT ANTONI · Museu d'Art Contemporani · Plaça de Catalunya · RONDA DE SANT PERE · Arc de Triomf

Poble Espanyol · Palau Nacional y Museu d'Art de Catalunya · Casa de Misericòrdia · Mercat Boqueria · BARRI GÒTIC · PASSEIG DE SANT JOAN

Museu Arqueològic · EL RAVAL · Catedral · Museu Història de la Ciutat · Parc de la Ciutadella

Museu Etnològic · Teatre Grec · Gran Teatre del Liceu · CR DE FERRAN · CR DE LA PRINCESA · Mercat del Born

Fundació Miró · Palau Güell · Plaça Reial · Casa de la Ciutat · Museu Picasso · RIBERA · Estació de França

Estadi Olimpic · Funicular · POBLE SEC · Santa Maria del Mar · Parc Zoològic

Parc del Migdia · AVINGUDA DE MIRAMAR · Museu Marítim Drassanes · Monument a Colom · PASSEIG DE COLOM · RONDA · LITORAL

MONTJUÏC · CRTA DE MIRAMAR · PO DE JOSEP CARNER · Museu Oceanogràfic · Moll d'Espanya · L'Aquàrium · LA BARCELONETA

Museu Militar · Cable Car · Moll de Barcelona · Cable Car

Castell de Montjuïc · RONDA LITORAL · World Trade Centre

EL PORT · Dàrsena San Beltran · Moll del Contradicte · Dàrsena del Morrot · Moll de Ponent

0 METRES 500 · 0 YARDS 500 · *Mediterranean Sea*

---

**pay & display**
Indicates that parking must be paid for. Times are Mon-Fri, 9am to 2pm and from 5 to 9pm. On Saturdays from 9am to 2pm.

**no parking**
*ambos lados*
= both sides
*reservado minusválido*
= disabled parking

**guarded parking**

P · ZONA DE ESTACIONAMIENTO LIMITADO Y CONTROLADO TICKET DE CONTROL OBLIGATORIO · HORARIO LUNES A VIERNES de 9 a 14h de 17 a 21h SABADOS de 9h a 14h

ATENCION VIA URBANA · **50** · VELOCIDAD CONTROLADA POR RADAR

**Spanish speed limits**
In built-up areas the limit is 50kph, ordinary roads 90kph, dual carriageways (*autovías*) and motorways (*autopistas*) 120kph.

P · 24 HORAS · PARKING · VIGILADO

# Barcelona District

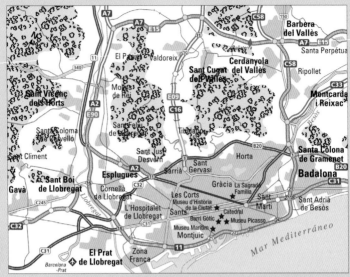

**exit**

*European route*

*motorway*     exit 181

*toll*

**prepaid motorway toll**
Do not choose this lane
unless you have a
special in-car device.

**change of direction**
To turn left, pull off to
the right and a bridge
takes you back over
the road to go left.

**alternative route
to motorway**

**non-motorway
traffic**

Toll charges can be
expensive. You pay
on completion of
each sector covered.

**access to motorway**
(A-7 and European route E-15)

# Shopping

In Spain there is a tendency to use small, local shops more (on a daily basis), particularly for bread, meat and fish. Many shops are closed during the 'siesta' hours of 2pm–5pm and remain closed on Saturday afternoons. They are, however, often open later in the evening than is usual in the UK. Very large department stores and supermarkets stay open all day. Sunday opening is not common.

Check out the local markets, particularly for fresh products. They are busy,, lively and well worth visiting. Most large towns have a daily market, smaller towns a weekly one.

**off-license**

There are several types of lottery. The national lottery (3 times a week) is similar to the UK's, with a 6-number pick. Buy the tickets from kiosks and shops with this sign.

**gifts**

**baker's**

**fish shop**

**general grocer's** Small shops open 10am–2pm and 5pm–8.30pm.

**main shopping area**

**bookshop**
*tienda = shop*

*i* *Smaller supermarkets can be found within the city limits and larger ones on the outskirts of town. Big supermarkets or hypermarkets include* **Carrefour**, **Eroski** *and* **Alcampo**. *In these, you can find everything you need, normally including petrol. Out-of-town supermarkets provide free parking. By and large, all supermarkets offer a good range of products. You usually have to get someone to weigh the fruit for you at the fruit & veg section. Plastic bags are free. Larger supermarkets have cash dispensers.*

**supermarket sign**

**ALCANTARILLA
SUPERMERCADO
SUPERMARKET**

**Scanner to
check prices**

Trolleys
generally take
a 1 euro coin.

**locker- and present-wrapping area**
Leave bags in a locker at the entrance
or with an attendant who will give
you a token to return as you leave.

**10 items or less checkout**

Caja Rápida **10** MÁXIMO UNIDADES POR CARRO

**where can I buy...?**
¿dónde puedo comprar...?
*don-de pwe-do kom-prar...*

**do you have...?**
¿tiene...?
*tyen-e...*

**I am looking for...**
estoy buscando...
*es-toy boos-kan-do...*

**is there a market?**
¿hay mercado?
*aee mer-ka-do*

**have you change for the trolley?**
¿tiene cambio para el carro?
*tyen-e kamb-yo pa-ra el kar-ro*

**batteries**
pilas
*peel-as*

**how much is it?**
¿cuánto es?
*kwan-to es*

**a present**
un regalo
*oon re-ga-lo*

**which day?**
¿qué día?
*ke dee-ya*

**can I pay with this card?**
¿puedo pagar con esta tarjeta?
*pwe-do pa-gar kon es-ta tar-khe-ta*

**a tin-opener**
un abrelatas
*oon a-bre-la-tas*

**a good wine**
un buen vino
*oon bwen bee-no*

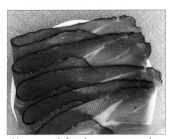

*Weights and measures are all in metric. At, for example, a deli counter you would ask for the number of grammes required (e.g. 250g); for wine or water, the number of bottles or litres. You can also buy cheap wine in cartons. Almost all products other than fresh ones are prepacked so you only need to ask for the product by name.*

You can ask for cheese or meat by slices (**lonchas**) rather than by weight. **Jamón serrano** is cured ham; cooked ham is **jamón de York**.

Eggs are sold by the dozen and half-dozen (**dozena y media dozena**). It may be difficult to get free-range (**huevos de campo**).

Health foods (**productos dietéticos**) are available in large supermarkets and specialist shops (**herbolisterías**) but they are not very widespread.

Baker's sell fresh bread, milk, juice and other basic items.

When ordering bread ask for **una barra** (French stick), **bollos** (rolls) or **un pan** (round country loaf).

Milk is almost always UHT. Go by the wording, not the colour which may vary.

skimmed milk
(**leche desnatada**)

semi-skimmed milk
(**leche semidesnatada**)

whole milk
(**leche entera**)

**a piece of that cheese**
un trozo de ese queso
*oon **tro**-tho de **e**-se **ke**-so*

**a little more please**
un poco más por favor
*oon **po**-ko mas por fa-**bor***

**a little less please**
un poco menos por favor
*oon **po**-ko **me**-nos por fa-**bor***

**that's enough thanks**
basta gracias
***bas**-ta **grath**-yas*

**10 slices of cooked ham**
diez lonchas de jamón de York
*dyeth **lon**-chas de kha-**mon** de york*

**200 grams of chorizo**
doscientos gramos de chorizo
*dos-**thyen**-tos **gra**-mos de cho-**ree**-tho*

**a carton of milk**
un cartón de leche
*oon kar-**ton** de **le**-che*

**a bottle of mineral water**
una botella de agua mineral
***oo**-na bo-**tel**-ya de **a**-gwa mee-ne-**ral***

| **still** | **fizzy** |
|---|---|
| sin gas | con gas |
| *seen gas* | *kon gas* |

| **a tin of...** | **a roll of...** |
|---|---|
| una lata de... | un rollo de... |
| *oo-na **la**-ta de...* | *oon **rol**-yo de...* |

| **a jar of...** | **a bag of...** |
|---|---|
| un tarro de... | una bolsa de... |
| *oon **tar**-ro de...* | *oo-na **bol**-sa de...* |

**a bottle of...**
una botella de...
***oo**-na bo-**tel**-ya de...*

**a packet of...**
un paquete de...
*oon pa-**ke**-te de...*

**that's all thanks**
nada más gracias
***na**-da mas **grath**-yas*

Gluten-free flour (**harina**)
for bread and pastry.

nutrition

no added
sweetener
(**sacarosa**)
or salt (**sal**)

low in
sodium

unsaturated
vegetable
fat

no sugar

**Bio** generally
indicates
organic
produce.

*Valor nutricional medio por 100g*
*Average nutritional value per 100g*

| | Valor | |
|---|---|---|
| energy | energético KJ | 42 / 177 |
| protein | Proteínas | 1,3g |
| fat | Grasos | 1,6g |
| carbohydrates | Hidratos de Carbono | 0,1g |

*Here is a list of everyday foods you might need.*

**Everyday Foods** comestibles *ko-mes-teeb-les*

**biscuits** las galletas *gal-ye-tas*

**bread** el pan *pan*

**bread roll** el panecillo *pa-ne-theel-yo*

**bread** *(sliced)* el pan de molde
  pan de *mol-de*

**butter** la mantequilla *man-te-kee-lya*

**cereal** los cereales *the-re-a-les*

**cheese** el queso *ke-so*

**chicken** el pollo *pol-yo*

**coffee** el café *ka-fe*

**cream** la nata *na-ta*

**cottage cheese** el requesón
  *re-ke-son*

**crisps** las patatas fritas
  *pa-ta-tas free-tas*

**eggs** los huevos *we-bos*

**fish** el pescado *pes-ka-do*

**flour** la harina *a-ree-na*

**ham** *(cooked)* el jamón de York
  *kha-mon de york*

**ham** *(cured)* el jamón serrano
  *kha-mon ser-ra-no*

**herbal tea** la infusión *een-foo-syon*

**honey** la miel *myel*

**jam** la mermelada *mer-me-la-da*

**juice** el zumo *thoo-mo*

**margarine** la margarina *mar-ga-ree-na*

**marmalade** la mermelada de naranja
  *mer-me-la-da de na-ran-kha*

**meat** la carne *kar-ne*

**milk** la leche *le-che*

**mustard** la mostaza *mos-ta-tha*

**oil** el aceite *a-the-ee-te*

**orange juice** el zumo de naranja
  *thoo-mo de na-ran-kha*

**pasta** la pasta *pas-ta*

**pepper** la pimienta *pee-myen-ta*

**rice** el arroz *ar-roth*

**salt** la sal *sal*

**sausage** la salchicha *sal-cheech-a*

**sugar** el azúcar *a-thoo-kar*

**stock cubes** las pastillas de caldo
  *pas-teel-yas de kal-do*

**tea** el té *te*

**tomatoes** *(tin)* la lata de tomates
  *la-ta de tom-a-tes*

**tuna** *(tin)* el atún *a-toon*

**vinegar** el vinagre *bee-na-gre*

**yoghurt** el yogur *yo-goor*

## Fruit fruta froo-ta

**apples** las manzanas man-**tha**-nas

**apricots** los albaricoques
  al-ba-ree-**ko**-kes

**bananas** los plátanos **pla**-ta-nos

**cherries** las cerezas the-**re**-thas

**figs** los higos ee-gos

**grapefruit** el pomelo po-**me**-lo

**grapes** las uvas oo-bas

**lemon** el limón lee-**mon**

**melon** el melón me-**lon**

**nectarines** las nectarinas
  nek-ta-**ree**-nas

**oranges** las naranjas na-**ran**-khas

**peaches** los melocotones
  melo-ko-**to**-nes

**pears** las peras **pe**-ras

**pineapple** la piña **peen**-ya

**plums** las ciruelas thee-**rwe**-las

**raspberries** las frambuesas
  fram-**bwe**-sas

**strawberries** las fresas **fre**-sas

**watermelon** la sandía san-**dee**-a

## Vegetables verduras ver-**doo**-ras

**artichokes** las alcachofas al-ka-**cho**-fas

**aubergines** las berenjenas
  be-ren-**khen**-as

**asparagus** los espárragos
  es-**par**-ra-gos

**carrots** las zanahorias tha-na-o-ryas

**cauliflower** la coliflor ko-lee-**flor**

**celery** el apio a-**pee**-o

**courgettes** los calabacines
  kala-ba-**thee**-nes

**cucumber** el pepino pe-**pee**-no

**french beans** las judías verdes
  khoo-**dee**-yas **ber**-des

**garlic** el ajo a-kho

**leeks** los puerros **pwer**-ros

**lettuce** la lechuga le-**choo**-ga

**mushrooms** los champiñones
  cham-peen-**yo**-nes

**onions** las cebollas the-**bol**-yas

**peas** los guisantes gee-**san**-tes

**peppers** los pimientos pee-**myen**-tos

**potatoes** las patatas pa-**ta**-tas

**radishes** los rábanos **ra**-ba-nos

**spinach** las espinacas espee-na-kas

**spring onions** las cebolletas
  theb-ol-**ye**-tas

**tomatoes** los tomates to-**ma**-tes

**turnip** el nabo **na**-bo

*Spain's most famous department store is **El Corte Inglés**. It is not the cheapest place to shop, but it is sometimes open on Sundays, and there is a branch in all major towns.*

Spain's most famous department store.

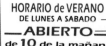

HORARIO de VERANO — summer opening
DE LUNES A SABADO — Monday to Saturday
**ABIERTO** — open
de 10 de la mañana
a 10 de la noche — from 10 in the morning to 10 at night
DOMINGOS Y FESTIVOS CERRADO TODO EL DIA — Sundays and holidays closed all day
MERCANCIA PROTEGIDA ELECTRONICAMENTE

pay here

sold out

Sales usually take place in Jan/Feb and again in Jul/Aug.

**grandes almacenes**
*gran-des al-ma-**then**-es*
department store

**sótano**
*so-ta-no*
basement

**planta baja**
*plan-ta ba-kha*
ground floor

**primera planta**
*pree-me-ra plan-ta*
first floor

**departamento**
*de-par-ta-men-to*
department

**aparatos eléctricos**
*a-pa-ra-tos e-lek-tree-kos*
electrical goods

**joyas**
*kho-yas*
jewellery

**señoras**
*sen-yo-ras*
ladies'

**caballeros**
*ka-bal-ye-ros*
men's

keywords keywords keywords keywords

**which floor is the...?**
¿en qué planta está...?
*en ke plan-ta es-ta...*

**can I try this on?**
¿puedo probarme esto?
*pwe-do pro-bar-me es-to*

**food department**
alimentación
*a-lee-men-tath-yon*

**where is the changing room?**
¿dónde está el probador?
*don-de es-ta el pro-ba-dor*

**shoe department**
zapatería
*tha-pa-te-ree-ya*

talking

*There is a good selection of clothes and shoe shops in Spain. It is essential to produce your receipt if you want a refund and you may well be offered another product or credit note instead of getting your money back.*

Ascensores a: — lifts to the 2nd, 3rd and 4th floors
2ª, 3ª y 4ª Planta ←

Aseos — toilets

ESTA USTED EN LA PLANTA — you are on the 1st floor
1ª

in-store guide

**PROBADORES**

changing rooms

**ZAPATOS**

shoes

**CONFECCIONES**

clothes

**50%**
**TODO A MITAD DE PRECIO**
**TODO A MITAD DE PRECIO**

everything at half price

100 % Seda

100% silk

70 % lana
30 % algodon

70% wool 30% cotton

**do you have size...?**
¿tiene la talla...?
*tyen-e la **tal**-ya...*

**do you have this in my size?**
¿tiene esto en mi talla?
*tyen-e **es**-to en mi **tal**-ya*

**it is too big**
es demasiado grande
*es de-mas-**ya**-do **gran**-de*

**I need a larger/smaller size**
necesito una talla más grande/pequeña
*ne-thes-**ee**-to **oo**-na **tal**-ya mas **gran**-de/pe-**ken**-ya*

**do you have this...?**
¿lo tiene...?
*lo **tyen**-e...*

**do you have shoe size...?**
¿tiene el número...?
*tyen-e el **noo**-me-ro...*

**I take shoe size 40...**
uso el cuarenta...
*oo-so el kwa-**ren**-ta...*

**it is too small**
es demasiado pequeño
*es de-mas-**ya**-do pe-**ken**-yo*

**in black/brown**
en negro/marrón
*en **neg**-ro/mar-**ron***

**in other colours**
en otros colores
*en **o**-tros ko-**lo**-res*

*If you simply want to buy stamps, it is easier to buy them from tobacconists (**estancos**) or kiosks. A few of the big hypermarkets have post offices on site, which have the same opening times as the supermarket. Within the European Union, the rate for sending postcards is the same as a standard-sized letter. They go by air automatically, but postcards do generally take a little longer than letters, perhaps up to a week. For destinations outside the EU, check at the Post Office.*

Spanish Post Office logo. For letters and parcels, go to a window marked **Admisión Polivalente**; there you can also buy envelopes, phonecards and send telegrams and faxes. For sending something big, go to the section marked **Admisión Masiva**.

When sending normal letters or cards, find a yellow postbox. If you have a choice, use the slot marked **Extranjero** (*Overseas*).

Red boxes are for urgent mail with a different tariff.

**collection times**

Mon-Fri 5pm
Sat 1pm

**where is the post office?**
¿dónde está Correos?
*don-de es-ta kor-re-os*

**do you have stamps?**
¿tiene sellos?
*tyen-e sel-yos*

**10 stamps please**
diez sellos por favor
*dyeth sel-yos por fa-bor*

**for postcards**
para postales
*pa-ra po-sta-les*

**for letters**
para cartas
*pa-ra kar-tas*

**to Europe**
para Europa
*pa-ra e-oo-ro-pa*

**to America**
para América
*pa-ra a-me-ree-ka*

**to Australia**
para Australia
*pa-ra ows-tral-ya*

**I want to send this registered**
quiero mandar esto certificado
*kyer-o man-dar es-to ther-tee-fee-ka-do*

**I want to send this parcel**
quiero mandar este paquete
*kyer-o man-dar es-te pa-ke-te*

**priority mail**
correo urgente
*kor-re-o oor-khen-te*

**surface**
por correo normal
*por kor-re-o nor-mal*

**airmail**
por avión
*por a-byon*

talking talking talking

keywords keywords keywords

**carrete**
kar-re-te
film

**pila**
pee-la
battery

**en mate**
en ma-te
matt

**en brillo**
en breel-yo
glossy

**video-cámara**
bee-de-o-ka-ma-ra
camcorder

**cintas**
theen-tas
tapes

**copias**
kop-yas
prints

**Horario de Apertura**

**Lunes a Viernes:**
**de 8:30 a 20:30 h.**

**Sábados:**
**de 9:30 a 14:00 h.**

**Domingos y Festivo :**
**ERRADO**

**BUZONES**

letterboxes

PRODUCTOS
**Kodak**
DE VENTA AQUI
**REVELADO**

Opening hours of a main post office. The quietest time to visit is 2pm–5pm. In smaller towns they often open only in the mornings.

You can also buy stamps at *estancos* and kiosks. The *timbres* sign means *stamps*.

As a rule, you can't take photos in art galleries, museums, etc.

Buy films in specialist photographic shops for the best prices. In tourist areas, outlets doing fast developing sell films at much higher prices. For camcorder equipment, go to good photographic shops, as the choice will be better and prices lower.

talking talking talking

**where can I buy film?**
¿dónde venden carretes?
don-de ben-den kar-re-tes

**a colour film**
un carrete en color
oon kar-re-te en ko-lor

**with ... pictures**
de ... fotos
de ... fo-tos

**can you develop this film?**
¿me pueden revelar este carrete?
me pwe-den re-be-lar es-te kar-re-te

**can you take a picture of us?**
¿podría hacernos una foto?
pod-ree-ya a-ther-nos oo-na fo-to

**tapes for the camcorder**
cintas para esta video-cámara
theen-tas pa-ra es-ta bee-de-o-ka-ma-ra

**a slide film**
un carrete de diapostivas
oon kar-re-te de dee-a-po-see-tee-bas

**24**
veinticuatro
beyn-tee-kwat-ro

**36**
treintayseis
treyn-ta-ee-seyss

**when will the photos be ready?**
¿para cuándo estarán las fotos?
pa-ra kwan-do es-ta-ran las fo-tos

**can I video here?**
¿puedo usar la cámara de u vídeo aquí?
pwe-do oo-sar la-ka-ma-ra de bee-de-yo a-kee

# Phones

*Payphones take coins, phonecards and occasionally credit cards. You can buy a range of phonecards in post offices, tobacconist's (**tabacos**), kiosks and some small supermarkets. There are a range of phonecards. Shops selling phonecards have a sign displayed.*

Where you see this sign, you can buy phonecards.

Phonecards (**tarjetas telefónicas**) come in denominations of 6 and 12 euros.

---

**do you have phonecards?**
¿tiene tarjetas telefónicas?
**tyen**-e tar-**khe**-tas te-le-**fo**-nee-kas

**a phonecard**
una tarjeta telefónica
**oo**-na tar-**khe**-ta te-le-**fo**-nee-ka

**6 euros**
de seis euros
de seyss e-**oo**-ros

**12 euros**
de doce euros
de **doth**-e e-**oo**-ros

**Mr Alvarez please**
con el Señor Alvarez por favor
kon el sen-**yor** **al**-ba-reth por fa-**bor**

**hello** (answering the phone)
diga
**dee**-ga

**can I speak to María?**
¿puedo hablar con María?
**pwe**-do a-**blar** kon ma-**ree**-a

**it's Caroline**
soy Caroline
soy ka-ro-**leen**

**can I have an outside line please?**
¿me da línea por favor?
me da **lee**-ne-a por fa-**bor**

**extension...**
extensión...
es-tens-**yon**...

**I'd like to make a reverse charge call**
quiero hacer una llamada a cobro revertido
**kyer**-o a-**ther** **oo**-na lya-**ma**-da a **ko**-bro re-ber-**tee**-do

**what is your phone number?**
¿cuál es su número de teléfono?
kwal es soo **noo**-me-ro de te-**le**-fo-no

**my phone number is...**
mi número es...
mee **noo**-me-ro es...

talking talking talking talking

keywords keywords keywords

**tarjeta telefónica**
*tar-khe-ta*
*te-le-fo-nee-ka*
phonecard

**móvil**
*mo-beel*
mobile

**código**
*ko-dee-go*
code

**información telefónica**
*een-for-math-yon*
*te-le-fo-nee-ka*
directory enquiries

**páginas amarillas**
*pa-khee-nas*
*a-ma-reel-yas*
yellow pages

Insert coins or a telephone card

(Pulsa *01 para enviar un sms, e-mail, fax = press *01 to send a text message, an email a fax)

If you see lit up on the display *solo llamadas gratuitas* it means free calls only, i.e. emergency numbers or the operator.

Most bars have a public phone, which usually only takes coins.

TELEFONO PUBLICO

Larger cities usually have a phone centre (*locutorio*) where you phone from a booth and pay afterwards (by credit card or cash).

There is no shortage of public phones.

talking

**I will call back...**
le volveré a llamar...
*le bol-be-re a lya-mar...*

**later**
más tarde
*mas tar-de*

**tomorrow**
mañana
*man-ya-na*

**do you have a mobile phone?**
¿tiene móvil?
*tyen-e mo-beel*

**is it switched on?**
¿está encendido?
*es-ta en-then-dee-do*

**what is your mobile phone number?**
¿cuál es su número de móvil?
*kwal es soo noo-me-ro de mo-beel*

**my mobile number is...**
mi número de móvil es...
*mee noo-me-ro de mo-beel es...*

*There are a lot of internet cafés in Spain, particularly in student and tourist areas. Rates vary but typically you can expect to pay around 2 euros an hour. Staff are quite likely to have some knowledge of English and are generally quite helpful.*

internet café sign

**INTERNET**
OFERTAS DE BONOS

5 Horas por 12 €uros
(Te sale 25 minutos por 1 €uro)

15 Horas por 30 €uros
(Te sale 30 minutos por 1 €uro)

30 Horas por 50 €uros
(Te sale 36 minutos por 1 €uro)

Todos los bonos valen para un mes
incluido IVA

National and local tourist and what's-on information can be accessed via the internet.

Many places offer deals where you buy a number of hours in advance, which works out cheaper. However, check how many days you have to use up your hours – some offers are not as good as they look.

**ordenador**
*or-den-a-dor*
computer

**pantalla**
*pan-tal-ya*
screen

**ratón**
*ra-ton*
mouse

**teclado**
*tek-la-do*
keyboard

**anexo**
*a-neks-o*
attachment

**descargar**
*des-kar-gar*
download

**what is your e-mail address?**
¿cuál es su dirección de email?
*kwal es soo dee-rekth-yon de ee-meyl*

**my e-mail address is...**
mi dirección de email es...
*mee dee-rekth-yon de ee-meyl es...*

**caroline.smith@anycompany.co.uk**
caroline punto smith arroba anycompany punto co punto uk
*caroline poon-to smith ar-ro-ba anycompany poon-to co poon-to oo-ka*

**can I send an e-mail?**
¿puedo mandar un email?
*pwe-do man-dar oon ee-meyl*

**did you get my e-mail?**
¿le llegó mi email?
*le lyeg-o mee ee-meyl*

**can I send and receive e-mail here?**
¿puedo mandar y recibir email aquí?
*pwe-do man-dar ee reth-ee-beer ee-meyl a-kee*

**how much does an hour of netsurfing cost?**
¿cuánto es una hora de internet?
*kwan-to es oo-na o-ra de een-ter-net*

*Main post offices offer fax services. The cost is around 2 euros per page within Spain, and 6 euros to Europe. Faxes to North America can cost 12 euros per page. You usually also have to pay to receive a fax (around 50 cents a page). It is worth checking out internet cafés and shops and offices which carry the* **FAX PÚBLICO** *signs. These outlets would almost certainly be cheaper.*

prices

**keywords**

**mandar**
man-*dar*
send

**recibir**
reth-ee-*beer*
receive

**confirmar**
kon-feer-*mar*
confirm

**portada**
por-*ta*-da
cover page

**iniciar**
ee-neeth-*yar*
start

**error**
er-*ror*
error

| | |
|---|---|
| *date sent:* | **Fecha de envío:** |
| *time sent:* | **Hora de envío:** |
| *no. of pages including this:* | **Número de páginas incluida la portada:** |

| | |
|---|---|
| A | *to* |
| **Nombre:** | *name* |
| **Organización o depto.:** | *organisation or department* |
| **CC:** | *copy* |
| **Teléfono:** | *telephone no.* |
| **Fax:** | *fax* |

| | |
|---|---|
| ❑ **Urgente** | *urgent* |
| ❑ **Para revisar** | *to view* |
| ❑ **Se ruega comentar** | *please comment* |
| ❑ **Se ruega contestación** | *please reply* |

**talking**

**I want to send a fax**
quiero mandar un fax
*kyer*-o man-*dar* oon faks

**can I send a fax from here?**
¿puedo mandar un fax desde aquí?
*pwe*-do man-*dar* oon faks *des*-de a-kee

**how much is it to send a fax?**
¿cuánto cuesta mandar un fax?
*kwan*-to *kwes*-ta man-*dar* oon faks

**what is your fax number?**
¿cuál es su número de fax?
*kwal* es soo *noo*-me-ro de faks

**I'm trying to send a fax**
estoy intentando mandar un fax
es-*toy* een-ten-*tan*-do man-*dar* oon faks

**do you have a fax?**
¿tiene fax?
*tyen*-e faks

**can I receive a fax here?**
¿puedo recibir un fax aquí?
*pwe*-do reth-ee-*beer* oon faks a-kee

**it has ... pages**
tiene ... hojas
*tyen*-e ... *o*-khas

**please confirm your number**
confirme su número por favor
kon-*feer*-me soo *noo*-me-ro por fa-*bor*

**did you get my fax?**
¿le llegó mi fax?
le lyeg-*o* mee faks

# Out & About

*Normally you have to pay to enter galleries and museums, but minors, the unemployed and senior citizens sometimes get free admission. There are 3 dates worth mentioning when admission in some museums is free. These are: May 18th (International Museum Day), October 12th (Spanish National Holiday), and December 6th (Constitution Day). You can sometimes also get a discount with an International Student Card.*

Tourist information offices can help with local attractions, accommodation, transport, etc. There is usually at least one English speaker in the office.

You can get free maps from tourist offices.

There are no special deals to visit art galleries and museums except for the 3-gallery ticket to visit the Reina Sofía gallery, the Thyssen gallery and the Prado in Madrid.

**Museo Nacional Centro de Arte Reina Sofía**

the best **MADRID**

Most museums close one day a week, normally Monday. In this sign the museum is closed Tuesday.

**HORARIO**
De 10:00 a 21:00.
Domingos de 10:00 a 14:30
Martes Cerrado

Larger museums will have guided tours.

**VISITAS GUIADAS**

**PUNTO DE ENCUENTRO**

*meeting point*

**espectáculo**
*es-pek-ta-koo-lo*
show

**exposición**
*eks-po-seeth-yon*
exhibition

**excursión**
*eks-koors-yon*
trek, ramble

**cata de vinos**
*ka-ta de bee-nos*
wine tasting

**parque de atracciones**
*par-ke de at-rak-thyo-nes*
fun fair

**iglesia**
*ee-gles-ya*
church

**catedral**
*ka-ted-ral*
cathedral

**castillo**
*kas-teel-yo*
castle

**ayuntamiento**
*a-yoon-ta-myen-to*
town hall

In some larger museums, scanners are used to check bags. The large museums usually have cafeterias, gift shops and disabled access.

put in the scanner — **ENTREGAR AL SCANNER**
- **Mochilas** — rucksacks
- **Camaras** — cameras
- **Bolsos/as** — bags

**general signs**

exit — **SALIDA / EXIT**
bookshop — **LIBRERIA**
tickets — **TAQUILLAS**
cloakroom — **GUARDARROPA**
lecture theatre — **SALON DE ACTOS**
exhibitions — **EXPOSICIONES**

**CONSERVE SU ENTRADA HASTA LA SALIDA**

*keep your entry ticket until you leave*

**excuse me, where is the tourist office?**
¡oiga por favor! ¿dónde está la oficina de turismo?
*oy-ga por fa-bor don-de es-ta la o-fee-thee-na de too-rees-mo*

**do you have...?**
¿tiene...?
*tyen-e...*

**a town guide**
un mapa de la ciudad
*oon ma-pa de la thyoo-dad*

**leaflets in English**
folletos en inglés
*fol-ye-tos en een-gles*

**we'd like to visit...**
queríamos visitar...
*ke-ree-a-mos bee-see-tar...*

**how do we get there?**
¿cómo se llega hasta allí?
*ko-mo se lyeg-a as-ta al-yee*

**when can we visit the...?**
¿cuándo se puede ir a ver el/la...?
*kwan-do se pwe-de eer a ber el/la...*

**when does it close?**
¿cuándo cierra?
*kwan-do thyer-ra*

**is there a tour of the town?**
¿se puede hacer una visita guiada a la ciudad?
*se pwe-de a-ther oo-na bee-see-ta gee-a-da a la thyoo-dad*

Public sports facilities and accessibility are somewhat limited. On the coast, the possibilities are considerably greater than inland (e.g. hiring bikes, surfboards, pony trekking, etc.) National parks in Spain generally have walking and cycling trails. However, it is best not to leave the routes. If you are staying in a good hotel, you will probably have access to a swimming pool, tennis courts and a gym. Public swimming pools exist, but opening hours vary. You must wear a cap at all indoor pools, but usually don't have to in outdoor ones.

**diving forbidden**

**depth 2 metres**
It is not unusual for there to be no shallow end, so not all pools are suitable for children.

**PROFUNDIDAD 2.0 M**

**VESTUARIO**

**changing rooms**

Most tourist beaches have a lifeguard and a flag system. They are cleaned regularly and have shower (but not changing) facilities.

BUEN TIEMPO
GOOD WEATHER

PRECAUCIÓN
PRECAUTION

PELIGRO
DANGER

*police beach patrols*

*restricted swimming areas*

Prices for renting a sun lounger (**hamaca**) are per person per day.

**where can we...?**
¿dónde se puede...?
*don-de se pwe-de...*

**play tennis**
jugar al tenis
*khoo-gar al te-nees*

**go windsurfing**
hacer surfing
*a-ther soor-feeng*

**how much is it to...?**
¿cuánto cuesta...?
*kwan-to kwes-ta...*

**hire bikes**
alquilar bicis
*al-kee-lar bee-thees*

**per hour/day**
por hora/día
*por o-ra/dee-ya*

**is there a swimming pool?**
¿hay piscina?
*aee pees-thee-na*

**play golf**
jugar al golf
*khoo-gar al golf*

**go waterskiing**
hacer esquí acuático
*a-ther e-skee a-kwa-tee-ko*

**go riding**
montar a caballo
*mon-tar a ka-bal-yo*

**can we hire equipment?**
¿se puede alquilar el equipo?
*se pwe-de al-kee-lar el e-kee-po*

**where can we hire beach umbrellas?**
¿dónde se alquilan sombrillas?
*don-de se al-kee-lan som-breel-yas*

Spain's national parks offer trekking. Walks are well signposted and graded according to difficulty.

Sierra de Grazalema

Golf facilities, particularly on the Costa del Sol, are good, but can be expensive. You usually do not need to be a club member to play a round.

Signs are fairly easily understood and are given in English at the course (*campo de golf*).

**VISITANTES**

**away supporters**

**GOL**

**enclosure behind the goal**

**TRIBUNA**

side enclosures

**local football stadium**
Football is Spain's most popular spectator sport. The season runs Aug–May.

malaga FC club shop

The easiest way to buy tickets is direct from the stadium ticket booth an hour before kick-off. However, for big games you should try to buy a ticket in advance. Violence at matches is rare.

**we'd like to see a football match**
nos gustaría ver un partido de fútbol
*nos goos-ta-**ree**-ya ber oon par-**tee**-do de **foot**-bol*

**where can we get tickets?**
¿dónde se sacan las entradas?
***don**-de se **sa**-kan las en-**tra**-das*

**how do we get to the stadium?**
¿cómo se va al estadio?
***ko**-mo se ba al es-**tad**-yo*

**who is playing?**
¿quién juega?
*kyen **khwe**-ga*

**how much are they?**
¿cuánto cuestan?
***kwan**-to **kwes**-tan*

**what time is the match?**
¿a qué hora es el partido?
*a ke **o**-ra es el par-**tee**-do*

# Accommodation

*Accommodation is divided into several different categories: hotels, **pensiones** and **hostales**. There is not much difference between the latter two. They are usually owned by a live-in proprietor, like very large guest-houses. They do not provide meals.*

**RESERVAS HOTELES Y PENSIONES** — viajes brújula sa

You can find booking agencies at larger railway stations and airports.

The hotel star system goes from 1 to 5. For a 1 or 2 star **hostal**, accommodation will be basic,

sometimes with shared wash and WC facilities, but usually clean. For 3-star, expect en-suite and probably TV. For facilities such as meals, mini-bars and sports facilities, you should choose a hotel.

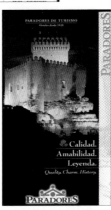

PARADORES DE TURISMO — Hoteles desde 1928

Calidad. Amabilidad. Leyenda.

*Quality. Charm. History.*

PARADORES

In addition to hotels, **hostales** and **pensiones**, there is a network of **paradores**, good quality hotels, usually set in gardens or the hotel itself being a monument or listed building.

## Booking in advance

The Spanish Tourist Office will be able to provide information on different types of accommodation. You can either book through them or phone up yourself once you have decided on where you want to stay.

**I want to book a room**
quiero reservar una habitación
*kyer-o re-ser-bar oo-na a-bee-tath-yon*

**single/double**
individual/doble
*een-dee-bee-dwal/dob-le*

**for ... nights**
para ... noches
*pa-ra ... no-ches*

**from ... to...**
del ... al...
*del ... al...*

**my name is...**
soy...
*soy...*

**I will fax to confirm**
se lo confirmaré por fax
*se lo kon-feer-ma-re por faks*

**my credit card number is...**
el número de mi tarjeta de crédito es...
*el noo-me-ro de mee tar-khe-ta de kre-dee-to es...*

**please can you fax me to confirm my booking?**
¿puede mandarme un fax para confirmar la reserva?
*pwe-de man-dar-me oon faks pa-ra kon-feer-mar la re-ser-ba*

*Pensiones* and *hostales*
are types of budget
accommodation. Both tend to
be family-run establishments.
Price often only includes bed.

There are also **HR, Hostal/
Hotel Residencial**, which take
long-term guests.

**reception**

**registration form**
You need to show your passport when
checking in. It may be kept overnight or
for the duration of your stay. If you need
it back, just ask. Reception staff often fill
out the registration form for you and just
ask you to sign it. If you do have to fill it
out yourself, it will probably be in English
as well as Spanish.

You only get room service in hotels.
There should be instructions in English by
your room phone regarding room service.

---

**do you have a ... room?**
¿tiene una habitación...?
**tyen**-e **oo**-na a-bee-tath-**yon**...

**can I see the room?**
¿puedo ver la habitación?
**pwe**-do ber la a-bee-tath-**yon**

| **single** | **double** | **double-bedded** | **family** |
|---|---|---|---|
| individual | doble | de matrimonio | familiar |
| een-dee-bee-**dwal** | **dob**-le | de mat-ree-**mon**-yo | fa-meel-**yar** |

**with ensuite bath**
con baño
kon **ban**-yo

**with shower**
con ducha
kon **doo**-cha

**for tonight**
para esta noche
pa-ra **es**-ta **no**-che

**for one night**
para una noche
pa-ra **oo**-na **no**-che

**for ... nights**
para ... noches
pa-ra ... **no**-ches

**is breakfast included?**
¿es con desayuno?
es kon de-sa-**yoo**-no

**how much is half board?**
¿cuánto cuesta con media pensión?
**kwan**-to **kwes**-ta kon **med**-ya pen-**syon**

**with full board?**
¿con pensión completa?
kon pen-**syon** kom-**ple**-ta

**can I have my passport back?**
¿me puede devolver el pasaporte?
me **pwe**-de de-bol-**ber** el pa-sa-**por**-te

*talking talking talking*

In self-catering accommodation, if you are using gas it will probably be bottled rather than from a mains supply. It is a good idea to turn this off every night, by flicking the switch on the top of the bottle. Plugs are 2-pinned and 220 volt/50 Hz, the same as the rest of continental Europe. Be careful: some places still operate 125 or 110 volt (in such cases the sockets should be labelled), in which case you will need a transformer for British appliances.

ALQUILER DE APARTAMENTOS

If you arrive in Spain with no accommodation and want to go self-catering, look for the signs **Alquiler de apartamentos** (apartments to rent).

Rubbish is collected from bins in the streets daily (usually at night). Recycling bins are often available. This one takes all kinds of glass (**vidrio**). There is no distinction between which colours.

Recycling is now part of Spanish life.

*only containers and packaging (plastic, tins, etc.)*

**paper recycling**

*only paper and cardboard*

**battery recycling containers**

*only biodegradable material*

**líquido**
**lavavajillas**
*lee-kee-do*
*la-ba-ba-kheel-yas*
washing-up liquid

**detergente**
*de-ter-khen-te*
washing powder

**jabón**
*kha-bon*
soap

**abrelatas**
*a-bre-la-tas*
tin-opener

**velas**
*be-las*
candles

**cerillas**
*ther-eel-yas*
matches

**bombona de**
**gas/butano**
*bom-bo-na de*
*gas/boo-ta-no*
gas cylinder

You can get leaflets about youth hostels from the local Spanish tourist office.

Youth hostels in Spain vary greatly in quality and service. You can book in advance in most of them. Visit www.europeanhostels.com for more information.

eating hours
breakfast (**desayuno**)
lunch (**almuerzo**)
dinner (**cena**)

**HORARIO DE COMEDOR**

| | | |
|---|---|---|
| DESAYUNO: | 8'30H. | A  10'00H. |
| ALMUERZO: | 14'00H. | A  15'00H. |
| CENA: | 20'30H. | A  21'30H. |

**there is/are no...**
no hay...
*no aee...*

**how does ... work?**
¿cómo funciona ...?
*ko-mo foonth-yo-na...*

**can you show us how this works?**
¿nos enseña cómo funciona?
*nos en-sen-ya ko-mo foonth-yo-na*

**the cooker**
la cocina
*la ko-thee-na*

**the dishwasher**
el lavavajillas
*el la-ba-ba-kheel-yas*

**the washing machine**
la lavadora
*la la-ba-dor-a*

**the microwave**
el microondas
*el meek-ro-on-das*

**who do I contact if there are problems?**
¿a quién aviso si hay algún problema?
*a kyen a-bee-so see aee al-goon prob-le-ma*

**when is the rubbish collected?**
¿cuándo recogen la basura?
*kwan-do re-ko-khen la ba-soo-ra*

**where do we leave the rubbish?**
¿dónde se deja la basura?
*don-de se de-kha la ba-soo-ra*

**can you give us another key?**
¿nos puede dar otra llave?
*nos pwe-de dar o-tra lya-be*

# Camping

*Campsites in Spain are given either 1st-class (1ª), 2nd-class (2ª) or 3rd-class (3ª) ratings. Even the third grade sites usually have hot showers, a cafeteria and electrical hook-ups. The first-grade sites often have heated swimming pools, laundry service, restaurants, etc. You usually pay per tent, per person and per car/caravan. Sites can get very busy in July and August, when it is advisable to book in advance. In tourist areas, staff will probably speak English. Prices in cafés and shops on sites can be a little on the high side.*

Tourist offices have information on local campsites and should also be able to help with bookings.

### camping sign

Remember the limit is 10km/h not 10mph.

no dogs

no vehicles between 11pm and 7am.

no sounding horn

---

**we are looking for a campsite**
estamos buscando un camping
*es-ta-mos boos-kan-do oon kam-peen*

**have you any vacancies?**
¿tienen sitio?
*tyen-en seet-yo*

**we want to stay for ... nights**
queremos quedarnos ... noches
*ke-re-mos ke-dar-nos ... no-ches*

**where should we pitch the tent?**
¿dónde ponemos la tienda?
*don-de se po-ne-mos la tyen-da*

**how much is it?**
¿cuánto cuesta?
*kwan-to kwes-ta*

**per tent**
por tienda
*por tyen-da*

**per caravan**
por caravana
*por ka-ra-ba-na*

**where are...?**
¿dónde están...?
*don-de es-tan...*

**the showers**
las duchas
*las doo-chas*

**the toilets**
los servicios
*los ser-beeth-yos*

**is there a restaurant on the campsite?**
¿hay restaurante en el camping?
*a-ee res-tow-ran-te en el kam-peen*

**do you have a more sheltered site?**
¿tienen algún sitio más resguardado?
*tyen-en al-goon seet-yo mas res-gwar-da-do*

**can we camp here overnight?**
¿podemos acampar aquí para pasar la noche?
*po-de-mos a-kam-par a-kee pa-ra pa-sar la no-che*

site price list

launderette/dry cleaners

laundry service at campsite

## Speed restrictions for caravans and trailers

| | |
|---|---|
| built up area | 50 km/h (C/T) |
| ordinary roads | 80 km/h (C/T) |
| dual carriageway | 90 km/h (C); |
| | 80 km/h (T) |
| motorway | 90 km/h (C); |
| | 80 km/h (T) |

C = caravans
T = trailers

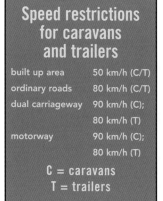

**is there a launderette near here?**
¿hay alguna lavandería automática por aquí cerca?
*aee al-goo-na la-ban-de-ree-ya ow-to-ma-tee-ka por a-kee ther-ka*

**where can I do some washing?**
¿dónde puedo lavar algo de ropa?
*don-de pwe-do la-bar al-go de ro-pa*

**can I do some washing?**
¿puedo lavar algo de ropa?
*pwe-do la-bar al-go de ro-pa*

**can I borrow an iron?**
¿me pueden dejar una plancha?
*me pwe-den de-khar oo-na plan-cha*

**when will my things be ready?**
¿para cuándo estarán mis cosas?
*pa-ra kwan-do es-ta-ran mees ko-sas*

talking talking

*Access for the disabled in Spain is poor and needs to be checked out carefully before your trip. The British organisation RADAR is worth contacting for their publication on travel abroad for disabled people. You can also visit their website **www.radar.org.uk**. It also has links to other useful sites. In Spain, wheelchair access to buses exists but the number of buses and routes covered is limited. Although public buildings may well have ramps, once you are inside, you may find that the toilet facilities are on the first floor only.*

Some buses have wheelchair access: check for the sign at the door.

Large supermarkets usually have trolleys for the disabled.

EXCEPTO/EXCEPT FOR

Ramp to get on to the beach.

Disabled parking is clearly signed but once parked, you may find general accessibility difficult.

**are there any disabled toilets?**
¿hay aseos para minusválidos?
*aee a-**se**-os **pa**-ra mee-noos-**ba**-lee-dos*

**is there a wheelchair-accessible entrance?**
¿hay acceso para sillas de ruedas?
*aee ak-**the**-so **pa**-ra **seel**-yas de **rwed**-as*

**is it possible to visit ... with a wheelchair?**
¿se puede entrar en ... con silla de ruedas?
*se **pwe**-de en-**trar** en ... kon **seel**-ya de **rwed**-as*

**is there a reduction for the disabled?**
¿hay descuento para minusválidos?
*aee des-**kwen**-to **pa**-ra mee-noos-**ba**-lee-dos*

**I need a bedroom on the ground floor**
necesito una habitación en la planta baja
*neth-es-**ee**-to **oo**-na a-bee-ta-th**yon** en la **plan**-ta **ba**-kha*

**I use a wheelchair**
uso silla de ruedas
*oo-so **seel**-ya de **rwe**-das*

**where is the lift?**
¿dónde está el ascensor?
***don**-de es-**ta** el as-then-**sor***

talking talking

# With Kids

*In Spain children are welcome almost everywhere. They will often be out with the family until very late at night. Children under 4 go free on trains and buses. On trains, they pay only 60% of the adult fare if between 4 and 11 years old. All children must be secured in the car at all times, using any of a variety of seatbelts/chairs, etc.*

**keywords keywords keywords**

**niño**
*neen-yo*
child

**asiento del bebé**
*as-yen-to del be-be*
baby seat

**trona**
*tro-na*
high chair

**cuna**
*koo-na*
cot

**parque infantil**
*par-ke een-fan-teel*
play park

**pañales**
*pan-ya-les*
nappies

The best place to buy baby food, nappies, etc, is in supermarkets, hypermarkets or chemists'.

Most large super-markets have little play trolleys for children (**carritos para niños**).

Hypermarkets and larger motorway services often have play areas and baby-changing facilities.

**talking talking talking**

**where can I change the baby?**
¿dónde puedo cambiar al niño?
*don-de pwe-do kamb-yar al neen-yo*

**a child's ticket**
un billete de niño
*oon beel-ye-te de neen-yo*

**do you have...?**
¿tiene...?
*tyen-e...*

**a high chair**
una trona
*oo-na tro-na*

**a cot**
una cuna
*oo-na koo-na*

**do you sell nappies?**
¿vende pañales?
*ben-de pan-ya-les*

**baby wipes**
toallitas infantiles
*to-al-yee-tas een-fan-tee-les*

**baby food**
potitos
*po-tee-tos*

**is there a children's menu?**
¿hay un menú para niños?
*aee oon me-noo pa-ra neen-yos*

**a small portion**
una ración pequeña
*oo-na rath-yon pe-ken-ya*

**is there a play park near here?**
¿hay algún parque infantil por aquí cerca?
*aee al-goon par-ke een-fan-teel por a-kee ther-ka*

# Health

*The old E111 form has been replaced with a new European Health Insurance Card – apply at the post office or online at **www.dh.gov.uk**. As well as pharmacies, Spain has **parafarmacias** (pa-ra-far-**math**-yas) which sell many of the same things but cheaper.*

If you need to see a doctor, simply visit the nearest clinic and ask for an appointment. Make sure you are being treated as a National Health patient and not privately. You usually need to go in the morning (9am) to get a ticket for an appointment later that day. It is not usual to phone or book from one day to the next. Many doctors speak some English, but don't take this for granted.

All dental provision is private. Simply book an appointment, but it is advisable to get a quote in advance for any work to be done.

pharmacy

Chemists sell medical items for which you often don't need a doctor's prescription. A chemist's is a good place to seek advice for minor ailments and suggested non-prescription medicines (including some antibiotics).

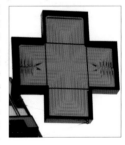

**where is there a chemist?**
¿dónde hay una farmacia?
*don-de aee oo-na far-math-ya*

**have you something for...?**
¿tiene algo para...?
*tyen-e al-go pa-ra...*

**an upset stomach**
la indigestión
*la een-dee-khest-yon*

**sunburn**
las quemaduras del sol
*las ke-ma-doo-ras del sol*

**diarrhoea**
la diarrea
*la dee-ar-re-a*

**a headache**
el dolor de cabeza
*el do-lor de ka-be-tha*

**I have cystitis**
tengo cistitis
*ten-go thees-tee-tees*

**I need antibiotics**
necesito antibióticos
*neth-e-see-to an-tee-bee-yo-tee-kos*

talking

**first aid**

Each town has a 'duty chemist'. Every chemist will list the duty chemist rota (**Farmacia de Guardia**) in their window or posted nearby. You can also find this list in local newspapers, including English language ones.

**I am not well**
me encuentro mal
*me en-kwen-tro mal*

**he/she is not well**
no se encuentra bien
*no se en-kwen-tra byen*

**I need to see a doctor**
necesito un médico
*neth-e-see-to oon med-ee-ko*

**we need a doctor to come out**
necesitamos que venga un médico
*neth-e-see-ta-mos ke ben-ga oon med-ee-ko*

**please call the doctor**
llame al médico por favor
*lyam-e al med-ee-ko por fa-bor*

**my child is ill**
mi hijo está enfermo
*mee ee-kho es-ta en-fer-mo*

**I have a pain here**
me duele aquí
*me dwe-le a-kee*

**I am on this medication**
estoy tomando estos medicamentos
*es-toy to-man-do es-tos me-dee-ka-men-tos*

**I'm pregnant**
estoy embarazada
*es-toy em-ba-ra-tha-da*

**I am on the pill**
estoy tomando la píldora
*es-toy to-man-do la peel-do-ra*

**I'm breastfeeding**
estoy dando el pecho
*es-toy dan-do el pech-o*

**I have an infected finger**
tengo el dedo infectado
*ten-go el ded-o een-fek-ta-do*

**I'm diabetic**
soy diabético/a
*soy dee-a-be-tee-ko/a*

**I'm allergic to...**
soy alérgico/a a...
*soy a-ler-khee-ko/a a...*

**I've high blood pressure**
tengo la tensión alta
*ten-go la ten-syon al-ta*

**is this covered by Social Security?**
¿esto lo cubre la Seguridad Social?
*es-to lo koob-re la se-goo-ree-dad soth-yal*

**I need a receipt for my insurance**
necesito un recibo para el seguro
*neth-e-see-to oon re-thee-bo pa-ra el se-goo-ro*

**how much will it cost?**
¿cuánto va a costar?
*kwan-to ba a kos-tar*

**I need a dentist**
necesito un dentista
*ne-thes-ee-to oon den-tees-ta*

**I have toothache**
me duelen las muelas
*me dwe-len las mwe-las*

**can you repair my dentures?**
¿puede arreglarme la dentadura postiza?
*pwe-de ar-reg-lar-me la den-ta-doo-ra pos-tee-tha*

**I need a temporary filling**
necesito un empaste provisional
*neth-e-see-to oon em-pas-te pro-bee-syo-nal*

**I have an abscess**
tengo un absceso
*ten-go oon ab-thes-o*

talking talking talking talking talking talking talking

*Accident and Emergency (**Urgencias**) operate pretty much the same as in the UK. You will need to complete a registration form at reception and this will be in Spanish only.*

**road sign to hospital**

The ambulance service is private. Contact numbers are available in local phone directories, tourist information offices and chemist's. For the emergency ambulance, call 061.

**accident & emergency**

**to all wards**

**Pabellón A**

***Pabellón** means section*

## If you need to go to hospital

Make sure you take with you your health insurance card and passport. If you do not do this, you will be charged as a private patient and will be unlikely to get your money back.

**will he/she have to go to hospital?**
¿tendrá que ir al hospital?
*ten-**dra** ke eer al os-pee-**tal***

**where is the hospital?**
¿dónde está el hospital?
***don**-de es-**ta** el os-pee-**tal***

**I need to go to casualty**
necesito ir a urgencias
*neth-s-**see**-to eer a oor-**khenth**-yas*

**please take me to the nearest hospital**
por favor me lleva al hospital más cercano
*por fa-**bor** me **lyeb**-a al os-pee-**tal** mas ther-**ka**-no*

**when are visiting hours?**
¿cuáles son las horas de visita?
***kwal**-es son las **o**-ras de bee-**see**-ta*

**which ward?**
¿qué planta?
*ke **plan**-ta*

**can you explain what is the matter?**
¿me puede explicar qué pasa?
*me **pwe**-de eks-plee-**kar** ke **pa**-sa*

# Emergency

*i* *There are several police forces in Spain: **Guardia Civil** (for countryside, roads and borders), **Policía Nacional** (for provincial capitals and large towns) and **Policía Municipal/local** (for local bylaws). The **Guardia Civil** deal with traffic accidents and offences, but local parking offences fall to the **Policía Municipal**. The Basque Country, Catalonia and Galicia also have their own police. All carry guns. The emergency number for the local police is 092. If you have to report an accident or crime, you will have to fill in a form in Spanish.*

**help!**
¡socorro!
*so-**kor**-ro*

**can you help me?**
¿me puede ayudar?
*me **pwe**-de a-yoo-**dar***

**please call...**
por favor llame a...
*por fa-**bor** lya-me a...*

**the police**
la policía
*la po-lee-**thee**-a*

**an ambulance**
una ambulancia
***oo**-na am-boo-**lanth**-ya*

**fire!**
¡fuego!
***fwe**-go*

**please call the fire brigade**
por favor llame a los bomberos
*por fa-**bor** lya-me a los bom-**be**-ros*

**my ... has been stolen**
me han robado...
*me an ro-**ba**-do...*

**I want to report a theft**
quiero denunciar un robo
***kyer**-o de-noon-**thyar** oon **ro**-bo*

**here are my insurance details**
aquí tienen mis datos del seguro
*a-**kee** tyen-en mees **da**-tos del se-**goo**-ro*

**where is the police station/the hospital?**
¿dónde está la comisaría/el hospital?
***don**-de es-**ta** la kom-ee-sa-**ree**-a/el os-pee-**tal***

**I would like to phone...**
quería llamar a...
*kee-**ree**-ya lya-**mar** a...*

**my car has been broken into**
me han entrado en el coche
*me an en-**tra**-do en el **ko**-che*

**please give me your insurance details**
¿me puede dar sus datos del seguro
*me **pwe**-de dar soos **da**-tos del se-**goo**-ro*

**I need a report for my insurance**
necesito un informe para el seguro
*neth-e-**see**-to oon een-for-me **pa**-ra el se-**goo**-ro*

# Food
# &
# Drink

# Spanish Food

*It is very easy to find something to eat in Spain almost any time and anywhere. Food is not particularly expensive and eating snacks rather than full meals is common and popular. Breakfast is normally light, consisting of coffee/milk with bread and olive oil or butter. The main meal is still eaten at lunchtime (2–3pm) and this is very much a family event. Lunches are usually 3-course meals, with the second course often being a piece of meat with no accompaniment. When people eat in the evening, either at home or out, their meal may not start until 10pm or later. Traditional Spanish food uses lots of fresh produce – meat, salads, fish and olive oil. In the north and interior there is more emphasis on stews, using lentils, chickpeas and a lot of meat.*

Bars serve drinks, coffee and breakfasts Spanish-style. They may also offer **tapas**, **pinchos** (snacks) and **bocadillos** (sandwiches).

A **mesón** is a traditional-style tavern restaurant.

*Cafeterías* serve some dishes as well as toasted sandwiches and **pasteles** (cakes). **Platos combinados** consist normally of meat or fish with rice, potatoes or chips and vegetables, i.e. a full dish.

**Bodega** means wine cellar. It is rather like a wine bar which serves some food.

dining room

**Comedor**

breakfasts and meals

| | |
|---|---|
| small | PEQUEÑA |
| medium | MEDIANA |
| large | GRANDE |

At restaurants, be prepared to spend time at the table. You can order
à la carte or opt for the set menu, in which case you will be served more
quickly. But take into consideration the large portions generally served.
In Spain salads and vegetable dishes are considered as separate items and
normally brought to the table before the main dish. Bread is always provided
but not butter. Flexibility is often the key here. For example, if you want boiled
potatoes instead of chips, ask and they will probably be able to do it.

RESTAURANTE
EL ANCLA
**PESCAITOS - PESCADOS - MARISCOS Y CARNES**

fried fish          fish          shellfish          meat

It is normal to pay
for drinks as you
leave the bar.
However, in some
outdoor cafés, the
waiter will present
you with the bill as
he gives you the
drink and you are
expected to pay
there and then.

**where can we have a snack?**
¿dónde se puede comer algo?
*don*-de se **pwe**-de ko-**mer** **al**-go

**can you recommend a good restaurant?**
¿puede recomendarnos algún buen restaurante?
**pwe**-de re-ko-men-**dar**-nos al-**goon** bwen rest-ow-**ran**-te

**are there any vegetarian restaurants?**
¿hay algún restaurante vegetariano?
aee al-**goon** rest-ow-**ran**-te be-khe-tar-**ya**-no

**do we need to book a table?**
¿es necesario reservar mesa?
es neth-es-**ar**-yo re-ser-**bar** **me**-sa

**what dishes do you recommend?**
¿qué platos nos recomienda?
ke **pla**-tos nos re-kom-**yen**-da

**how do we get to the restaurant?**
¿cómo se va al restaurante?
**ko**-mo se ba al rest-ow-**ran**-te

talking talking talking

*i* There is no shortage of places to eat, from restaurants to **tapas** bars and pizzerias to cafés. If you want international cuisine, you'll find foreign restaurants on the coast, in major cities and in large hotels; Italian food is widely available. A popular and inexpensive alternative is the tapas bar – you'll find these wherever you go. Many offer a **Menú del día** which is a limited selection of basic fare in the form of a 3-course meal, often including bread and wine. At around 7 euros a head they are very good value. See pp. 84–85 for **tapas**.

Kiosks are good for soft drinks, crisps, sweets and ice creams.

Snacks are often sold on the street, especially in shopping areas and during fiestas.

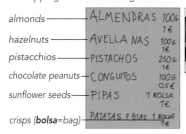

| | |
|---|---|
| almonds | ALMENDRAS 100G  1€ |
| hazelnuts | AVELLANAS 100G  1€ |
| pistacchios | PISTACHOS 250G  1€ |
| chocolate peanuts | CONGUITOS 100G  0,5€ |
| sunflower seeds | PIPAS 1 BOLSA  1€ |
| crisps (**bolsa**=bag) | PATATAS FRITAS 1 BOLSA  1€ |

Beach bars/restaurants are called **chiringuitos**.

## I'd like a ... please
quería un/una ... por favor
*ke-**ree**-ya oon/**oo**-na ... por fa-**bor***

**a white coffee**
un café con leche
*oon ka-**fe** kon **le**-che*

**an espresso**
un café solo
*oon ka-**fe** **so**-lo*

**a decaff coffee**
un café descafeinado
*oon ka-**fe** des-ka-feyn-**a**-do*

**a hot chocolate**
un chocolate
*oon cho-ko-**la**-te*

**a tea with milk (on the side)**
un té con leche (aparte)
*oon te kon **le**-che (a-**par**-te)*

**an orange juice (fresh)**
un zumo de naranja (natural)
*oon **thoo**-mo de na-**ran**-kha (na-too-**ral**)*

**an apple juice**
un zumo de manzana
*oon **thoo**-mo de man-**tha**-na*

**a red wine**
un tinto
*oon **teen**-to*

**a white wine**
un vino blanco
*oon **bee**-no **blan**-ko*

**a half lager**
una caña
*oo-na **kan**-ya*

**a bottle of mineral water**
una botella de agua mineral
*oo-na bo-**tel**-ya de **ag**-wa mee-ne-**ral***

**fizzy**
con gas
*kon gas*

**still**
sin gas
*seen gas*

talking talking

**GOFRES**

**HELADOS · GRANIZADOS**

**REFRESCOS ·**

waffles • ice creams
iced drinks • cold soft drinks

A popular breakfast dish is thick hot chocolate with *churros* (fried batter sticks) for dipping. It is also a popular snack in the late afternoon (*merienda*).

Ordering a tea with milk will often get you a teabag put into hot milk; tea with cold milk is *un té con leche fría aparte*. Coffee comes in many varieties; the most common is *café con leche* (*coffee with milk*); *café solo* (*black coffee*) is very strong and served in a very small cup. If you want decaffeinated coffee, be careful that you ask for *descafeinado de máquina* (*from the espresso machine*) or you are likely to get a cup of warm milk and a sachet of Nescafé.

Beer in Spain means lager. Local brews are very good. You can order a bottle (*un botellín*) or a draft beer (*una caña*), normally quite a small measure. In major cities and tourist areas, you can find UK-style pubs where there is a larger selection of imported but expensive beers and wines.

**can we eat?**
¿podemos comer?
*po-**de**-mos ko-**mer***

**what can we eat?**
¿qué podemos comer?
*ke po-**de**-mos ko-**mer***

**do you have a dish of the day?**
¿tiene un menú del día?
***tyen**-e oon me-**noo** del **dee**-ya*

**what is the dish of the day?**
¿cuál es el plato del día?
*kwal es el **pla**-to del **dee**-a*

**what sandwiches do you have?**
¿qué bocadillos tiene?
*ke bo-ka-**deel**-yos **tyen**-e*

**what cakes do you have?**
¿qué pasteles tiene?
*ke pas-**te**-les **tyen**-e*

**I would like ice cream**
quería un helado
*ke-**ree**-ya oon e-**la**-do*

**what flavours are there?**
¿qué sabores hay?
*ke sa-**bor**-es aee*

talking

*Sampling the many tastes and textures of Spanish food couldn't be easier: just stop at a bar (**bar**) and order **tapas**. Tapas seem to have originated in Andalusia, but they are a way of life in the whole of Spain and have become fashionable even outside the country. They have the advantage of allowing you to taste lots of dishes at once, because, even though they can just be appetizers such as cured ham (**jamón serrano**) or cheese, they are often small portions of main dishes. In fact almost any dish can be served as a **tapa**: for instance, meat balls in sauce (**albóndigas**), squid rings fried in batter (**calamares fritos**), tripe (**callos**) and many more. Often each person orders two or three different **tapas**, so if you are eating with a group of friends you will have a dozen or so mini dishes to share. Tapas are ideal as a quick snack or light meal – often very welcome when you consider how late the meals are served in Spain.*

**ESPECIALIDAD TAPAS**

In **tapas** bars, there are usually two sets of prices, the lower one for sitting at the bar and the other for sitting at a table. If you are at the bar, ordering **tapas** is simply a matter of pointing at what you want. If you only want a drink, particularly during the day, you may find you are asked if you want something to eat. A **tapa** is a small serving, sometimes very small. A **ración** is a larger amount (served on a slightly bigger plate) which you might order if there were a group of you eating together. You will also see the word **pincho** which is a kind of **tapa** served on a cocktail stick.

**Tortilla**

Spanish omelette cooked with fried sliced potatoes. This is often served as a **tapa**, but can also be ordered as a main dish. Variations can be cooked with tuna fish, asparagus and prawns.

A selection of **tapas**: toasted bread with sardines, tomatoes with anchovies and toasted bread with black pudding.

**croquetas**
*(fish or meat croquettes)*

**chorizo**
*(spicy salami-type sausage)*

**calamares fritos**
*(squid in batter)*

**chanquetes**
*(whitebait)*

**queso**
*(cheese)*

**almejas**
*(clams)*

**aceitunas**
*(olives)*

**gambas**
*(prawns)*

**jamón serrano**
*(cured ham)*

**patatas bravas**
*(fried potato cubes with spicy tomato sauce)*

### Tapas y Raciones

|   |           | TAPA | RACIÓN |
|---|-----------|------|--------|
| 1 | ESTOFADO  | 2,85 | 4,30   |

A *ración* is a larger serving of **tapas**.

**do you have tapas?**
¿tiene tapas?
*tyen-e ta-pas*

**what tapas do you have?**
¿qué tapas tiene?
*ke ta-pas tyen-e*

**a portion of that and that**
una ración de eso y eso
*oo-na rath-yon de es-o ee es-o*

**what tapas do you recommend?**
¿qué tapas nos recomienda?
*ke ta-pas nos re-kom-yen-da*

**what is this?**
¿qué es eso?
*ke es es-o*

talking

*i* *To get the bill, catch the waiter's attention either through eye contact or by slightly raising your hand. Service is rarely included and if sitting at a table, you are expected to add around 5%, something which is not automatic if you are at the bar. Smoking is banned in bars and restaurants as of 2006.*

Options are limited if you are vegetarian. Menus are predominantly meat- or fish-based and even 'vegetable' dishes, soups and salads need to be checked for ingredients. It's worth telling the waiter that you don't eat animal products (***no como productos animales***). Simply saying you are vegetarian may not help, as ham and chicken is often not considered meat. ***Tapas*** bars are probably your safest bet as you can see the food before you order it and there are often dishes which contain only one vegetable or item. In Madrid, Barcelona and some tourist areas you will find the occasional vegetarian restaurant.

**tomato salad with onions and olives**

***jarra de rosado***
*(carafe of rosé)*

***pimienta*** *(pepper)*

***sal*** *(salt)*

***cuenta*** *(bill)*
***propina*** *(tip)*

**I would like to book a table**
quería reservar una mesa
*ke-**ree**-ya re-ser-**bar** **oo**-na **me**-sa*

**for tonight**
para esta noche
*pa-ra **es**-ta **no**-che*

**for lunch**
para comer
*pa-ra ko-**mer***

**at 8.30**
a las ocho y media
*a las **o**-cho ee **med**-ya*

**in the name of Smith**
a nombre de Smith
*a **nomb**-re de smith*

**for 4 people**
para cuatro personas
*pa-ra **kwat**-ro per-**so**-nas*

**for tomorrow night**
para mañana por la noche
*pa-ra man-**ya**-na por la **no**-che*

**at 2 o'clock**
a las dos
*a las dos*

**at 9 o'clock**
a las nueve
*a las **nwe**-be*

**talking talking**

*Paella* has become a dish that is served all over Spain though it originated around Valencia. Different regions of Spain vary the *paella* according to the local produce. Vegetables, meat and chicken are found in the *paellas* of interior Spain. Valencia and Barcelona combine sea foods with chicken and vegetables. Saffron is another ingredient of the dish. The name comes from the iron *paellera* (*pan*) with two handles in which the rice is cooked and served. You can generally only order it for a minimum of two people.

**the menu please**
la carta por favor
la **kar**-ta por fa-**bor**

**the wine list please**
la carta de vinos por favor
la **kar**-ta de **bee**-nos por fa-**bor**

**do you have a children's menu?**
¿tienen menú para niños?
**tyen**-en me-**noo pa**-ra **neen**-yos

**for a starter I will have...**
de primero quiero...
de preem-**er**-o **kyer**-o...

**for a main dish I will have...**
de segundo quiero...
de se-**goon**-do **kyer**-o...

**what vegetarian dishes do you have?**
¿qué platos vegetarianos tienen?
ke **pla**-tos ve-khe-tar-**ya**-nos **tyen**-en

**what desserts do you have?**
¿qué postres tienen?
ke **post**-res **tyen**-en

**some tap water please**
¿me da agua del grifo?
me da **ag**-wa del **gree**-fo

**some more bread please**
más pan por favor
mas pan por fa-**bor**

**the bill please**
la cuenta por favor
la **kwen**-ta por fa-**bor**

**we would like to pay separately**
queremos pagar por separado
ke-**re**-mos pa-**gar** por se-pa-**ra**-do

talking talking talking talking talking

*i* Some menus exist in the form of a blackboard on the wall of the restaurant for dish-of-the-day-type meals. Other menus (**cartas**) include different categories of food: **tapas y raciones**, **platos combinados**, etc.

# PLATOS COMBINADOS

**Platos combinados** consist normally of meat or fish with rice, potatoes or chips and vegetables, i.e. a full dish.

If what you order isn't a **plato combinado** and you order, for example, a piece of fish, you will only get fish. The waiter will usually ask you if you want it with chips or vegetables.

**solomillo adobado**
*marinated sirloin*
**patatas a lo pobre**
*potatoes cooked in garlic & parsley*

**filetes de rosada**
*rock fish*
**cogollos de lechugas**
*lettuce hearts*

**pechugas de pollo**
*chicken breasts*
**huevos fritos**
*fried eggs*

**potaje del dia**
*soup of the day*

*choice of smoked meats with gherkins & anchovies*

*dessert: cake, ice-cream or fruit*

*main meals (from 12.30 to 6pm)*

**PLATOS COMBINADOS (de 12'30 a 18'00 horas)**

1. **Solomillo adobado, huevos fritos, patatas a lo pobre y pimientos** .............9,05
2. **Filetes de rosada a la parilla, cogollos de lechugas, espárragos verdes con vinagreta**............8,45
3. **Pechugas de pollo a la plancha, croquetas, patatas fritas y salsa de tomate**............7,25
4. **Salteado de verduras de temporada, espárragos y jamón en juliana**............7,25
5. **Ensalada de pimientos con frituras de boquerones y adobo de rosada**............7,25
6. **Entrecot de ternera a la plancha con arroz blanco y rodajas de tomate**............10,85
7. **Huevos fritos con bacon, salchichas y pimientos fritos** ............7,25
8. **Escalope de ternera con ensaladilla rusa y pimientos del Piquillo**............10,25
9. **Cucharon potaje del día** ............6,00
10. **Selección de ahumados con pepinillos y anchoas** ............11,45

**POSTRE: Tarta, Helado o Fruta**............3,35

**menus**

*breakfasts and snacks*

***infusiones variadas***
*selection of herbal teas*

*glass of milk*

*coffee with cream*

*coffee with a dash
of brandy*

*tea*

**con suizo** *with a bun*

**con tostadas**
*with toast*

*sponge cake soaked
in wine
and syrup*

**ensaimada** *spiral bun*
**torta** *cake*

*full breakfast*

### DESAYUNOS Y MERIENDAS

| | |
|---|---:|
| Café, Descafeinado, Infusiones Varias | 1,40 |
| Chocolate | 1,70 |
| Vaso de Leche | 1,30 |
| Café Vienés | 2,40 |
| Café con Nata | 1,80 |
| Carajillo | 2,10 |
| Capuchino | 2,40 |
| Café Irlandés | 5,30 |
| Té Americano | 2,00 |
| Café o Te con Suizo | 2,10 |
| Café o Té con Tostadas | 3,35 |
| Borrachuelos | 2,90 |
| Croissant, Ensaimada, Torta o Suizo | 1,95 |
| Plum Cake | 2,80 |
| Desayuno Completo | 7,80 |

**jamón York**
*cooked ham*

**jamón serrano**
*cured ham*

| SÁNDWICH | | |
|---|---|---:|
| *toasted sandwich* | Vegetal | 3,75 |
| | Jamón y Queso | 3,90 |
| | J. York o Chorizo o Salchichón | 4,20 |

| BOCADILLO | | |
|---|---|---:|
| *sandwich usually* | Atún | 3,90 |
| *with french bread* | J. Serrano | 4,75 |
| | Pollo | 3,90 |

## La Carta

The menu will indicate the various types of dishes served, dividing them into categories, i.e. soups, starters, fish dishes, and so on, in more or less detail, according to the type of restaurant.

**Entremeses** *Starters (also* **entrantes fríos** *or* **calientes** *– starters, cold or hot)*

**Sopas** *Soups*

**Plato del día** *Dish of the day*

**Primer plato** *First course*

**Ensalada** *Salad*

**Verduras** *Vegetables*

**Huevos** *Egg dishes*

**Revueltos** *Scrambled eggs (generally cooked with something like mushrooms, asparagus or spinach)*

**Pastas** *Pasta dishes*

**Arroz** *Rice dishes. (Many rice dishes, such as paella, are normally only prepared for a minimum of two people)*

**Parrilladas** *Grilled food*

**Pescados** *Fish dishes*

**Carnes** *Meats*

**Postres** *Desserts*

**Quesos** *Cheeses*

# Wine

*In Britain when we think of Spanish wine we tend to think of Rioja, but there is far more to explore in Spain than big, beefy, powerfully alcoholic, oaky reds. No country is more diverse: there are wines to be found here that mirror those of Australia, California and Bordeaux, and many more with a unique character, totally Spanish. Quality is soaring as Spanish winemakers get to grips with new techniques and international taste. Dig deep and be adventurous.*

1994

## RIOJA
DENOMINACIÓN DE ORIGEN

## EL PORTICO

PRODUCTO DE ESPAÑA

CASA FUNDADA EN 1894
**BODEGAS PALACIO**

EMBOTELLADO POR
BODEGAS PALACIO S.A
EN LAGUARDIA. ALAVA    12,5% Vol.
(ESPAÑA)              750 ml.
R.E. Nº 8269- VI-1

**Rioja** The unoaked *sin crianza* style can be a revelation: silky, fruity, rich, modern, lacking the big oak attack of the *reserva* (3 years' ageing) and *gran reserva* (5 years). The *crianza* (1 year) is often the best bet. Watch out – Rioja quality is increasingly variable. Riojas are red blends, but single Tempranillo grape wines and Tempranillo/ Cabernet blends can be delicious. Some good whites too, particularly those lower in oak.

There are some very good Albariño whites under the Rias Baixas *DO*. Other wines to try are those from Navarra. An exciting but often pricey region: superb Tempranillos, Tempranillo/Cabernet and Tempranillo/ Merlot blends. Some world-class Chardonnays are emerging and other good whites. Try the Garnacha-based pinks, the *rosados*. Also try wines from Ribera del Duero. Spain's smartest *DO* has some wonderful wine. Tempranillo is called *Tinto Fino* here.

RIAS BAIXAS
DENOMINACION DE ORIGEN

## LAGAR de CERVERA
*Albariño*
1996

12%vol                    75 cl
ALC 12%VOL
EMBOTELLADO EN LA PROPIEDAD
LAGAR DE FORNELOS, S.A.
EL ROSAL · PONTEVEDRA · ESPAÑA

Like Navarra, there are single varietals, but Tempranillo blended with Merlot or Cabernet Sauvignon is often more successful. Whites are less exciting. No other Castilla region wines come close, though Rueda whites are good. Bierzo *DO* is improving fast.

## SANTARA

### CHARDONNAY

CONCA DE BARBERÀ
DENOMINACIÓN DE ORIGEN
1996

PRODUCED AND BOTTLED BY CONCAVINS & HUGH RYMAN S.A
BARBENA DE LA CONCA. PRODUCT OF SPAIN

13%alc./vol.
750 ML

Priorato, Tarragona, Costers del Segre and Conca de Barberà *DO* are all good wines to try from the Penedès region. Look out for the following regions. Aragón is one of the up-and-coming names: superb whites from Somontano, and improving reds from Cariñena, Campo de Borja and Calatayud. Valencia: wines are generally medium-mediocre in quality. Try the traditional sweet *moscatel de Valencia*. La Mancha: In the centre of Spain, this is traditionally the plonk zone, but modern approaches are improving quality. The best are everyday wines, not stars; Valdepeñas *DO* is the best of them.

*cosecha vintage*

*At 13% ABV, this quite a strong wine. A table wine would probably be about 11%; port is 20%.*

The **DO** (**denominación de origen**) system is based on regions (in this case Penedès). **DOC** (adding the word **calificada**), supposedly a higher level of quality, thus far only applies to Rioja wines and merely reflects tighter growing and making controls. Stick to **DO** and **DOC**, and avoid the lowlier **vino de la tierra** and **vino de mesa**. The really exciting wine areas are in the north and east, particularly from Navarra and Ribera del Duero.

There are three sherry towns: Jerez, El Puerto de Santa María and Sanlúcar. Avoid the cheapies. **Fino**: dry, lean, subtle and lemony from Jerez. **Amontillado**: an aged **Fino**, rich and nutty. **Manzanilla**: briny, dry, yeasty. **Palo Cortado**: a halfway house between **Amontillado** and **Oloroso**. **Oloroso**: rich, spicy, christmassy. Once opened you should finish the bottle within a week.

**the wine list please**
la carta de vinos por favor
la **kar**-ta de **bee**-nos por fa-**bor**

**what wines do you have?**
¿qué vinos tiene?
ke **bee**-nos **tyen**-e

**is there a local wine?**
¿hay un vino típico de esta zona?
aee oon **bee**-no **tee**-pee-ko de **es**-ta **tho**-na

**can you recommend a good wine?**
¿puede recomendarnos un vino bueno?
**pwe**-de re-ko-men-**dar**-nos oon **bee**-no **bwen**-o

**a glass of red wine please**
un tinto por favor
oon **teen**-to por fa-**bor**

**a glass of white wine please**
un vino blanco por favor
oon **bee**-no **blan**-ko por fa-**bor**

**a bottle of wine**
una botella de vino
**oo**-na bo-**tel**-ya de **bee**-no

**red wine**
vino tinto
**bee**-no **teen**-to

**white wine**
vino blanco
**bee**-no **blan**-ko

**a carafe of house wine**
una jarra de vino de la casa
**oo**-na **khar**-ra de **bee**-no de la **ka**-sa

**a dry sherry**
un fino
oon **fee**-no

*talking talking talking*

# Flavours of Spain

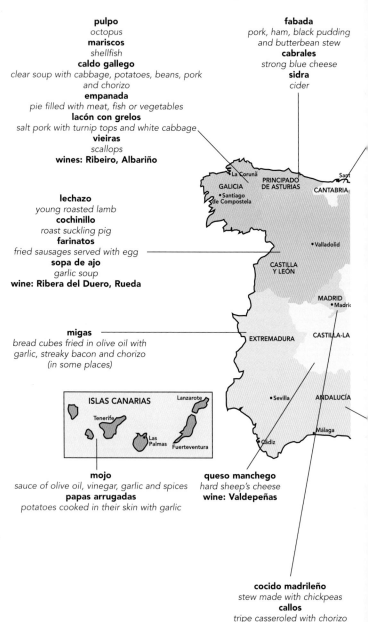

**pulpo**
*octopus*
**mariscos**
*shellfish*
**caldo gallego**
*clear soup with cabbage, potatoes, beans, pork and chorizo*
**empanada**
*pie filled with meat, fish or vegetables*
**lacón con grelos**
*salt pork with turnip tops and white cabbage*
**vieiras**
*scallops*
**wines: Ribeiro, Albariño**

**fabada**
*pork, ham, black pudding and butterbean stew*
**cabrales**
*strong blue cheese*
**sidra**
*cider*

**lechazo**
*young roasted lamb*
**cochinillo**
*roast suckling pig*
**farinatos**
*fried sausages served with egg*
**sopa de ajo**
*garlic soup*
**wine: Ribera del Duero, Rueda**

**migas**
*bread cubes fried in olive oil with garlic, streaky bacon and chorizo (in some places)*

**ISLAS CANARIAS**
Lanzarote
Tenerife
Las Palmas
Fuerteventura

**mojo**
*sauce of olive oil, vinegar, garlic and spices*
**papas arrugadas**
*potatoes cooked in their skin with garlic*

**queso manchego**
*hard sheep's cheese*
**wine: Valdepeñas**

La Coruña
PRINCIPADO DE ASTURIAS
GALICIA
Santiago de Compostela
CANTABRIA
Sant
Valladolid
CASTILLA Y LEÓN
MADRID
Madri
EXTREMADURA
CASTILLA-LA
Sevilla
ANDALUCÍA
Málaga
Cádiz

**cocido madrileño**
*stew made with chickpeas*
**callos**
*tripe casseroled with chorizo in a spicy paprika sauce*

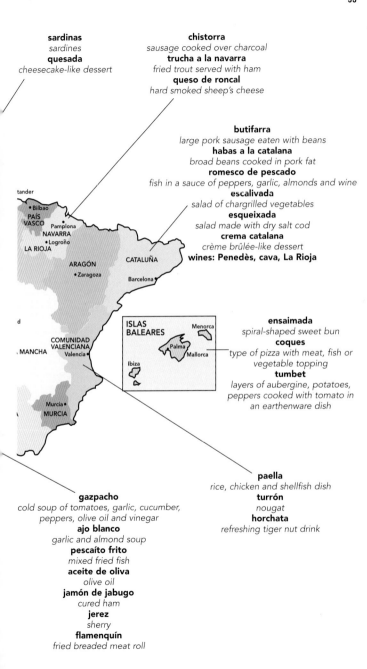

**sardinas**
*sardines*
**quesada**
*cheesecake-like dessert*

**chistorra**
*sausage cooked over charcoal*
**trucha a la navarra**
*fried trout served with ham*
**queso de roncal**
*hard smoked sheep's cheese*

**butifarra**
*large pork sausage eaten with beans*
**habas a la catalana**
*broad beans cooked in pork fat*
**romesco de pescado**
*fish in a sauce of peppers, garlic, almonds and wine*
**escalivada**
*salad of chargrilled vegetables*
**esqueixada**
*salad made with dry salt cod*
**crema catalana**
*crème brûlée-like dessert*
**wines: Penedès, cava, La Rioja**

tander
• Bilbao
**PAÍS VASCO**
Pamplona
**NAVARRA**
• Logroño
**LA RIOJA**
**ARAGÓN**
• Zaragoza
**CATALUÑA**
Barcelona •

d
**COMUNIDAD VALENCIANA**
**MANCHA**
Valencia •
Murcia •
**MURCIA**

**ISLAS BALEARES**
Menorca
Palma
Mallorca
Ibiza

**ensaimada**
*spiral-shaped sweet bun*
**coques**
*type of pizza with meat, fish or vegetable topping*
**tumbet**
*layers of aubergine, potatoes, peppers cooked with tomato in an earthenware dish*

**paella**
*rice, chicken and shellfish dish*
**turrón**
*nougat*
**horchata**
*refreshing tiger nut drink*

**gazpacho**
*cold soup of tomatoes, garlic, cucumber, peppers, olive oil and vinegar*
**ajo blanco**
*garlic and almond soup*
**pescaíto frito**
*mixed fried fish*
**aceite de oliva**
*olive oil*
**jamón de jabugo**
*cured ham*
**jerez**
*sherry*
**flamenquín**
*fried breaded meat roll*

*If you cannot eat certain things, it is as well warning the waiter before making your choice.*

talking talking talking talking talking talking talking

**I'm vegetarian**
soy vegetariano(a)
*soy ve-khe-tar-ya-no(a)*

**I don't eat meat/pork**
no como carne/cerdo
*no ko-mo kar-ne/ther-do*

**I don't eat fish/shellfish**
no como pescado/marisco
*no ko-mo pes-ka-do/ma-rees-ko*

**I'm allergic to shellfish**
soy alérgico(a) al marisco
*soy a-ler-khee-ko(a) al ma-rees-ko*

**I can't eat raw eggs**
no puedo comer huevos crudos
*no pwe-do ko-mer hwe-bos kroo-dos*

**I am on a diet**
estoy a dieta
*es-toy a dyet-a*

**I am allergic to peanuts**
soy alérgico(a) a los cacahuetes
*soy a-ler-khee-ko(a) a los ka-ka-we-tes*

**I can't eat liver**
no puedo comer hígado
*no pwe-do ko-mer ee-ga-do*

**I don't drink alcohol**
no bebo alcohol
*no be-bo al-kol*

**what is in this?**
¿qué lleva esto?
*ke lyeb-a es-to*

**is it raw?**
¿está crudo?
*es-ta kroo-do*

**is it made with unpasteurised milk?**
¿está hecho con leche sin pasteurizar?
*es-ta e-cho kon le-che seen past-e-oo-ree-thar*

**frito**
*free-to*
fried

**cocido**
*ko-thee-do*
boiled

**al vapor**
*al ba-por*
steamed

**asado**
*a-sa-do*
roast/baked

**pinchito moruno**
*peen-cheeto mo-roo-no*
kebab

**relleno**
*rel-ye-no*
stuffed

**a la plancha**
*a la plan-cha*
grilled

**ahumado**
*a-oo-ma-do*
smoked

**guisado**
*gee-sa-do*
stewed

**adobado**
*a-dob-a-do*
marinated

**en escabeche**
*en es-ka-be-che*
pickled

**escalfado**
*es-kal-fa-do*
poached

**azucarado**
*a-thoo-ka-ra-do*
sugared

**salado**
*sa-la-do*
salted

## Tapas

There are many different varieties of **tapas** depending on the region. This is a list of some of the most common **tapas** that can be found in any part of Spain. A larger portion of **tapas** is called a *ración*. A *pincho* is a **tapa** on a cocktail stick.

**asadillo/asadura de pimientos** *roasted red peppers marinated in olive oil and garlic*

**berenjenas fritas** *fried aubergines*

**boquerones en vinagre** *fresh anchovies marinated in garlic, parsley and olive oil*

**croquetas de carne/pescado** *meat/fish croquettes with bechamel*

**ensaladilla rusa** *potato salad with vegetables, tuna, hard-boiled eggs and mayonnaise*

**fritería de pescado** *assorted deep-fried fish*

**gambas al ajillo** *grilled shrimps sautéed in olive oil, garlic, parsley and dry white wine*

**gambas plancha** *grilled shrimps*

**japuta/Cazón en adobo** *marinated pomfret/dogfish*

**montadito de lomo** *grilled pork fillet marinated in paprika and garlic, served on toasted bread*

**patatas alioli** *potato in garlic and olive oil vinaigrette*

**patatas bravas** *fried potato cubes with a spicy tomato sauce*

**pinchitos morunos** *grilled skewers of pork tenderloin marinated in spices, garlic and olive oil*

**pincho de tortilla** *small portion of Spanish omelette*

**pulpo a la vinagreta** *octopus marinated in garlic, onions, peppers, olive oil and lemon juice*

**rabo de toro en salsa** *oxtail stew*

**salmorejo** *thick cold tomato soup made with tomatoes, bread, garlic and olive oil*

---

**...a la/al** *in the style of*

**...a la Navarra** *stuffed with ham*

**...a la parilla/plancha** *grilled*

**...a la romana** *fried in batter*

**...al horno** *baked/roast*

**aceite** *oil*
 **aceite de oliva** *olive oil*

**aceitunas** *olives*
 **aceitunas rellenas** *stuffed olives*

**acelgas** *Swiss chard*

**adobo, ...en** *marinated*

**agua** *water*
 **agua mineral** *mineral water*
 **agua con gas** *sparkling water*
 **agua sin gas** *still water*

**aguardiente** *a kind of clear brandy*

**ahumado** *smoked*

**ajetes** *garlic shoots*

**ajillo, ...al** *with garlic*

**ajo** *garlic*
 **ajo blanco** *kind of garlic, bread and almond soup served cold. Sometimes served with diced apple and raisins*
 **ajo de las manos** *sliced, boiled potatoes mixed with a garlic, oil and vinegar dressing, and flavoured with red chillies*

**albahaca** *basil*

**albaricoque** *apricot*

**albóndigas** *meatballs in sauce*

**alcachofas** *artichokes*

**alcachofas a la vinagreta** *artichokes served with a strong vinaigrette*

**alcachofas con jamón** *sautéed artichoke hearts with cured ham*

**alcachofas rellenas** *stuffed artichokes*

**alcaparras** *capers*

**aliño** *dressing*

**alioli/allioli** *olive oil and garlic mashed together into a creamy paste similar to mayonnaise. Served with meat, potatoes or fish*

**almejas** *clams*

**almejas a la marinera** *steamed clams cooked with parsley, wine and garlic*

**almendras** *almonds*

**alubias** *large white beans found in many stews*

**amontillado** *medium-dry to dry sherry*

**ancas de rana** *frogs' legs*

**anchoa** *anchovy*

**anguila** *eel*

**angulas** *baby eels, highly prized*

**angulas al ajillo** *baby eels cooked with garlic*

**angulas en cazuelita** *garlic-flavoured, fried baby eels seasoned with hot pepper*

**anís (seco** or **dulce)** *aniseed liqueur, dry or sweet, normally drunk as a long drink with water and ice*

**apio** *celery*

**arenque** *herring*

**arroz** *rice*

**arroz a banda** *a dish of rice and fish. The dish is served in two courses: first the rice cooked with saffron is served and then the fish that has been cooked in it*

**arroz a la cubana** *rice with fried egg and tomato sauce*

**arroz a la levantina** *rice with shellfish, onions, artichokes, peas, tomatoes and saffron*

**arroz a la marinera** *rice with seafood*

**arroz a la valenciana** *Valencian version of paella, sometimes cooked with eel*

**arroz a la zamorana** *rice with pork, peppers and garlic*

**arroz blanco** *boiled rice*

**arroz con costra** *rice with chicken, rabbit, sausages, chickpeas and pork meatballs baked in oven with egg topping*

**arroz con leche** *rice pudding flavoured with cinnamon*

**arroz con pollo** *rice with chicken, garnished with peas and peppers*

**arroz negro** *black rice (with squid in its own ink)*

**arroz santanderino** *rice cooked with salmon and milk*

**asado** *roasted*

**asadillo** *roasted sliced red peppers in olive oil and garlic*

*bacalao al pil-pil*

**asadillo/asadura de pimientos**
*roasted peppers*

**atún** *tuna (usually fresh)*
**atún con salsa de tomate**
*tuna fish in tomato sauce*

**avellana** *hazelnut*

**azafrán** *saffron*

**azúcar** *sugar*

**bacalao** *salt cod, cod*
**bacalao a la vizcaína** *salt cod
cooked with dried peppers,
onions and parsley*
**bacalao al ajo arriero** *salt cod
fried with garlic to which is
added vinegar, paprika and
parsley*
**bacalao al pil-pil** *a Basque
speciality – salt cod cooked in a
creamy garlic and olive oil sauce*
**bacalao con patatas** *salt cod
slowly baked with potatoes,
peppers, tomatoes, onions,
olives and bay leaves*
**bacalao de convento** *salt cod
cooked with spinach and potato*

**bajoques farcides** *peppers
stuffed with rice, pork, tomatoes
and spices*

**bandeja de quesos** *cheese
platter*

**barbacoa, ...a la** *barbecued*

**berenjena** *aubergine (eggplant)*

**berenjenas a la catalana**
*aubergines with tomato sauce,
Catalan style*
**berenjenas rellenas** *stuffed
aubergines (usually with mince)*
**berenjenas salteadas**
*aubergines sautéed with
tomatoes and onions*

**besugo** *red bream*

**bistec** *steak*

**bizcocho** *sponge*
**bizcocho borracho** *sponge
soaked in wine and syrup*

**blanco y negro** *a milky coffee
with ice*

**bocadillo** *sandwich (French
bread)*
**bocadillo (de...)** *sandwich*

**bogavante** *lobster*

**bonito** *tunny fish, lighter than
tuna, good grilled*

**boquerones** *fresh anchovies*
**boquerones fritos** *fried
anchovies*

**brandy** *Spanish brandy; if you
want what we would call brandy
ask for* **coñac**

**brasa, ...a la** *barbecued*

*buñuelos*

*butifarra*

**buñuelos** type of fritter. Savoury ones are filled with cheese, ham, mussels or prawns. Sweet ones can be filled with fruit
  **buñuelos de bacalao** salt cod fritters
**butifarra** special sausage from Catalonia
  **butifarra blanca** white sausage containing pork and tripe
  **butifarra negra** black sausage containing pork blood, belly and spices
**caballa** mackerel
**cabello de ángel** sweet pumpkin filling
**cabrito** kid (goat)
  **cabrito al horno** roast kid
**cacahuete** peanut
**cachelada** chopped boiled potatoes and cabbage with garlic, red pepper and fried bacon. Often served with **chorizo**
**café** coffee
  **café con leche** white coffee
  **café cortado** coffee with only a little milk

**café descafeinado** decaffeinated coffee
  **café helado** iced coffee
  **café solo** black coffee
**calabacines** courgettes
  **calabacines rellenos** stuffed courgettes
**calabaza guisada** stewed pumpkin
**calamares** squid
  **calamares a la romana** fried squid rings in batter
  **calamares en su tinta** squid cooked in its own ink
  **calamares fritos** fried squid
  **calamares rellenos** stuffed squid
**calçotada** roasted spring onion with olive oil and almonds, typical of Tarragona
**caldeirada** fish soup from Galicia
**caldereta** stew/casserole
  **caldereta de cordero** lamb casserole
  **caldereta de langosta** lobster stew
  **caldereta de pescado** fish stew
**caldo** clear soup
  **caldo de pescado** fish soup
  **caldo gallego** clear soup with green vegetables, beans, pork and **chorizo**
**caliente** hot

*callos a la madrileña*

**callos** tripe

**callos a la madrileña** fried tripe casseroled in a spicy paprika sauce with tomatoes and **chorizo**

**camarones** shrimps

**canela** cinnamon

**cangrejo** crab

**caracoles** snails
**caracoles de mar** winkles

**caracolillos** winkles

**carajillo** black coffee with brandy which may be set alight depending on regional customs

**cardo** cardoon, plant related to the artichoke

**carne** meat
**carne de buey** beef
**carne picada** minced meat

**carnero** mutton

**cassolada** pork and vegetable stew from Catalonia

**castaña** chestnut

**cava** champagne-style sparkling wine

**cazuela de fideos** legumes, meat and noodle stew

**cebolla** onion
**cebollas rellenas** stuffed onions
**cebollas rojas** red onions

**centollo** spider crab

**cerdo** pork
**cerdo asado** roast pork

**cerezas** cherries

**cerveza** beer

**champán** champagne

**champiñones** mushrooms

**chanfaina** a stew made from pig's liver and other parts

**chanquetes** whitebait

**chilindrón, ...al** sauce made with pepper, tomato, fried onions and meat (pork or lamb)

**chistorra** spicy sausage from Navarra

**chocolate** either chocolate (for eating) or a hot thick drinking chocolate **un chocolate**

**chorizo** spicy red sausage. The larger type is eaten like salami, the thinner type is cooked in various dishes

**choto** kid or calf
**choto albaicinero** kid fried with garlic, from Granada

**chuleta** chop
**chuleta de cerdo** pork chop
**chuleta de ternera** veal/beef chop

**chuletas de cordero** grilled lamb chops

**chuletón** large steak

**churrasco** barbecued steak

**churros** fried batter sticks sprinkled with sugar, usually eaten with thick hot chocolate

**ciervo** deer (venison)

**cigalas** king prawns

**cilantro** coriander

**ciruelas** plums

**coca (coques)** type of pizza with meat, fish or vegetables served in the Balearic Islands. They can also be sweet

**cochinillo** roast suckling pig

**cocido** stew made with various meats, vegetables and

chickpeas. There are regional variations of this dish and it is worth trying the local version
**cocido de lentejas** *thick stew of lentils and* **chorizo**
**cocido de pelotas** *a rich spicy stew with mince wrapped in cabbage leaves containing pork and chickpeas*

**coco** *coconut*

**cóctel de gambas** *prawn cocktail*

**codillo de cerdo** *pig's trotter*

**codornices asadas** *roast quail*

**codorniz** *quail*

**col** *cabbage*

**coles de Bruselas** *Brussels sprouts*

**coliflor** *cauliflower*

*cordero asado*

**cordero** *lamb*
**cordero al chilindrón** *lamb in a spicy pepper sauce*
**cordero asado** *roast lamb*
**cordero asado a la manchega** *spit-roasted young lamb*
**cordero relleno trufado** *lamb stuffed with truffles*

**costillas** *ribs*
**costillas de cerdo** *pork ribs*

**crema** *cream soup/cream*
**crema catalana** *similar to crème brûlée*
**crema de espárragos** *cream of asparagus*
**crema de tomate** *cream of tomato soup*

**crema** *generic name given to smooth liqueurs, e.g.* **crema de naranja** *(orange cream)*

**cremat** *coffee with brandy and rum, served in Catalonia*

**croquetas** *croquettes (made with thick bechamel sauce)*
**croquetas de camarones** *shrimp croquettes*

**crudo** *raw*

**cuajada** *cream-based dessert like junket, served with honey or sugar*

**comino** *cumin*

**coñac** *brandy*

**conchas finas** *large scallops*

**conejo** *rabbit*

**consomé** *consommé*
**consomé al jerez** *consommé with sherry*
**consomé de gallina** *chicken consommé*

**copa** *goblet*
**copa de helado** *ice cream sundae*

**coques** *see* **coca**
**coques de torró** *wafers filled with almonds, sold at Christmas in Majorca*

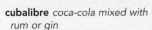

*dorada a la sal*

*ensalada de casa*

**cubalibre** *coca-cola mixed with rum or gin*

**cucurucho de helado** *ice cream cone*

**culantro** *coriander*

**dátiles** *dates*

**descafeinado** *decaffeinated*

**dorada** *sea bream*
  **dorada a la sal** *sea bream cooked in the oven, covered only with salt, forming a crust*
  **dorada al horno** *baked sea bream*

**dulce** *sweet*

**dulces** *cakes and pastries*

**embutido** *sausage, cold meat*

**empanada** *pastry/pie filled with meat or fish and vegetables*

**empanadilla** *pasty/small pie filled with meat or fish*

**empanado** *breadcrumbed and fried*

**ensaimada** *sweet spiral-shaped yeast bun from Majorca*

**ensalada (mixta/verde)** *(mixed/green) salad*
  **ensalada de la casa** *lettuce, tomato and onion salad (may include tuna)*
  **ensalada de huevos** *salad with hard boiled eggs*

**ensaladilla rusa** *diced cooked vegetables and potatoes in mayonnaise*

**entrecot** *entrecôte steak*

**entremeses** *starters*

*ensaimada*

**entremeses de fiambre** *cold meat hors d'œuvres*

**entremeses de pescado** *fish hors d'œuvres*

**escabeche, ...en** *pickled*

**escabeche de pescado** *fish marinated in oil and served cold*

**escalfado** *poached*

**escalivada** *salad of chargrilled or baked vegetables such as peppers and aubergines soaked in olive oil*

**escalope de ternera** *veal/beef escalope*

**escarola** *endive*

**escudella** *meat, vegetable and chickpea stew. Traditionally served as two courses: a soup and then the cooked meat and vegetables*

**escudilla de pages** *white bean, sausage, ham and pork soup*

**espárragos** *asparagus*

**espárragos con mahonesa** *asparagus with mayonnaise*

**espinacas gratinadas** *spinach au gratin*

**esqueixada** *salad made with salt cod*

**estofado** *braised/stewed*

**estofado de cordero** *lamb stew*

**estofado de ternera** *veal/beef stew*

**estragón** *tarragon*

**fabada asturiana** *pork, cured ham, black pudding, large butter beans or sausage stew with **chorizo** and **morcilla***

**fabes** *large white haricot beans*

**faisán** *pheasant*

**farinatos** *fried sausages served with eggs*

**fiambre** *cold meat*

**fiambre de tenera** *veal pâté*

**fiambres surtidos** *assorted cold meats*

**fideos** *noodles/thin ribbons of pasta (vermicelli)*

**fideos a la cazuela** *noodles cooked with pork, sausages, ham and **sofrito** (fried onions, garlic and tomato)*

**fideuà amb marisc** *seafood dish with fine pasta (vermicelli)*

**filete** *fillet steak*

**filete de ternera** *veal/beef steak*

**filete a la plancha** *grilled fillet steak*

**filetes de lenguado** *sole fillets*

**fino** *pale, very dry sherry*

*fabada*

*flamenquín*

**flamenquín** *fried breaded meat roll, containing cured or smoked ham and sometimes cheese; typical of southern Spain*

**flan** *crème caramel*

**frambuesas** *raspberries*

**fresas** *strawberries*
**fresas con nata** *strawberries and cream*

**frijoles** *beans (name used in the Canary Islands)*

**frío** *cold*

**frite** *pieces of lamb fried in olive oil and paprika*

**frito** *fried*

**fritura de pescado** *fried assortment of fish*

**fruta** *fruit*
**fruta del tiempo** *fruit in season*

**frutos secos** *nuts*

**galleta** *biscuit*

**gallina** *hen*

**gambas** *prawns*
**gambas a la plancha** *grilled prawns*
**gambas al ajillo** *grilled prawns with garlic*
**gambas al pil-pil** *sizzling prawns cooked with chillies*

**ganso** *goose*

**garbanzos** *chickpeas*
**garbanzos con espinacas** *chickpeas with spinach*

**garrotxa** *goat's cheese*

**gazpacho** *traditional cold tomato soup of southern Spain. There are many different recipes. Basic ingredients are water, tomatoes, garlic, fresh breadcrumbs, salt, vinegar and olive oil. Sometimes served with diced cucumbers, hard-boiled eggs and cured ham*
**gazpacho extremeño** *a version of gazpacho made with finely chopped green peppers and onions*

**ginebra** *gin*

**gofio** *toasted corn meal often rolled into balls and eaten as a bread substitute in the Canary Islands*

**gran reserva** *classification given to aged wines of exceptional quality*

**granada** *pomegranate*

**granizado** *fruit drink with crushed ice*

**gratinado** *au gratin*

**grelos** *young turnip tops*

**guindilla** chilli

**guisado** stew or casserole

**guisantes** peas

**guisantes a la española** boiled peas with cured ham, lettuce, carrots and onions

**gulas** the cheap alternative to **angulas**, made of fish (mainly haddock) and squid ink

**habas** broad beans

**habas a la catalana** broad beans cooked in pork fat often served with **chorizo**

**habas con jamón** broad beans with cured ham

**hamburguesa** hamburger

**helado** ice cream

**hervido** boiled

**hígado** liver

**hígado con cebolla** fried calf's liver with onions

**higos** figs

**higos secos** dried figs

**horchata de chufas** cool drink made with tiger nuts

**horno, ...al** baked (in oven)

**huevos** eggs

**huevos a la española** stuffed eggs with a cheese sauce

**huevos a la flamenca** baked eggs with tomatoes, peas, peppers, asparagus and **chorizo**

**huevos al plato** eggs baked in butter

**huevos con jamón** fried eggs and cured ham

**ibéricos** traditional Spanish gourmet products; a **surtido de ibéricos** means assorted products such as cured ham, cheese, **chorizo** and **salchichón**

**infusión** herbal tea

**intxaursalsa** whipped cream and walnut pudding

**jamón** ham

**jamón de Jabugo** Andalusian prime-quality cured ham from Jabujo, a small town in Huelva

**jamón de pata negra** prime cured ham (the best quality)

**jamón serrano** dark red cured ham

**jamón de York** cooked ham

**jengibre** ginger

**jerez** sherry

**jibia** cuttlefish

**judías** beans

**judías blancas** haricot beans

**judías verdes** green beans

**judías verdes a la castellana/española** boiled green beans mixed with fried parsley, garlic and peppers

**jurel** horse mackerel

**kokotxas** hake's cheek usually fried

**lacón con grelos** salted pork with young turnip tops and white cabbage

**langosta** lobster

**langosta a la catalana** potatoes with a lobster filling served with mayonnaise

**langostinos** king prawns

**langostinos a la plancha** grilled king prawns

**langostinos a la vinagreta** *casseroled crayfish with hardboiled eggs served in a vinaigrette sauce*

**laurel** *bay leaf*

**lechazo** *young lamb (roasted)*

**leche** *milk*

**leche caliente** *hot milk*

**leche fría** *cold milk*

**leche frita** *very thick custard dipped into an egg and breadcrumb mixture, fried and served hot in squares*

**leche merengada** *type of ice cream made with egg whites, sugar and cinnamon (can be drunk as a milkshake)*

**leche condensada** *condensed milk*

**leche evaporada** *evaporated milk*

**leche preparada** *boiled milk with sugar, cinnamon and lemon peel, usually drunk in summer as a milkshake*

**lechuga** *lettuce*

**legumbres** *fresh or dried pulses*

**lengua** *tongue*

**lenguado** *sole*

**lenguado a la romana** *sole fried in batter*

**lenguados fritos** *fried fillets of sole often served on a bed of mixed sautéed vegetables*

**lenguados rellenos** *fillets of sole stuffed with shrimps or prawns*

**lentejas** *lentils (very popular in Spain)*

**licor** *liqueur*

**liebre** *hare*

**liebre estofada** *stewed hare*

**limón** *lemon*

**limonada** *lemonade (normally canned and fizzy)*

**lomo** *loin of pork*

**longaniza** *spicy pork sausage*

**longaniza con judías blancas** *spicy pork sausage with white beans*

**lubina** *sea bass*

**lubina a la asturiana** *Asturian-style sea bass, with cider*

**lubina al horno** *baked sea bass with potatoes, onion, tomato and garlic*

**macarrones** *macaroni*

**macedonia de fruta** *fruit salad*

**magras con tomate** *slices of fried ham dipped into tomato sauce*

**mahonesa** *mayonnaise*

**maíz** *sweetcorn*

**majorero** *goat's cheese from Canary Islands*

**manitas de cerdo** *pig's trotters*

**mantequilla** *butter*

**manzana** *apple*

**manzanas rellenas** *stuffed baked apples*

**manzanilla** *camomile tea, or a very dry sherry from Sanlúcar de Barrameda*

**margarina** *margerine*

**marinado** *marinated*

**mariscada** *mixed shellfish*

**marisco** *shellfish ; seafood*

**marmitako** *tuna fish and potato stew*

**mayonesa** *mayonnaise*

**mazapán** *marzipan*

**medallón** *thick steak (medallion)*

**mejillones** *mussels*

**mejillones a la marinera** *mussels steamed in wine*

**mejillones al vapor** *mussels (steamed)*

**melocotón** *peach*

**melocotón en almíbar** *peaches in syrup*

*menestra*

**melón** melon
  **melón con jamón** melon and cured ham
**membrillo** quince jelly
**menestra de verduras** fresh vegetable stew often cooked with cured ham
**merluza** hake, one of the most popular fish in Spain
  **merluza a la asturiana** boiled hake served with mayonnaise and garnished with hard boiled eggs
  **merluza a la sidra** hake baked with clams, onions and cider

**merluza en salsa verde** hake with green sauce (with parsley)
**mermelada** jam
**mero** grouper
**miel** honey
**migas** breadcrumbs or croûtons usually fried in garlic and olive oil, sometimes with streaky bacon and **chorizo**
  **migas con jamón** ham with breadcrumbs
  **migas extremeñas** breadcrumbs fried with egg and spicy sausage
**mollejas** sweetbreads
**mojama** cured tuna fish, a delicacy
**mojo** a sauce made from olive oil, vinegar, garlic and different spices. Paprika is added for the red mojo. Predominantly found in the Canaries
  **mojo picón** spicy **mojo** made with chilli peppers
  **mojo verde** made with fresh coriander
**mollejas** sweetbreads
  **mollejas de ternera** calves' sweetbreads
**morcilla** black pudding
**moros y cristianos** rice, black beans and onions with garlic sausage

*migas*

*mojo de tomate*

**moscatel** *sweet dessert wine from the muscat grape wine*

**mostaza** *mustard*

**nabo** *turnip*

**naranja** *orange*

**naranjada** *orangeade*

**nata** *cream*

**natillas** *sort of custard*

**navajas** *razor clams*

**nécora** *sea crab*

**nectarinas** *nectarines*

**níspero** *medlar*

**nuez moscada** *nutmeg*

**olla** *stew made traditionally with white beans, beef and bacon*
  **olla gitana** *thick stew/soup made with chickpeas, pork and vegetables and flavoured with almonds and saffron*
  **olla podrida** *thick cured ham, vegetable and chickpea stew/soup*

**oloroso** *sweet, dark, full-bodied sherry*

**orejas de cerdo a la plancha** *grilled pigs' ears*

**ostras** *oysters*

**paella** *one of the most famous of Spanish dishes. Paella varies from region to region but usually consists of rice, chicken,*

*olla*

*shellfish, vegetables, garlic and saffron. The dish's name derives from the large shallow pan in which it is cooked. The traditional paella Valenciana contains rabbit, chicken and sometimes eel*
  **paella de mariscos** *rice and shellfish paella*

**pan** *bread*
  **pan de higos** *dried figs pressed together in the shape of a small cake*

**panades** *lamb pasties eaten at Easter in the Balearics*

**panchineta** *almond and custard tart*

**panecillo** *bread roll*

*paella*

**panelleta** *small cakes with pine nuts and almonds*

**papas arrugadas** *potatoes cooked in skins in salty water*

**parrilla, ...a la** *grilled*

**parrillada** *mixed grill (can be meat or fish)*

**parrillada de mariscos** *mixed grilled shellfish*

**pasas** *raisins*

**pasta** *pasta*

**pastel** *cake/pastry*

**pastel de carne** *meat pie*

**pastel de ternera** *veal/beef pie*

**patatas** *potatoes*

**patatas arrugadas** *potatoes cooked in their skins*

**patatas bravas** *fried diced potatoes mixed with a garlic, oil and vinegar dressing and flavoured with tomatoes and red chilli peppers*

**patatas con chorizo** *potatoes cooked with chorizo*

**patatas fritas** *chips/crisps*

**patatas nuevas** *new potatoes*

**pato** *duck*

**pato a la sevillana** *joints of wild duck cooked with sherry, onion, tomatoes, herbs and garlic, served in an orange and olive sauce*

**pavo** *turkey*

**pavo relleno** *stuffed turkey*

**pechuga de pollo** *chicken breast*

**pechugas en bechamel** *chicken breasts in bechamel sauce*

**Pedro Ximénez** *sweet, rich sherry-type dessert wine*

**pepino** *cucumber*

**pepitoria de pavo/pollo** *turkey/chicken fricassée*

**pera** *pear*

**percebes** *goose-neck barnacle, a Galician shellfish*

**perdices con chocolate** *partridges with a chocolate sauce*

**perdiz** *partridge*

**perejil** *parsley*

**pescado** *fish*

**pescaíto frito** *mixed fried fish*

**pez espada** *swordfish*

**picada** *sauce made of chopped parsley, almonds, pine nuts and garlic*

**pichones** *young pigeon*

**pimentón** *(sweet) paprika; (spicy) cayenne pepper*

**pimienta** *pepper (spice)*

**pimientos** *red and green peppers, one of the typical Spanish flavours*

**pimientos de piquillo** *pickled red peppers*

**pimientos morrones** *sweet red peppers*

**pimientos rellenos** *peppers stuffed with meat or fish*

**piña** *pineapple*

**pinchos** *small tapas*

**pinchos morunos** *pork grilled on a skewer. If you ask for a pinchito you can omit the word moruno, but if you say pincho you have to specify it and say moruno.*

**piperrada** *type of scrambled eggs with red and green peppers, tomato, onion, garlic and paprika. A typical dish from the Basque country.*

**pipirrana** *a salad of fish, roast red peppers, tomatoes, hard-boiled eggs and onions, from Andalusia*

**pisto manchego** *a mixture of sautéed peppers, onions, aubergines, tomatoes, garlic and parsley. Similiar to French ratatouille. Served hot or cold*

**plancha, ...a la** *grilled*

**plátano** *banana*

**platija** *plaice (flounder)*

**plato** *dish*

**plato del día** *dish of the day*

**plato combinado** *assorted food served together on one plate rather than as separate dishes as is more usual in Spain*

**pollo** *chicken*

**pollo al chilindrón** *chicken cooked with onion, ham, garlic, red pepper and tomatoes*

**pollo asado** *roast chicken*

**pollo con patatas** *chicken and chips*

**pollo en pepitoria** *breaded chicken pieces fried, then casseroled with herbs, almonds, garlic and sherry*

**pollo estofado** *chicken stewed with potatoes, mushrooms, shallots, bay leaves and mushrooms*

**pollo relleno** *stuffed chicken*

**polvorones** *very crumbly cakes made with almonds and often eaten with a glass of **anís***

*pulpo*

**pomelo** *grapefruit*

**porras** *fried sticks of batter; in some parts of Spain they are called **churros***

**postres** *desserts*

**potaje** *thick soup/stew often with pork and pulses*

**potaje murciano** *red bean, French bean and rice soup*

**pote** *thick soup with beans and sausage which has many regional variations*

**pote gallego** *thick soup made with cabbage, white kidney beans, potatoes, pork and sausage*

**primer plato** *starter, first course*

**puchero** *hotpot made from meat or fish*

**puchero canario** *salted fish and potatoes served with **mojo** sauce*

**puerros** *leeks*

**pulpo** *octopus*

**puré de garbanzos** *thick chickpea soup*

**puré de patatas** *mashed potatoes*

**queimada** *warm drink made with* **aguardiente** *(clear brandy) sweetened with sugar and flambéed, a speciality of Galicia*

**quesada** *dessert similar to cheesecake*

**queso** *cheese*

**queso de Burgos** *curd cheese from Burgos*

**queso de cabrales** *strong blue cheese from Asturias*

**queso curado/semicurado** *cured/semi-cured cheese. Cured cheese has a strong flavour*

**queso de Idiazábal** *smoked sheep's milk cheese from the Basque country*

**queso de Mahón** *strong hard cheese from Menorca*

**queso de oveja** *mild sheep's cheese from León*

**rábanos** *radishes*

**rabo de toro** *bull's tail, usually cooked in a stew*

**rancio** *dessert wine*

**ración** *small taster portion/a kind of* **tapa**. *You can also ask for* **media ración** *(also written ½* **ración***) in many bars and restaurants*

**rape** *monkfish*

**rape a la marinera** *monkfish cooked with wine*

**raya** *skate*

**rebozado** *in batter*

**refresco de fruta** *fruit drink with ice*

**rehogado** *lightly fried*

**relleno** *stuffed*

**queso de Roncal** *hard, smoked sheep's cheese*

**queso de tetilla** *soft, white cheese made in the form of a woman's breast*

**queso fresco** *green cheese*

**queso manchego** *hard sheep's curd cheese from La Mancha*

**queso rallado** *grated cheese*

**remolacha** *beetroot*

**repollo** *cabbage*

**requesón** *cottage cheese*

**reserva** *wines of good quality that have been aged, but not as long as* **gran reserva**

**revuelto** *scrambled eggs often cooked with another ingredient*
**revuelto de champiñones** *scrambled eggs with mushrooms*
**revuelto de espárragos** *scrambled eggs with asparagus*
**revuelto de espinacas** *scrambled eggs with spinach*
**revuelto de gambas** *scrambled eggs with prawns*
**revuelto de morcilla** *scrambled eggs with black pudding*
**riñones al jerez** *kidneys in sherry sauce*
**rodaballo** *turbot*
**romana, ...a la** *fried in batter (generally squid –* **calamares***)*
**romero** *rosemary*
**romesco** *sauce made traditionally with olive oil, red pepper and bread. Other ingredients are often added, such as almonds and garlic*
**romesco de pescado** *fish in a sauce of peppers, olive oil and bread with almonds*
**ron** *rum*
**rosco** *type of doughnut*
**roscón de reyes** *a large bun-like cake in the shape of a ring, similar to Italian panettone and eaten at Epiphany*
**sal** *salt*
**salchicha** *sausage*
**salchichón** *salami-type sausage*
**salmón** *salmon*
**salmón a la parilla** *grilled salmon*
**salmón a la ribereña** *salmon fried with ham cooked with cider*
**salmón ahumado** *smoked salmon*
**salmonete** *red mullet*
**salmonete frito** *fried red mullet*
**salpicón** *chopped seafood or meat with tomato, onion, garlic and peppers*
**salsa** *sauce*
**salsa de tomate** *tomato sauce*

**salsa romesco** *sauce made of almonds and hazelnuts with mild chilli. Often served with fish and chicken*
**salsa verde** *garlic, olive oil and parsley sauce often served with fish*
**salteado** *sautéed*
**samfaina** *a dish of peppers, aubergines and tomatoes to which meat is often added*
**sandía** *watermelon*
**sándwich** *sandwich (usually toasted)*
**sangría** *red wine mixed with fruit, lemonade, sugar and ice often with cinnamon added.* **Sangría** *is always made of red wine but you can also find* **sangría de champán** *'champagne sangría'*
**sardinas** *sardines*
**sardinas a la santanderina** *sardines cooked with tomato, Santander style*
**sardinas asadas** *barbecued sardines*
**sardinas frescas/fritas** *fresh/fried sardines*
**sardinas rebozadas** *sardines cooked in batter*
**sargo** *type of bream*
**seco** *dry*
**sepia** *cuttlefish*
**sesos** *brains*
**sesos a la romana** *brains fried in batter*
**sesos fritos** *fried brains*
**setas** *wild mushrooms*
**sidra** *cider*
**sifón** *soda water*
**sobrasada** *a paprika-flavoured pork sausage from Mallorca*
**sofrito** *basic sauce made with slowly fried onions, garlic and tomato*
**solomillo** *sirloin*
**solomillo de ternera** *veal/beef sirloin*

*sopa*

**sopa** *soup*
 **sopa castellana** *or* **sopa de ajo**
 *garlic soup with bread. May
 contain poached egg or cured
 ham*
 **sopa de arroz** *rice soup*
 **sopa de cebolla** *onion soup*
 **sopa de cocido** *meat soup*
 **sopa de fideos** *noodle soup*
 **sopa de gallina** *chicken soup*
 **sopa de rabo** *oxtail/bull's tail
 soup*
 **sopa mallorquina** *tomato, onion
 and pepper soup thickened with
 breadcrumbs*
 **sopa de mariscos** *shellfish soup*
 **sopa de pescado** *fish soup*
 **sopa de pollo** *chicken soup*
 **sopa de verduras** *vegetable
 soup*
**sorbete** *sorbet*
 **sorbetes de frutas** *fruit sorbets*
**suquet** *fish, potato and tomato
 stew*
**suspiros** *meringues*
 **suspiros de monja** *meringues
 served with thick custard*
**tapas** *appetizers; snacks*
**tarta** *cake or tart*

**tarta de manzana** *apple tart*
**tarta de Santiago** *flat almond
 cake*
**tarta helada** *ice-cream cake*
**té** *tea*
 **té con leche** *tea with milk*
 **té con limón** *tea with lemon*
 **té helado** *iced tea*
**ternasco** *young lamb*
**ternera** *veal/beef*
 **ternera con naranja** *veal/beef
 cooked with orange*
 **ternera rellena** *stuffed veal/beef*
**tisana** *herbal tea*
**tocinillo (de cielo)** *sweet made
 with egg yolk and sugar*
**tocino** *bacon*
**tomates** *tomatoes*
 **tomates rellenos** *stuffed
 tomatos*
**tomillo** *thyme*
**toronja** *grapefruit*
**torrija** *bread dipped in milk and
 then fried and sprinkled with
 sugar and cinnamon*
**tortilla (española)** *traditional
 potato and onion omelette,
 often served as a tapa*
 **tortilla de
 champiñones**
 *mushroom
 omelette*

**tortilla de chorizo**
 *chorizo omelette*
**tortilla de espárragos**
 *asparagus omelette*
**tortilla de jamón** *cured ham
 omelette*

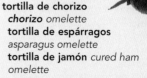

**tortilla murciana** *tomato and pepper omelette*

**trucha** *trout*
  **trucha a la navarra** *trout stuffed with cured ham*
  **trucha con almendras** *fried trout with almonds*

**tumbet** *layers of peppers, aubergine and tomato cooked with potato in an earthenware dish. Originally from Majorca*

**turrón** *nougat*
  **turrón de Alicante,**
  **turrón duro** *hard nougat*
  **turrón de Jijona,**
  **turrón blando** *soft nougat*

**txangurro** *spider crab*

**uvas** *grapes*

**vapor, ...al** *steamed*

**verduras** *vegetables*
  **verduras con patatas** *boiled potatoes with greens*

**vermú** *vermouth*

**vieiras** *scallops*
  **vieiras de Santiago** *scallops served in their shell, cooked in brandy, topped with breadcrumbs and grilled*

**vinagre** *vinegar*

**vinagreta** *vinaigrette*

**vino** *wine*
  **vino blanco** *white wine*
  **vino clarete** *rosé*
  **vino de jerez** *sherry*
  **vino de mesa** *table wine*

**vino rosado** *rosé wine*
  **vino tinto** *red wine*

**yemas** *small cakes that look like egg yolks*

**yogur** *yoghurt*

**zanahorias** *carrots*

**zarzuela de mariscos** *mixed seafood with wine and saffron*

**zarzuela de pescado** *fish stew*

**zumo** *juice*
  **zumo de fruta** *fruit juice*
  **zumo de albaricoque** *apricot juice*
  **zumo de lima** *lime juice*
  **zumo de melocotón** *peach juice*
  **zumo de naranja** *orange juice*
  **zumo de naranja natural** *fresh orange juice*
  **zumo de piña** *pineapple juice*
  **zumo de tomate** *tomato juice*

**zurrukutuna** *salt cod cooked with green peppers*

## A

**a(n)** un(a)
**abbey** la abadía
**able: to be able** poder
**abortion** el aborto
**about** *(concerning)* sobre
  *about 2 o'clock* alrededor de
  las dos
**above** arriba ; por encima
**abroad** en el extranjero
**abscess** el absceso
**accelerator** el acelerador
**accent** *(pronunciation)* el acento
**to accept** aceptar
  *do you accept this card?* ¿acepta esta
  tarjeta?
**access** el acceso
  *wheelchair access* el acceso para sillas
  de ruedas
**accident** el accidente
**accident & emergency department**
  las urgencias
**accommodation** el alojamiento
**to accompany** acompañar
**account** *(bank, etc)* la cuenta
**account number** el número de cuenta
**to ache** doler
  *my head aches* me duele la cabeza
  *it aches* duele
**acid** el ácido
**actor/actress** el actor/la actriz
**adaptor** el adaptador
**address** la dirección
  *what's the address?* ¿cuál es la
  dirección?
**address book** la agenda
**admission charge/fee** el precio
  de entrada
**to admit** *(to hospital)* ingresar
**adult** el/la adulto(a)
  *for adults* para adultos
**advance: in advance** por adelantado
**advertisement** el anuncio
**to advise** aconsejar
**A&E** las urgencias
**aeroplane** el avión
**aerosol** el aerosol
**afraid: to be afraid of** tener miedo de
**after** después
**afternoon** la tarde
  *this afternoon* esta tarde
  *in the afternoon* por la tarde
  *tomorrow afternoon* mañana por
  la tarde
**aftershave** el aftershave
**again** otra vez
**against** contra

**age** la edad
**agency** la agencia
**ago: a week ago** hace una semana
**to agree** estar de acuerdo
**agreement** el acuerdo
**AIDS** el sida
**air** el aire
  *by air* en avión
**air ambulance** avión sanitario ;
  ambulancia aérea
**airbag** *(in car)* el airbag
**air bed** el colchón inflable
**air conditioning** el aire acondicionado
**air-conditioning unit** el aparato de aire
  acondicionado
**air freshener** el ambientador
**airline** la linea aérea
**air mail: by airmail** por avión
**airplane** el avión
**airport** el aeropuerto
**airport bus** el autobús del aeropuerto
**air ticket** el billete de avión
**aisle** el pasillo
**alarm** la alarma
**alarm clock** el despertador
**alcohol** el alcohol
**alcohol-free** sin alcohol
**alcoholic** alcohólico(a)
  *is it alcoholic?* ¿tiene alcohol?
**all** todo(a)/todos(as)
**allergic to** alérgico(a) a
  *I'm allergic to...* soy alérgico(a) a...
**allergy** la alergia
**to allow** permitir
  *it's not allowed* no está permitido
**all right** *(agreed)* de acuerdo
  *(OK)* vale
  *are you all right?* ¿está bien?
**almost** casi
**alone** solo(a)
**alphabet** el alfabeto
**already** ya
**also** también
**altar** el altar
**always** siempre
**a.m.** de la mañana
**amber** *(traffic light)* amarillo ; *(substance)*
  ámbar
**ambulance** la ambulancia
**America** Norteamérica
**American** norteamericano(a)
**amount** el total
**anaesthetic** la anestesia
  *local anaesthetic* la anestesia local
  *general anaesthetic* la anestesia
  general

anchor el ancla
ancient antiguo(a)
and y
angina la angina (de pecho)
angry enfadado(a)
animal el animal
aniseed el anís
ankle el tobillo
anniversary el aniversario
to announce anunciar
announcement el anuncio
annual anual
another otro(a)
  *another beer, please* otra cerveza,
  por favor
answer la respuesta
to answer responder
answerphone el contestador
  (automático)
antacid el antiácido
antibiotic el antibiótico
antifreeze el anticongelante
antihistamine el antihistamínico
anti-inflammatory antiinflamatorio(a)
antiques las antigüedades
antique shop el anticuario
antiseptic el antiséptico
any alguno(a)
  *have you any pears?* ¿tiene peras?
anyone alguien
anything algo
anywhere en cualquier parte
apartment el apartamento
appendicitis la apendicitis
apple la manzana
application form el impreso de
  solicitud
appointment *(meeting)* la cita
  *(dentist, hairdresser)* la hora
approximately aproximadamente
apricot el albaricoque
April abril
apron el delantal
architect el/la arquitecto(a)
architecture la arquitectura
arm el brazo
armbands *(to swim)* los manguitos
  de nadar
armchair el sillón
to arrange organizar
to arrest detener
arrival la llegada
to arrive llegar
art el arte
art gallery la galería de arte
arthritis la artritis

artificial artificial
artist el/la artista
ashtray el cenicero
to ask *(question)* preguntar
  *(ask for something)* pedir
asparagus el espárrago
aspirin la aspirina
asthma el asma
  *I have asthma* tengo asma
at a ; en
  *at home* en casa
  *at 8 o'clock* a las ocho
  *at once* ahora mismo
  *at night* por la noche
Atlantic Ocean el Océano Atlántico
attack *(terrorist)* el atentado
  *(medical)* el ataque
to attack atacar
attractive atractivo(a)
aubergine la berenjena
auction la subasta
audience el público
August agosto
aunt la tía
au pair el/la au pair
Australia Australia
Australian australiano(a)
author el/la autor(a)
automatic automático(a)
automatic car el coche automático
auto-teller el cajero automático
autumn el otoño
available disponible
avalanche la avalancha
avenue la avenida
average medio(a)
to avoid *(issue)* evitar
  *(obstacle)* esquivar
awake: *to be awake* estar despierto(a)
away: *far away* lejos
awful espantoso(a)
awning *(for caravan etc)* toldo
axle *(in car)* el eje

## B

baby el bebé
baby food los potitos
baby milk la leche infantil
baby's bottle el biberón
babyseat *(in car)* el asiento del bebé
babysitter el/la canguro
baby wipes las toallitas infantiles
back *(of body)* la espalda
backpack la mochila
bacon el beicon/bacon

**bad** *(weather, news)* mal/malo(a)
  *(fruit and vegetables)* podrido(a)
**badminton** el bádminton
**bag** la bolsa
**baggage** el equipaje
**baggage allowance** el equipaje permitido
**baggage reclaim** la recogida de equipajes
**bail bond** la fianza
**bait** *(for fishing)* el cebo
**baked** al horno
**baker's** la panadería
**balcony** el balcón
**bald** *(person)* calvo(a)
  *(tyre)* gastado(a)
**ball** *(large: football, etc)* el balón
  *(small: golf, tennis, etc)* la pelota
**ballet** el ballet
**balloon** el globo
**banana** el plátano
**band** *(rock)* el grupo
**bandage** la venda
**bank** el banco
  *(river)* la ribera
**bank account** la cuenta bancaria
**banknote** el billete
**bar** el bar
**bar of chocolate** la tableta de chocolate
**barbecue** la barbacoa
  *to have a barbecue* hacer una barbacoa
**barber's** la barbería
**to bark** ladrar
**barn** el granero
**barrel** *(wine/beer)* el barril
**basement** el sótano
**basil** la albahaca
**basket** la cesta
**basketball** el baloncesto
**bat** *(baseball, cricket)* el bate
  *(creature)* el murciélago
**bath** el baño
  *to have a bath* bañarse
**bathing cap** el gorro de baño
**bathroom** el cuarto de baño
  *with bathroom* con baño
**battery** *(radio, camera, etc)* la pila
  *(in car)* la batería
**bay** *(along coast)* la bahía
**Bay of Biscay** el golfo de Vizcaya
**to be** estar ; ser
**beach** la playa
  *private beach* la playa privada
  *sandy beach* la playa de arena
  *nudist beach* la playa nudista

**beach hut** la caseta de playa
**bean** la alubia
**beard** la barba
**beautiful** hermoso(a)
**beauty salon** el salón de belleza
**because** porque
**to become** hacerse ; convertirse en ; llegar a ser
**bed** la cama
  *double bed* la cama de matrimonio
  *single bed* la cama individual
  *sofa bed* el sofá-cama
  *twin beds* las camas individuales
**bed and breakfast** alojamiento y desayuno
**bed clothes** la ropa de cama
**bedroom** el dormitorio
**bee** la abeja
**beef** la ternera
**beer** la cerveza
**before** antes de
  *before breakfast* antes de desayunar/del desayuno
**to begin** empezar
**behind** detrás de
  *behind the house* detrás de la casa
**beige** beige ; beis
**to believe** creer
**bell** *(church)* la campana
  *(door bell)* el timbre
**to belong to** pertenecer a
  *(club)* ser miembro de
**below** debajo ; por debajo
**belt** el cinturón
**bend** *(in road)* la curva
**berth** la litera
**beside** *(next to)* al lado de
  *beside the bank* al lado del banco
**best** el/la mejor
**bet** la apuesta
**to bet on** apostar por
**better** mejor
  *better than* mejor que
**between** entre
**bib** el babero
**bicycle** la bicicleta
  *by bicycle* en bicicleta
**bicycle pump** bomba de bicicleta
**bicycle repair kit** la caja de herramientas
**bidet** el bidé
**big** grande
  *bigger than* mayor que
**bike** *(pushbike)* la bicicleta
  *(motorbike)* la moto
**bike lock** el candado de la bicicleta
**bikini** el bikini

**bill** la factura
*(in restaurant)* la cuenta
**bin** el cubo ; la papelera
**bin liner** la bolsa de la basura
**binoculars** los prismáticos
**bird** el pájaro
**biro** el boli
**birth** el nacimiento
**birth certificate** la partida de nacimiento
**birthday** el cumpleaños
*happy birthday!* ¡feliz cumpleaños!
*my birthday is on...* mi cumpleaños es el...
**birthday card** la tarjeta de cumpleaños
**birthday present** el regalo de cumpleaños
**biscuits** las galletas
**bit:** *a bit of* un poco de
**bite** *(insect)* la picadura
*(animal)* la mordedura
**to bite** morder
*(insect)* picar
**bitten** *(by animal)* mordido(a)
*(by insect)* picado(a)
**bitter** *(taste)* amargo(a)
**black** negro(a)
**black ice** la capa invisible de hielo en la carretera
**blank** *(disk, tape)* virgen
**blanket** la manta
**bleach** *(household)* la lejía
**to bleed** sangrar
**blender** *(for food)* la licuadora
**blind** *(person)* ciego(a)
**blind** *(for window)* la persiana
*(roman)* el estor
**blister** la ampolla
**blocked** *(road)* cortado(a)
*(pipe)* obstruido(a)
**blond** *(person)* rubio(a)
**blood** la sangre
**blood group** el grupo sanguíneo
**blood pressure** la presión sanguínea
**blood test** el análisis de sangre
**blouse** la blusa
**blow-dry** el secado a mano
**blowout** *n (of tyre)* reventón
**blue** azul
*dark blue* azul marino
*light blue* azul claro
**blunt** *(knife, blade)* desafilado(a)
**boar** el jabalí
**to board** *(train, etc)* subir
**boarding card/pass** la tarjeta de embarque
**boarding house** la pensión

**boat** *(large)* el barco
*(small)* la barca
**boat trip** la excursión en barco
**body** el cuerpo
**to boil** hervir
**boiled** hervido(a)
**boiler** la caldera
**bomb** la bomba
**bone** el hueso
*(fish bone)* la espina
**bonfire** la hoguera
**bonnet** *(car)* el capó
**book** el libro
**to book** reservar
**booking** la reserva
**booking office** *(train)* la ventanilla de billetes
**bookshop** la librería
**boot** *(car)* el maletero
**boots** las botas
**border** *(of country)* la frontera
**boring** aburrido(a)
**born:** *I was born in...* nací en...
**to borrow** pedir prestado
**boss** el/la jefe(a)
**both** ambos(as)
**bottle** la botella
*a bottle of wine* una botella de vino
*a half-bottle of...* media botella de…
**bottle opener** el abrebotellas
**bottom** *(of pool, garden)* el fondo
**bowl** *(for soup, etc)* el bol
**bow tie** la pajarita
**box** la caja
**box office** la taquilla
**boxer shorts** los calzoncillos
**boy** el chico
**boyfriend** el novio
**bra** el sujetador
**bracelet** la pulsera
**brain** el cerebro
**brake** el freno
**to brake** frenar
**brake cable** cable de freno
**brake fluid** el líquido de frenos
**brake light** la luz de freno
**brake pads** las pastillas de freno
**branch** *(of tree)* la rama
*(of bank, etc)* la sucursal
**brand** *(make)* la marca
**brass** el latón
**brave** valiente
**bread** el pan
*wholemeal bread* el pan integral
*French bread* la barra de pan
*sliced bread* el pan de molde

**bread roll** el panecillo
**to break** romper
**breakable** frágil
**breakdown** (car) la avería
  (nervous) la crisis nerviosa
**breakdown van** la grúa
**breakfast** el desayuno
**breast** el pecho
**to breast-feed** amamantar
**to breathe** respirar
**brick** el ladrillo
**bride** la novia
**bridegroom** el novio
**bridge** el puente
**briefcase** la cartera
**bright** (colour) vivo(a)
**Brillo pad**® el nanas®
**to bring** traer
**Britain** Gran Bretaña
**British** británico(a)
**broadband** n banda ancha
**broccoli** el brócoli
**brochure** el folleto
**broken** roto(a)
  *my leg is broken* me he roto la pierna
**broken down** (car, etc) averiado(a)
**bronchitis** la bronquitis
**bronze** el bronce
**brooch** el broche
**broom** (brush) la escoba
**brother** el hermano
**brother-in-law** el cuñado
**brown** marrón
**bruise** el moratón ; el cardenal
**brush** el cepillo
**to brush** cepillar
**bubble bath** el baño de espuma
**bucket** el cubo
**buckle** la hebilla
**buffet car** el coche comedor
**to build** construir
**building** el edificio
**bulb** (electric) la bombilla
**bull** el toro
**bullfight** la corrida de toros
**bullfighter** el torero
**bullring** la plaza de toros
**bumbag** la riñonera
**bumper** (car) el parachoques
**bunch** (of flowers) el ramo
  (grapes) el racimo
**bungee jumping** el banyi
**buoy** la boya
**bureau de change** la oficina de cambio
**burger** la hamburguesa
**burglar** el/la ladrón/ladrona

**burglar alarm** la alarma antirrobo
**to burn** quemar
**burnt** (food) quemado(a)
**to burst** reventar
**bus** el autobús
**bus pass** el bonobús
**bus station** la estación de autobuses
**bus stop** la parada de autobús
**bus ticket** el billete de autobús
**business** el negocio
  *on business* de negocios
**business card** la tarjeta de visita
**business centre** centro de negocios
**business class** la clase preferente
**businessman/woman**
  el hombre/la mujer de negocios
**business trip** el viaje de negocios
**busy** ocupado(a)
**but** pero
**butcher's** la carnicería
**butter** la mantequilla
**butterfly** la mariposa
**button** el botón
**to buy** comprar
**by** (via) por
  (beside) al lado de
  *by air* en avión
  *by bus* en autobús
  *by car* en coche
  *by train* en tren
  *by ship* en barco
**bypass** (road) la carretera
  de circunvalación

## C

**cab** (taxi) el taxi
**cabaret** el cabaré
**cabin** (on boat) el camarote
**cabin crew** la tripulación de cabina
**cablecar** el teleférico
**café** el café
  *internet café* el cibercafé
**cafetiere** la cafetera
**cake** (big) la tarta
  (little) el pastel
**cake shop** la pastelería
**calculator** la calculadora
**calendar** el calendario
**call** (telephone) la llamada
  *a long distance call* una conferencia
**to call** (phone) llamar por teléfono
**calm** tranquilo(a)
**camcorder** la videocámara
  (digital) la cámara digital
**camera** la cámara

camera case la funda de la cámara
camera shop la tienda de fotografía
camera phone teléfono con cámara
to camp acampar
camping gas el camping gas
camping stove el hornillo de gas
campsite el camping
to can (to be able) poder
  I can puedo
  we can podemos
  I cannot no puedo
  we cannot no podemos
can la lata
can opener el abrelatas
Canada (el) Canadá
Canadian canadiense
canal el canal
to cancel anular ; cancelar
cancellation la cancelación
cancer el cáncer
candle la vela
canoe la canoa
canoeing: to go canoeing hacer
  piragüismo
cap (hat) la gorra
  (diaphragm) el diafragma
capital (city) la capital
car el coche
car alarm la alarma de coche
car ferry el transbordador ; el ferry
car hire el alquiler de coches
car insurance el seguro del coche
car keys las llaves del coche
car park el aparcamiento
car parts los accesorios para el coche
car port puerto del coche
car radio la radio del coche
car seat (child) el asiento para niños
car wash el lavado (automático) de
  coches
carafe la jarra
caravan la caravana
carburettor el carburador
card (greetings, business) la tarjeta
  playing cards las cartas
cardboard el cartón
cardigan la chaqueta de punto
careful cuidadoso(a)
  be careful! ¡cuidado!
carpet (rug) la alfombra
  (fitted) la moqueta
carriage (railway) el vagón
carrot la zanahoria
to carry llevar
carton la caja
  (of cigarettes) el cartón
case (suitcase) la maleta

cash el dinero en efectivo
to cash (cheque) cobrar
cash desk la caja
cash dispenser el cajero automático
cashier el/la cajero(a)
cashpoint el cajero automático
casino el casino
casserole la cazuela
cassette el casete
cassette player el radiocasete
castanets las castañuelas
castle el castillo
casualty department urgencias
cat el gato
cat food la comida para gatos
catalogue el catálogo
to catch (bus, train, etc) coger
cathedral la catedral
Catholic católico(a)
cauliflower la coliflor
cave la cueva
cavity (in tooth) la caries
CD el CD
CD player el lector de CD
CD ROM CD-ROM
ceiling el techo
cellar la bodega
cemetery el cementerio
cent el céntimo
centimetre el centímetro
central central
central heating la calefacción central
central locking (car) el cierre
  centralizado
centre el centro
century el siglo
ceramic la cerámica
cereal los cereales
certain (sure) seguro(a)
certificate el certificado
chain la cadena
chair la silla
chairlift el telesilla
chalet el chalet
chambermaid la camarera
champagne el champán
change el cambio
  (small coins) el suelto
  (money returned) la vuelta
to change cambiar
  (clothes) cambiarse
  (train) hacer transbordo
  to change money cambiar dinero
changing room el probador
chapel la capilla
charcoal el carbón vegetal

**charge** *(fee)* el precio
  *(electrical)* la carga
  **I've run out of charge** no tengo batería charge
**to charge** *(money)* cobrar
  *(battery)* cargar
  **please charge it to my account** cárguelo a mi cuenta, por favor
  **I need to charge my phone** necesito cargar el teléfono
**charger** *(for battery)* el cargador
**charter flight** el vuelo chárter
**chatroom** sala de chat
**cheap** barato(a)
**cheaper** más barato(a)
**cheap rate** la tarifa baja
**to check** revisar ; comprobar
**to check in** *(at airport)* facturar el equipaje
  *(at hotel)* registrarse
**check-in** la facturación
**cheek** la mejilla
**cheers!** ¡salud!
**cheese** el queso
**chef** el chef
**chemist's** la farmacia
**cheque** el cheque
**cheque book** el talonario
**cheque card** la tarjeta bancaria
**cherry** la cereza
**chest** *(of body)* el pecho
**chewing gum** el chicle
**chicken** el pollo
**chickenpox** la varicela
**child** *(boy)* el niño
  *(girl)* la niña
**children** *(infants)* los niños
  **for children** para niños
**child seat** *(car)* el asiento de niños
**chilli** la guindilla ; el chile
**chimney** la chimenea
**chin** la barbilla
**china** la porcelana
**chips** las patatas fritas
**chiropodist** podólogo(a)
**chocolate** el chocolate
**chocolates** los bombones
**to choose** escoger
**chop** *(meat)* la chuleta
**chopping board** la tabla de cortar
**christening** el bautizo
**Christian name** el nombre de pila
**Christmas** la Navidad
  **Merry Christmas!** ¡Feliz Navidad!
**Christmas card** la tarjeta de Navidad
**Christmas Eve** la Nochebuena

**church** la iglesia
**cigar** el puro
**cigarette** el cigarrillo
**cigarette lighter** el mechero
**cigarette paper** el papel de fumar
**cinema** el cine
**circle** *(theatre)* el anfiteatro
**circuit breaker** el cortacircuitos
**circus** el circo
**cistern** la cisterna
**city** la ciudad
**city centre** el centro de la ciudad
**class: first class** primera clase
  **second class** segunda clase
**clean** limpio(a)
**to clean** limpiar
**cleaner** *(person)* el/la encargado/a de la limpieza
**cleanser** *(for face)* la crema limpiadora
**clear** claro(a)
**client** el/la cliente
**cliff** *(along coast)* el acantilado
  *(in mountains)* el precipicio
**to climb** *(mountains)* escalar
**climbing boots** las botas de escalar
**Clingfilm®** el rollo de plástico transparente
**clinic** la clínica
**cloakroom** el guardarropa
**clock** el reloj
**close by** muy cerca
**to close** cerrar
**closed** *(shop, etc)* cerrado(a)
**cloth** *(rag)* el trapo
  *(fabric)* la tela
**clothes** la ropa
**clothes line** el tendedero
**clothes peg** la pinza
**clothes shop** la tienda de ropa
**cloudy** nublado(a)
**club** el club
**clutch** *(in car)* el embrague
**coach** *(bus)* el autocar
**coach station** la estación de autobuses
**coach trip** la excursión en autocar
**coal** el carbón
**coast** la costa
**coastguard** el/la guardacostas
**coat** el abrigo
**coat hanger** la percha
**cockroach** la cucaracha
**cocktail** el cóctel
**cocktail bar** bar de cóctel
**cocoa** el cacao
**code** el código

**coffee** el café
  *black coffee* el café solo
  *white coffee* el café con leche
  *cappuccino* el capuchino
  *decaffeinated coffee*
  el (café) descafeinado
**coil** *(IUD)* el DIU
**coin** la moneda
**Coke**® la Coca Cola®
**colander** el colador
**cold** frío(a)
  *I'm cold* tengo frío
  *it's cold* hace frío
  *cold water* el agua fría
**cold** *(illness)* el resfriado
  *I have a cold* estoy resfriado(a)
**cold sore** la calentura
**collar** el cuello
**collar bone** la clavícula
**colleague** el/la compañero(a) de trabajo
**to collect** recoger
**collection** la recogida
**colour** el color
**colour-blind** daltónico(a)
**colour film** *(for camera)* el carrete
  en color
**comb** el peine
**to come** venir
  *(to arrive)* llegar
**to come back** volver
**to come in** entrar
  *come in!* ¡pase!
**comedy** la comedia
**comfortable** cómodo(a)
**company** *(firm)* la empresa
**compartment** el compartimento
**compass** la brújula
**to complain** reclamar
**complaint** la reclamación ; la queja
**complete** completo(a)
**to complete** terminar
**compulsory** obligatorio(a)
**computer** el ordenador
**computer disk** *(floppy)* el disquete
**computer game** el juego de ordenador
**computer program** el programa de
  ordenador
**concert** el concierto
**concert hall** la sala de conciertos
**concession** el descuento
**concussion** la conmoción cerebral
**conditioner** el suavizante
**condom** el condón
**conductor** *(on bus)* el/la cobrador(a)
  *(on train)* el/la revisor(a)
**conference** el congreso

**to confirm** confirmar
  *please confirm* por favor, confirme
**confirmation** *(flight, booking)*
  la confirmación
**congratulations!** ¡enhorabuena!
**connection** *(train, etc)* el enlace
**constipated** estreñido(a)
**consulate** el consulado
**to consult** consultar
**to contact** ponerse en contacto con
**contact lens** la lentilla
**contact lens cleaner** la solución
  limpiadora para lentillas
**to continue** continuar
**contraceptive** el anticonceptivo
**contract** el contrato
**convenient: is it convenient?**
  ¿le viene bien?
**convulsions** las convulsiones
**to cook** cocinar
**cooked** preparado(a)
**cooker** la cocina
**cookies** las galletas
**cool** fresco(a)
**cool-box** la nevera portátil
**copper** el cobre
**copy** *(duplicate)* la copia
  *(of book)* el ejemplar
**to copy** copiar
**coral** el coral
**cordless phone** el teléfono inalámbrico
**cork** el corcho
**corkscrew** el sacacorchos
**corner** la esquina
**cornflakes** los copos de maíz
**corridor** el pasillo
**cortisone** la cortisona
**cosmetics** los cosméticos
**cost** *(price)* el precio
**to cost** costar
  *how much does it cost?* ¿cuánto
  cuesta?
**costume** *(swimming)* el bañador
**cot** la cuna
**cottage** la casita de campo
**cotton** el algodón
**cotton buds** los bastoncillos
**cotton wool** el algodón hidrófilo
**couchette** la litera
**to cough** toser
**cough** la tos
**cough mixture** el jarabe para la tos
**cough sweets** los caramelos para la tos
**counter** *(in shop)* el mostrador
  *(in bar)* la barra

**country** (not town) el campo
(nation) el país
**countryside** el campo
**couple** (2 people) la pareja
 *a couple of...* un par de ...
**courgette** el calabacín
**courier service** el servicio de mensajero
**course** (of study) el curso
(of meal) el plato
**cousin** el/la primo(a)
**cover charge** (in restaurant) el cubierto
**cow** la vaca
**crafts** la artesanía
**craft fair** feria de artesanía(s)
**craftsperson** el/la artesano(a)
**cramps** los calambres
**cranberry juice** el zumo de arándanos
**crash** (car) el accidente
**to crash** (car) chocar
**crash helmet** el casco protector
**cream** (lotion) la crema
(on milk) la nata
 *soured cream* la nata cortada
 *whipped cream* la nata montada
**credit** n (on mobile phone) saldo
**credit card** la tarjeta de crédito
**crime** el delito
**crisps** las patatas fritas
**cross** (crucifix) la cruz
**to cross** (road) cruzar
**cross country skiing** el esquí de fondo
**crossing** (sea) la travesía
**crossroads** el cruce
**crossword puzzle** el crucigrama
**crowd** la multitud
**crowded** concurrido(a)
**crown** la corona
**cruise** el crucero
**crutches** las muletas
**to cry** (weep) llorar
**crystal** el cristal
**cucumber** el pepino
**cufflinks** los gemelos
**cul-de-sac** el callejón sin salida
**cup** la taza
**cupboard** el armario
**currant** la pasa (de Corinto)
**currency** la moneda
**current** la corriente
**curtain** la cortina
**cushion** el cojín
**custom** (tradition) la costumbre
**customer** el/la cliente
**customs** (control) la aduana
**customs declaration** la declaración
aduanera

**cut** el corte
**to cut** cortar
**cutlery** los cubiertos
**to cycle** ir en bicicleta
**cycle track** el carril bici
**cycling** el ciclismo
**cyst** el quiste
**cystitis** la cistitis

## D

**daily** (each day) cada día ; diario
**dairy produce** los productos lácteos
**dam** la presa
**damage** el/los daño(s)
**damp** húmedo(a)
**dance** el baile
**to dance** bailar
**danger** el peligro
**dangerous** peligroso(a)
**dark** oscuro(a)
 *after dark* por la noche
**date** la fecha
**date of birth** la fecha de nacimiento
**daughter** la hija
**daughter-in-law** la cuñada
**dawn** el amanecer
**day** el día
 *every day* todos los días
 *per day* al día
**dead** muerto(a)
**deaf** sordo(a)
**dear** (on letter) querido(a)
(expensive) caro(a)
**debt** la deuda
**debit card** la tarjéta de débito
**decaffeinated coffee**
 el descafeinado
 *have you decaff?*
 ¿tiene descafeinado?
**December** diciembre
**deck chair** la tumbona
**to declare** declarar
 *nothing to declare* nada que declarar
**deep** profundo(a)
**deep freeze** el ultracongelador
**deer** el ciervo
**to defrost** descongelar
**to de-ice** descongelar
**delay** el retraso
 *how long is the delay?*
 ¿cuánto lleva de retraso?
**delayed** retrasado(a)
**delicatessen** la charcutería
**delicious** delicioso(a)
**demonstration** la manifestación

**dental floss** el hilo dental
**dentist** el/la dentista
**dentures** la dentadura postiza
**deodorant** el desodorante
**department** (gen) el departamento
  (in shop) la sección
**department store** los grandes
  almacenes
**departure lounge** la sala de embarque
**departures** las salidas
**deposit** la fianza
**to describe** describir
**description** la descripción
**desk** (in hotel, airport) el mostrador
**dessert** el postre
**details** los detalles
  (personal) los datos personales
**detergent** el detergente
**detour** el desvío
**to develop** (photos) revelar
**diabetes** la diabetes
**diabetic** diabético(a)
  *I'm diabetic* soy diabético(a)
**to dial** marcar
**dialling code** el prefijo
**dialling tone** el tono de marcar
**diamond** el diamante
**diapers** los pañales
**diaphragm** el diafragma
**diarrhoea** la diarrea
**diary** la agenda
**dice** los dados
**dictionary** el diccionario
**to die** morir
**diesel** el diesel ; el gasóleo
**diet** la dieta
  *I'm on a diet* estoy a dieta
  *special diet* la dieta especial
**different** distinto(a)
**difficult** difícil
**digital camera** la cámara digital
**digital radio** la radio digital
**to dilute** diluir
**dinghy** el bote
**dining room** el comedor
**dinner** (evening meal) la cena
  *to have dinner* cenar
**diplomat** el/la diplomático(a)
**direct** (train, etc) directo(a)
**directions** (instructions) las instrucciones
  *to ask for directions* preguntar el
  camino
**directory** (phone) la guía telefónica
**directory enquiries** la información
  telefónica
**dirty** sucio(a)

**disability** la discapacidad
**disabled** discapacitado(a) ;
  minusválido(a)
**to disagree** no estar de acuerdo
**to disappear** desaparecer
**disaster** el desastre
**disco** la discoteca
**discount** el descuento
**to discover** descubrir
**disease** la enfermedad
**dish** el plato
**dishtowel** el paño de cocina
**dishwasher** el lavavajillas
**dishwasher powder** el detergente
  para lavavajillas
**disinfectant** el desinfectante
**disk** (floppy) el disquete
**to dislocate** (joint) dislocarse
**disposable** desechable
**distance** la distancia
**distant** distante ; lejano(a)
**distilled water** el agua destilada
**district** el barrio
**to disturb** molestar
**ditch** la cuneta
**to dive** tirarse al agua
**diversion** el desvío
**divorced** divorciado(a)
**DIY shop** la tienda de bricolaje
**dizzy** mareado(a)
**to do** hacer
**doctor** el/la médico(a)
**documents** los documentos
**dog** el perro
**dog food** la comida para perros
**dog lead** la correa del perro
**doll** la muñeca
**dollar** el dólar
**domestic** (flight) nacional
**donor card** la tarjeta de donante
**door** la puerta
**doorbell** el timbre
**double** doble
**double bed** la cama de matrimonio
**double room** la habitación doble
**doughnut** el donut
**down:** *to go down* bajar
**to download** descargar
**downstairs** abajo
**Down's syndrome** síndrome (de) Down
  *he/she has Down's syndrome* tiene
  síndrome (de) Down
**dozen** la docena
**drain** el desagüe
**draught** (of air) la corriente
  *there's a draught* hay corriente

**draught lager** la cerveza de barril
**to draw** dibujar
**drawer** el cajón
**drawing** el dibujo
**dress** el vestido
**to dress** *(to get dressed)* vestirse
**dressing** *(for food)* el aliño
*(for wound)* el vendaje
**dressing gown** la bata
**drill** *(tool)* la taladradora
**drink** la bebida
**to drink** beber
**drinking water** el agua potable
**to drive** conducir
**driver** el/la conductor(a)
**driving licence** el carné de conducir
**drought** la sequía
**to drown** ahogarse
**drug** la droga
*(medicine)* la medicina
**drunk** borracho(a)
**dry** seco(a)
**to dry** secar
**dry-cleaner's** la tintorería ; la limpieza en seco
**due: when is it due?** ¿para cuándo está previsto?
**dummy** *(for baby)* el chupete
**during** durante
**dust** el polvo
**duster** el trapo del polvo
**dustpan and brush** el cepillo y recogedor
**duty-free** libre de impuestos
**duvet** el edredón nórdico
**duvet cover** la funda nórdico
**DVD** el DVD
**DVD player** el reproductor de DVD
**dye** el tinte
**dynamo** la dinamo

# E

**each** cada
**ear** *(outside)* la oreja
*(inside)* el oído
**earache** el dolor de oído(s)
*I have earache* me duele el oído
**earlier** antes
**early** temprano
**to earn** ganar
**earphones** los auriculares
**earplugs** los tapones para los oídos
**earrings** los pendientes
**earth** la tierra
**earthquake** el terremoto

**east** el este
**Easter** la Pascua ; la Semana Santa
**easy** fácil
**to eat** comer
**ecological** ecológico(a)
**eco-tourism** ecoturismo
**egg** el huevo
*fried egg* el huevo frito
*hard-boiled egg* el huevo duro
*scrambled eggs* los huevos revueltos
*soft-boiled egg* el huevo pasado por agua
**eggplant** la berenjena
**either... or...** o... o...
**elastic band** la goma
**elastoplast**® la tirita
**elbow** el codo
**electric** eléctrico(a)
**electric blanket** la manta eléctrica
**electric razor** la maquinilla de afeitar
**electric toothbrush** el cepillo de dientes eléctrico
**electrician** el/la electricista
**electricity** la electricidad
**electricity meter** el contador de electricidad
**electric point** el enchufe
**electric shock** la descarga eléctrica
**electronic** electrónico(a)
**electronic organizer** el agenda electrónica *(f)*
**elevator** el ascensor
**e-mail** el email
*to e-mail s.o.* mandar un email a alguien
**e-mail address** el email
**embassy** la embajada
**emergency** la emergencia
**emergency exit** la salida de emergencia
**empty** vacío(a)
**end** el fin
**engaged** *(to marry)* prometido(a)
*(toilet, phone)* ocupado(a)
**engine** el motor
**England** Inglaterra
**English** inglés/inglesa
*(language)* el inglés
**Englishman/-woman** el inglés/la inglesa
**to enjoy** *(to like)* gustar
*I enjoy swimming* me gusta nadar
*I enjoy dancing* me gusta bailar
*enjoy your meal!* ¡qué aproveche!
**to enjoy oneself** divertirse
**enough** bastante
*that's enough* ya basta
**enquiry desk** la información

to enter entrar en
entertainment el entretenimiento
entrance la entrada
entrance fee el precio de entrada
envelope el sobre
epileptic epiléptico(a)
epileptic fit el ataque epiléptico
equal igual
equipment el equipo
eraser la goma (de borrar)
error el error
escalator la escalera mecánica
to escape escapar
espadrilles las alpargatas
essential imprescindible
estate agent's la agencia inmobiliaria
euro el euro
euro cent el céntimo
Europe Europa
European el/la europeo(a)
European Union la Unión Europea
even (not odd) par
evening la tarde
  this evening esta tarde
  tomorrow evening mañana por la tarde
  in the evening por la tarde
evening dress (man's)
  el traje de etiqueta
  (woman's) el traje de noche
evening meal la cena
every cada
everyone todo el mundo ; todos
everything todo
everywhere en todas partes
examination el examen
example: for example por ejemplo
excellent excelente
except excepto
excess baggage el exceso de equipaje
exchange el cambio
to exchange cambiar
exchange rate el tipo de cambio
exciting emocionante
excursion la excursión
excuse: excuse me! perdón
exercise el ejercicio
exhaust pipe el tubo de escape
exhibition la exposición
exit la salida
expenses los gastos
expensive caro(a)
expert el/la experto(a)
to expire (ticket, etc) caducar
to explain explicar

explosion la explosión
to export exportar
express (train) el expreso
express: to send a letter express
  enviar una carta por correo urgente
extension (electrical) el alargador
extra (in addition) de más
  (more) extra ; adicional
eye el ojo
eyebrows las cejas
eye drops el colirio
eyelashes las pestañas
eyeliner el lápiz de ojos
eye shadow la sombra de ojos

# F

fabric la tela
face la cara
face cloth la toallita
facial la limpieza de cutis
facilities las instalaciones
fact el hecho
factor (sunblock) factor
  factor 25 factor 25
factory la fábrica
to fade desteñir
to faint desmayarse
fainted desmayado(a)
fair (hair) rubio(a)
  (just) justo(a)
fair (funfair) la feria
fake falso(a)
fall (autumn) el otoño
to fall caer ; caerse
  he/she has fallen se ha caído
false teeth la dentadura postiza
family la familia
famous famoso(a)
fan (electric) el ventilador
  (hand-held) el abanico
  (football, etc) el/la hincha
  (jazz, etc) el/la aficionado(a)
fan belt la correa del ventilador
fancy dress el disfraz
far lejos
  is it far? ¿está lejos?
  how far is it? ¿a cuánto está?
farm la granja
farmer el/la granjero(a)
farmers' market mercado agrícola
farmhouse la granja
fashionable de moda
fast rápido(a)
  too fast demasiado rápido
to fasten (seatbelt, etc) abrocharse

**fat** *(plump)* gordo(a)
  *(in food, on person)* la grasa
  **saturated fats** las grasas saturadas
  **unsaturated fats** las grasas insaturadas
**father** el padre
**father-in-law** el suegro
**fault** *(defect)* el defecto
  **it's not my fault** no tengo la culpa
**favour** el favor
**favourite** favorito(a) ; preferido(a)
**to fax** mandar por fax
**fax** el fax
  **by fax** por fax
**fax number** el número de fax
**February** febrero
**to feed** dar de comer
**to feel** sentir
  **I don't feel well** no me siento bien
  **I feel sick** estoy mareado(a)
**feet** los pies
**felt-tip pen** el rotulador
**female** mujer
**ferry** el ferry ; el transbordador
**festival** el festival
**to fetch** *(to bring)* traer
  *(to go and get)* ir a buscar
**fever** la fiebre
**few** pocos(as)
  **a few** algunos(as)
**fiancé(e)** el/la novio(a)
**field** el campo
**to fight** luchar
**file** *(computer)* el fichero
  *(nail)* la lima
**to fill** llenar
  *(form)* rellenar
  **fill it up, please!** *(car)* lleno, por favor
**fillet** el filete
**filling** *(in tooth)* el empaste
**film** *(at cinema)* la película
  *(for camera)* el carrete
**Filofax®** el agenda Filofax® *(f)*
**filter** el filtro
**to find** encontrar
**fine** *(to be paid)* la multa
**finger** el dedo
**to finish** acabar
**finished** terminado(a)
**fire** *(flames)* el fuego
  *(blaze)* el incendio
  **fire!** ¡fuego!
**fire alarm** la alarma de incendios
**fire brigade** los bomberos
**fire engine** el coche de bomberos
**fire escape** la salida de incendios
**fire exit** la salida de incendios

**fire extinguisher** el extintor
**fireplace** la chimenea
**fireworks** los fuegos artificiales
**firm** *(company)* la empresa
**first** primero(a)
**first aid** los primeros auxilios
**first aid kit** el botiquín de primeros auxilios
**first class** de primera clase
**first name** el nombre de pila
**fish** *(food)* el pescado
  *(alive)* el pez
**to fish** pescar
**fisherman** el pescador
**fishing permit** la licencia de pesca
**fishing rod** la caña de pescar
**fishmonger's** la pescadería
**fit** *(seizure)* el ataque
**to fit** *(clothes)* quedar bien
  **it doesn't fit** no queda bien
**to fix** arreglar
  **can you fix it?** ¿puede arreglarlo?
**fizzy** con gas
**flag** la bandera
**flames** las llamas
**flash** *(for camera)* el flash
**flashlight** la linterna
**flask** *(thermos)* el termo
**flat** *(apartment)* el piso
**flat** llano(a)
  *(battery)* descargado(a)
  *(beer)* sin gas
  **it's flat** ya no tiene gas
**flat tyre** la rueda pinchada
**flavour** el sabor
  **which flavour?** ¿qué sabor?
**flaw** el defecto
**fleas** las pulgas
**flesh** la carne
**flex** el cable eléctrico
**flight** el vuelo
**flip flops** las chancletas
**flippers** las aletas
**flood** la inundación
  **flash flood** la riada
**floor** *(of building)* el piso
  *(of room)* el suelo
  **which floor?** ¿qué piso?
  **on the ground floor** en la planta baja
  **on the first floor** en el primer piso
  **on the second floor** en el segundo piso
**floorcloth** la bayeta
**floppy disk** disquete
**florist's shop** la floristería
**flour** la harina
**flower** la flor

**flu** la gripe
**fly** la mosca
**to fly** volar
**fly sheet** el toldo impermeable
**fog** la niebla
**foggy: it's foggy** hay niebla
**foil** *(tinfoil)* el papel de estaño
**to fold** doblar
**to follow** seguir
**food** la comida
**food poisoning** la intoxicación por alimentos
**foot** el pie
  **on foot** a pie
**football** el fútbol
**football match** el partido de fútbol
**football pitch** el campo de fútbol
**football player** el/la futbolista
**footpath** *(in country)* el sendero
**for** para ; por
  **for me** para mí
  **for you** para usted/ti
  **for him/her/us** para él/ella/nosotros
**forbidden** prohibido(a)
**forehead** la frente
**foreign** extranjero(a)
**foreign currency** la moneda extranjera
**foreigner** el/la extranjero(a)
**forest** el bosque
**forever** para siempre
**to forget** olvidar
**fork** *(for eating)* el tenedor
  *(in road)* la bifurcación
**form** *(document)* el impreso
**formal dress** el traje de etiqueta
**fortnight** quince días
**forward** adelante
**foul** *(football)* la falta
**fountain** la fuente
**four-wheel drive** la tracción a cuatro ruedas
**fox** el zorro
**fracture** la fractura
**fragile** frágil
**fragrance** el perfume
**frame** *(picture)* el marco
**France** Francia
**free** *(not occupied)* libre
  *(costing nothing)* gratis
**free-range** de granja
**freezer** el congelador
**French** francés/francesa
  *(language)* el francés
**French bean** la judía verde
**French fries** las patatas fritas
**frequent** frecuente

**fresh** fresco(a)
**fresh water** el agua dulce
**Friday** el viernes
**fridge** el frigorífico
**fried** frito(a)
**friend** el/la amigo(a)
**frisbee®** el frisbee®
**frog** la rana
**from** de ; desde
  **from Scotland** de Escocia
  **from England** de Inglaterra
**front** la parte delantera
  **in front of** delante de
**front door** la puerta de la calle
**frost** la helada
**frozen** congelado(a)
**fruit** la fruta
  **dried fruit** la fruta seca
**fruit juice** el zumo (de fruta)
**fruit salad** la macedonia
**to fry** freir
**frying pan** la sartén
**fuel** *(petrol)* la gasolina
**fuel gauge** el indicador de la gasolina
**fuel tank** el depósito de gasolina
**fuel pump** *(in car)* el surtidor de gasolina
**full** lleno(a)
  *(occupied)* ocupado(a)
**full board** pensión completa
**fumes** *(of car)* los gases
**fun** la diversión
**funeral** el funeral
**funfair** la feria
**funny** *(amusing)* divertido(a)
**fur** la piel
**furnished** amueblado(a)
**furniture** los muebles
**fuse** el fusible
**fuse box** la caja de fusibles
**future** el futuro

## G

**gallery** la galería
**gallon = approx. 4.5 litres**
**game** el juego
  *(animal)* la caza
**garage** el garaje
  *(for repairs)* el taller
  *(for petrol)* la gasolinera
**garden** el jardín
**garlic** el ajo
**gas** el gas
**gas cooker** la cocina de gas
**gas cylinder** la bombona de gas
**gastritis** la gastritis

**gate** (airport) la puerta
**gay** (person) gay
**gear** la marcha
  **first gear** la primera
  **second gear** la segunda
  **third gear** la tercera
  **fourth gear** la cuarta
  **neutral** el punto muerto
  **reverse** la marcha atrás
**gearbox** la caja de cambios
**gear cable** el cable de cambio
**generous** generoso(a)
**gents** (toilet) los servicios de caballeros
**genuine** auténtico(a)
**German** alemán/alemana
  (language) el alemán
**German measles** la rubeola
**Germany** Alemania
**to get** (to obtain) conseguir
  (to receive) recibir
  (to bring) traer
**to get in** (vehicle) subir (al)
**to get out** (of vehicle) bajarse de
**gift** el regalo
**gift shop** la tienda de regalos
**girl** la chica
**girlfriend** la novia
**to give** dar
**to give back** devolver
**glacier** el glaciar
**glass** (for drinking) el vaso
  (substance) el cristal
  **a glass of water** un vaso de agua
  **a glass of wine** un vaso de vino
**glasses** (spectacles) las gafas
**glasses case** la funda de gafas
**gloves** los guantes
**glue** el pegamento
**gluten** el gluten
**GM-free** no transgénico(a)
**to go** ir
  **I'm going to ...** voy a...
  **we're going to ...** vamos a...
  **to go home** irse a casa
**to go back** volver
**to go in** entrar (en)
**to go out** salir
**goat** la cabra
**God** Dios
**goggles** (for swimming) las gafas
  de natación
  (for skiing) las gafas de esquí
**gold** el oro
**golf** el golf
**golf ball** la pelota de golf
**golf clubs** los palos de golf
**golf course** el campo de golf

**good** bueno(a)
  **very good** muy bueno
**good afternoon** buenas tardes
**goodbye** adiós
**good day** buenos días
**good evening** buenas tardes
  (when dark) buenas noches
**good morning** buenos días
**good night** buenas noches
**goose** el ganso
**gram(me)** el gramo
**grandchild** el/la nieto(a)
**granddaughter** la nieta
**grandfather** el abuelo
**grandmother** la abuela
**grandparents** los abuelos
**grandson** el nieto
**grapefruit** el pomelo
**grapes** las uvas
**grass** la hierba
**grated** (cheese, etc) rallado(a)
**grater** (for cheese, etc) el rallador
**greasy** grasiento(a)
**great** (big) grande
  (wonderful) estupendo(a)
**Great Britain** Gran Bretaña
**green** verde
**green card** la carta verde
**greengrocer's** la frutería
**greetings card** la tarjeta de felicitación
**grey** gris
**grill** el grill
  (barbecue) la parrilla
**to grill** gratinar
  (on barbecue) asar a la parrilla
**grilled** gratinado(a)
  (on barbecue) a la parrilla
**grocer's** la tienda de alimentación
**ground** el suelo
**ground floor** la planta baja
  **on the ground floor** en la planta baja
**groundsheet** el suelo (de tela)
  impermeable
**group** el grupo
**guarantee** la garantía
**guard** (on train) el/la jefe(a) de tren
**guava** la guayaba
**guest** el/la invitado(a)
  (in hotel) el/la huésped
**guesthouse** la pensión
**guide** (tour guide) el/la guía
**to guide** guiar
**guidebook** la guía turística
**guided tour** la visita con guía
**guitar** la guitarra
**gun** la pistola

gym el gimnasio
gym shoes las zapatillas de deporte
gynaecologist el/la ginecólogo(a)

# H

haemorrhoids las hemorroides
hail el granizo
hair el pelo
hairbrush el cepillo del pelo
haircut el corte de pelo
hairdresser el/la peluquero(a)
hairdryer el secador de pelo
hair dye el tinte de pelo
hair gel la gomina
hairgrip la horquilla
hair mousse la espuma del pelo
hair spray la laca
half medio(a)
  *half an hour* media hora
half board media pensión
half fare el billete reducido para niños
half-price a mitad de precio
ham el jamón
  *(cooked)* el jamón de York
  *(cured)* el jamón serrano
hamburger la hamburguesa
hammer el martillo
hand la mano
handbag el bolso
hand luggage el equipaje de mano
hand-made hecho(a) a mano
handicapped minusválido(a)
handkerchief el pañuelo
handle *(of cup)* el asa
  *(of door)* el pomo
handlebars el manillar
hands-free kit *(for phone)* el equipo
  manos libres
hands-free phone el teléfono de
  manos libres
handsome guapo(a)
hang gliding el vuelo con ala delta
hangover la resaca
to hang up *(phone)* colgar
to happen pasar
  *what happened?* ¿qué ha pasado?
happy feliz
  *happy birthday!* ¡feliz cumpleaños!
harbour el puerto
hard duro(a)
  *(difficult)* difícil
hard disk el disco duro
hardware shop la ferretería
to harm *(person)* hacer daño a
  *(crops, etc)* dañar

harvest la cosecha
hat el sombrero
to have tener
  *I have...* tengo
  *I don't have...* no tengo...
  *we have...* tenemos...
  *we don't have...* no tenemos...
  *do you have...?* ¿tiene...?
to have to tener que
hay fever la alergia al polen
he él
head la cabeza
headache el dolor de cabeza
  *I have a headache* me duele la cabeza
headlights los faros
headphones los auriculares
head waiter el maître
health la salud
health food shop la tienda de dietética
healthy sano(a)
to hear oír
hearing aid el audífono
heart el corazón
heart attack el infarto
heartburn el ardor de estómago
heater el calentador
heating la calefacción
to heat up *(food)* calentar
heavy pesado(a)
heel *(of foot)* el talón
  *(of shoe)* el tacón
heel bar la tienda de reparación
  de calzado en el acto
height la altura
helicopter el helicóptero
hello hola
  *(on phone)* ¿diga?
helmet *(for bike, etc)* el casco
help! ¡socorro!
to help ayudar
  *can you help me?* ¿puede ayudarme?
hem el dobladillo
hepatitis la hepatitis
her su
herb la hierba
herbal tea la infusión
here aquí
  *here is...* aquí tiene...
  *here is my passport* aquí tiene
  mi pasaporte
hernia la hernia
hi! ¡hola!
to hide *(something)* esconder
  *(oneself)* esconderse
high alto(a)
high blood pressure la tensión alta

**high chair** la silla alta para niños
**high tide** la marea alta
**hill** la colina
**hill-walking** el montañismo
**him** él
**hip** la cadera
**hip replacement** la prótesis de cadera
**hire** *(bike, boat, etc)* el alquiler
  *car hire* el alquiler de coches
  *bike hire* el alquiler de bicicletas
  *boat hire* el alquiler de barcas
**to hire** alquilar
**hired car** el coche de alquiler
**his** su
**historic** histórico(a)
**history** la historia
**to hit** pegar
**to hitchhike** hacer autostop ;
  hacer dedo
**HIV positive** seropositivo(a)
**hobby** el hobby ; el pasatiempo
**to hold** tener
  *(to contain)* contener
**hold-up** *(traffic jam)* el atasco
**hole** el agujero
**holiday** las vacaciones
  *(public)* la fiesta
  *on holiday* de vacaciones
**holiday rep** el/la guía turístico(a)
**home** la casa
  *at home* en casa
**homesick: to be homesick** tener
  morriña
  *I'm homesick* tengo morriña
**homeopathic** homeopático(a)
**homeopathy** homeopatía
**homosexual** homosexual
**honest** sincero(a)
**honey** la miel
**honeymoon** la luna de miel
**hood** *(jacket)* la capucha
**hook** *(fishing)* el anzuelo
**to hope** esperar
  *I hope so/not* espero que sí/no
**horn** *(car)* el claxon
**hors d'oeuvre** los entremeses
**horse** el caballo
**horse racing** la hípica
**horse riding** la equitación
**hosepipe** la manguera
**hospital** el hospital
**hostel** el hostal
**hot** caliente
  *I'm hot* tengo calor
  *it's hot (weather)* hace calor
  *hot water* el agua caliente

**hot-water bottle** la bolsa de agua
  caliente
**hotel** el hotel
**hour** la hora
  *half an hour* media hora
**house** la casa
**housewife/husband** la/el ama(o)
  de casa
**house wine** el vino de la casa
**housework** las tareas domésticas
**how** *(in what way)* cómo
  *how much?* ¿cuánto?
  *how many?* ¿cuántos?
  *how are you?* ¿cómo está?
**hungry: to be hungry** tener hambre
**to hunt** cazar
**hunting permit** el permiso de caza
**hurry: I'm in a hurry** tengo prisa
**to hurt** *(injure)* hacer daño
  *my back hurts* me duele la espalda
  *that hurts* eso duele
**husband** el marido
**hut** *(bathing/beach)* la caseta
  *(mountain)* el refugio
**hydrofoil** el hidrodeslizador
**hypodermic needle** la aguja
  hipodérmica

# I

**I** yo
**ice** el hielo
  *(cube)* el cubito
  *with/without ice* con/sin hielo
**ice box** la nevera
**icecream** el helado
**ice lolly** el polo
**ice rink** la pista de patinaje
**to ice skate** patinar sobre hielo
**ice skates** los patines de hielo
**iced tea** el té helado
**idea** la idea
**identity card** el carné de identidad
**if** si
**ignition** el encendido
**ignition key** la llave de contacto
**ill** enfermo(a)
**illness** la enfermedad
**immediately** inmediatamente ;
  en seguida
**immersion heater** el calentador
  eléctrico
**immigration** la inmigración
**immobilizer** *(on car)* el inmobilizador
**immunisation** la inmunización
**to import** importar

important importante
impossible imposible
to improve mejorar
in dentro de ; en
  *in 10 minutes* dentro de diez minutos
  *in London* en Londres
in front of delante de
inch la pulgada = approx. 2.5 cm
included incluido(a)
inconvenient inoportuno(a)
to increase aumentar
indicator *(in car)* el intermitente
indigestion la indigestión
indigestion tablets las pastillas para
  la indigestión
indoors dentro
infection la infección
infectious contagioso(a)
information la información
information desk la información
ingredients los ingredientes
inhaler *(for medication)* el inhalador
injection la inyección
to injure herir
injured herido(a)
injury la herida
ink la tinta
inn la pensión
inner tube la cámara
inquiries información
inquiry desk la información
insect el insecto
insect bite la picadura de insecto
insect repellent el repelente contra
  insectos
inside dentro de
instant coffee el café instantáneo
instead of en lugar de
instructor el/la instructor(a)
insulin la insulina
insurance el seguro
insurance certificate la póliza de
  seguros
to insure asegurar
insured asegurado(a)
iPod® iPod®
to intend to pensar
internet access:
  *do you have internet access?*
  ¿tiene acceso a Internet?
interesting interesante
international internacional
internet el/la Internet
  *internet café* el cibercafé
interpreter el/la intérprete
interval *(theatre, etc)* el descanso ;
  el intermedio

interview la entrevista
into en
  *into town* al centro
to introduce to presentar a
invitation la invitación
to invite invitar
invoice la factura
Ireland Irlanda
Irish irlandés/irlandesa
iron *(for clothes)* la plancha
  *(metal)* el hierro
to iron planchar
ironing board la tabla de planchar
ironmonger's la ferretería
island la isla
it lo/la
Italian italiano(a)
  *(language)* el italiano
Italy Italia
itch el picor
to itch picar
  *it itches* pica
item el artículo
itemized bill la factura detallada
IUD el DIU

# J

jack *(for car)* el gato
jacket la chaqueta
jam *(food)* la mermelada
jammed *(stuck)* atascado(a)
January enero
jar *(honey, jam, etc)* el tarro
jaundice la ictericia
jaw la mandíbula
jealous celoso(a)
jeans los vaqueros
jelly *(dessert)* la gelatina
jellyfish la medusa
jet ski la moto acuática
jetty el embarcadero
Jewish judío(a)
jeweller's la joyería
jewellery las joyas
job el empleo
to jog hacer footing
to join *(club, etc)* hacerse socio de
to join in participar en
joint *(body)* la articulación
to joke bromear
joke la broma
journalist el/la periodista
journey el viaje
judge el/la juez(a)
jug la jarra

**juice** el zumo
 *a carton of juice* un brik de zumo
**July** julio
**to jump** saltar
**jumper** el jersey
**jump leads** *(for car)* los cables
 de arranque
**junction** *(road)* la bifurcación
**June** junio
**jungle** la jungla
**just:** *just two* sólo dos
 *I've just arrived* acabo de llegar

## K

**to keep** *(to retain)* guardar
**kennel** la caseta (del perro)
**kettle** el hervidor (de agua)
**key** la llave
 *card key* *(used in hotel)* la llave tarjeta
**keyboard** el teclado
**keycard** *(electronic key eg in hotel)*
 la tarjeta-llave
**keyring** el llavero
**to kick** dar una patada a
**kid** *(child)* el/la crío(a)
**kidneys** los riñones
**to kill** matar
**kilo(gram)** el kilo(gramo)
**kilometre** el kilómetro
**kind** *(person)* amable
**kind** *(sort)* la clase
 *what kind?* ¿qué clase?
**king** el rey
**kiosk** el quiosco
**kiss** el beso
**to kiss** besar
**kitchen** la cocina
**kitchen paper** el papel de cocina
**kite** la cometa
**kiwi fruit** el kiwi
**knee** la rodilla
**knee highs** las medias cortas
**knickers** las bragas
**knife** el cuchillo
**to knit** hacer punto
**to knock** *(on door)* llamar
**to knock down** *(car)* atropellar
**to knock over** *(vase, glass)* tirar
**knot** el nudo
**to know** *(have knowledge of)* saber
 *(person, place)* conocer
 *I don't know* no sé
**to know how to** saber
 *to know how to swim* saber nadar
**kosher** kosher

## L

**label** la etiqueta
**lace** *(fabric)* el encaje
**laces** *(for shoes)* los cordones
**ladder** la escalera (de mano)
**ladies** *(toilet)* los servicios de señoras
**lady** la señora
**lager** la cerveza (rubia)
 *bottled lager* la cerveza (rubia)
 de botella
 *draught lager* la cerveza (rubia)
 de barril
**lake** el lago
**lamb** el cordero
**lamp** la lámpara
**lamppost** la farola
**lampshade** la pantalla (de lámpara)
**land** el terreno
**to land** aterrizar
**landlady** la dueña (de la casa)
**landlord** el dueño (de la casa)
**landslide** el desprendimiento de tierras
**lane** el carril
**language** el idioma ; la lengua
**language school** la escuela/academia
 de idiomas
**laptop** el ordenador portátil
**laptop bag** el maletín de ordenador
 portátil
**large** grande
**last** último(a)
 *the last bus* el último autobús
 *the last train* el último tren
 *last night* anoche
 *last week* la semana pasada
 *last year* el año pasado
 *last time* la última vez
**late** tarde
 *the train is late* el tren viene con
 retraso
 *sorry I'm late* siento llegar tarde
**later** más tarde
**to laugh** reírse
**launderette** la lavandería automática
**laundry service** el servicio de
 lavandería
**lavatory** *(in house)* el wáter
 *(in public place)* los servicios
**law** la ley
**lawn** el césped
**lawyer** el/la abogado(a)
**laxative** el laxante
**layby** la zona de descanso
**lead** *(electric)* el cable
**lead** *(metal)* el plomo
**lead-free** sin plomo

**leaf** la hoja
**leak** *(of gas, liquid)* la fuga
  *(in roof)* la gotera
**to leak:** *it's leaking (radiator, etc)*
  está goteando
**to learn** aprender
**learning disability:**
  *he/she has a learning disability* tiene
  problemas de aprendizaje
**lease** *(rental)* el alquiler
**leather** el cuero
**to leave** *(a place)* irse de
  *(leave behind)* dejar
  *when does the train leave?*
  ¿a qué hora sale el tren?
**leek** el puerro
**left:** *on/to the left* a la izquierda
**left-handed** *(person)* zurdo(a)
**left-luggage** *(office)* la consigna
**left-luggage locker** la consigna
  automática
**leg** la pierna
**legal** legal
**leisure centre** el polideportivo
**lemon** el limón
**lemonade** la gaseosa
**lemongrass** limonaria
**to lend** prestar
**length** la longitud
**lens** *(photographic)* el objetivo
  *(contact lens)* la lentilla
**lesbian** lesbiana
**less** menos
  *less than* menos de que
**lesson** la clase
**to let** *(to allow)* permitir
  *(to hire out)* alquilar
**letter** la carta
  *(of alphabet)* la letra
**letterbox** el buzón
**lettuce** la lechuga
**level crossing** el paso a nivel
**library** la biblioteca
**licence** el permiso
  *(driving)* el carné de conducir
**lid** la tapa
**lie** *(untruth)* la mentira
**to lie down** acostarse
**lifebelt** el salvavidas
**lifeboat** el bote salvavidas
**lifeguard** el/la socorrista
**life insurance** el seguro de vida
**life jacket** el chaleco salvavidas
**life raft** la balsa salvavidas
**lift** *(elevator)* el ascensor
  *can you give me a lift?* ¿me lleva?

**lift pass** *(on ski slopes)* el forfait
**light** *(not heavy)* ligero(a)
**light** la luz
  *have you a light?* ¿tiene fuego?
**light bulb** la bombilla
**lighter** el encendedor ; el mechero
**lighthouse** el faro
**lightning** el relámpago
**like** *(similar to)* como
**to like** gustar
  *I like coffee* me gusta el café
  *I don't like...* no me gusta...
  *I'd like to...* me gustaría...
  *we'd like to...* nos gustaría...
**lilo**® la colchoneta hinchable
**lime** *(fruit)* la lima
**line** *(row, queue)* la fila
  *(telephone)* la línea
**linen** el lino
**lingerie** la lencería
**lips** los labios
**lip-reading** la lectura de labios
**lip salve** el cacao para los labios
**lipstick** la barra de labios
**liqueur** el licor
**list** la lista
**to listen to** escuchar
**litre** el litro
**litter** *(rubbish)* la basura
**little** pequeño(a)
  *a little...* un poco...
**to live** vivir
  *I live in Edinburgh* vivo
  en Edimburgo
  *he lives in a flat* vive en un piso
**liver** el hígado
**living room** el salón
**loaf** el pan de molde
**local** de la región ; del país
**lock** *(on door, box)* la cerradura
  *the lock is broken* la cerradura está
  rota
**to lock** cerrar con llave
**locker** *(luggage)* la consigna
**locksmith** el/la cerrajero(a)
**log** *(for fire)* el leño
**log book** *(car)* los papeles del coche
**lollipop** la piruleta ; el chupón
**London** Londres
  *in London* en Londres
  *to London* a Londres
**long** largo(a)
  *for a long time* (por) mucho tiempo
**long-sighted** hipermétrope
**to look after** cuidar
**to look at** mirar
**to look for** buscar

**loose** suelto(a)
  *it's come loose* se ha soltado
**lorry** el camión
**to lose** perder
**lost** perdido(a)
  *I've lost...* he perdido...
  *I'm lost* me he perdido
**lost property office**
  la oficina de objetos perdidos
**lot:** *a lot of* mucho
**lotion** la loción
**lottery** la lotería
**loud** *(sound, voice)* fuerte
  *(volume)* alto(a)
**loudspeaker** el altavoz
**lounge** el salón
**love** el amor
**to love** *(person)* querer
  *I love swimming* me encanta nadar
  *I love you* te quiero
**lovely** precioso(a)
**low** bajo(a)
**low-alcohol** con baja graduación
**low-fat** bajo(a) en calorías
**low tide** la marea baja
**luck** la suerte
**lucky:** *to be lucky* tener suerte
**luggage** el equipaje
**luggage allowance** el equipaje
  permitido
**luggage rack** el portaequipajes
**luggage tag** la etiqueta
**luggage trolley** el carrito
**lump** *(swelling)* el bulto
  *(on head)* el chichón
**lunch** la comida
**lunch break** la hora de la comida
**lung** el pulmón
**luxury** de lujo

# M

**machine** la máquina
**mad** loco(a)
**magazine** la revista
**maggot** el gusano
**magnet** el imán
**magnifying glass** la lupa
**maid** *(in hotel)* la camarera
**maiden name** el apellido de soltera
**mail** el correo
  *by mail* por correo
**main** principal
**main course** *(of meal)* el plato principal
**main road** la carretera principal
**Majorca** Mallorca

**make** *(brand)* la marca
**to make** hacer
**make-up** el maquillaje
**male** masculino(a)
**mallet** el mazo
**man** el hombre
**to manage** *(be in charge of)* dirigir
**manager** el/la gerente
**mango** el mango
**manicure** la manicura
**manual** *(gear change)* manual
**many** muchos(as)
**map** *(of region, country)* el mapa
  *(of town)* el plano
**marble** el mármol
**March** marzo
**margarine** la margarina
**marina** el puerto deportivo
**mark** *(stain)* la mancha
**market** el mercado
  *where is the market?* ¿dónde está
  el mercado?
  *when is the market?* ¿cuándo hay
  mercado?
**market place** la plaza (del mercado)
**marmalade** la mermelada de naranja
**married** casado(a)
  *I'm married* estoy casado(a)
  *are you married?* ¿está casado(a)?
**to marry** casarse con
**marsh** la marisma
**mascara** el rímel®
**masher** *(potato)* el pasapurés
**mass** *(in church)* la misa
**massage** el masaje
**mast** el mástil
**masterpiece** la obra maestra
**match** *(game)* el partido
**matches** las cerillas
**material** *(cloth)* la tela
**to matter** importar
  *it doesn't matter* no importa
  *what's the matter?* ¿qué pasa?
**mattress** el colchón
**May** mayo
**mayonnaise** la mayonesa
**maximum** máximo(a)
**Mb** *(megabyte)* Mb
**meal** la comida
**to mean** querer decir
  *what does this mean?* ¿qué quiere
  decir esto?
**measles** el sarampión
**to measure** medir
**meat** la carne
**mechanic** el/la mecánico(a)

**medical insurance** el seguro médico
**medical treatment** el tratamiento
  médico
**medicine** la medicina
**medieval** medieval
**Mediterranean** el Mediterráneo
**medium rare** *(meat)* medio(a) hecho(a)
**to meet** *(by chance)* encontrarse con
  *(by arrangement)* ver
  *I'm meeting her tomorrow*
  he quedado con ella mañana
**meeting** la reunión
**meeting point** el punto de reunión
**megabyte** el megabyte
**melon** el melón
**to melt** derretir
**member** *(of club, etc)* el/la socio(a)
**membership fee** la cuota de socio
**memory** el recuerdo
**memory card** *or* **stick** la tarjeta de
  memoria
**men** los hombres
**to mend** arreglar
**meningitis** la meningitis
**menu** la carta
  **set menu** el menú del día
**message** el mensaje
**metal** el metal
**meter** el contador
**metre** el metro
**metro** *(underground)* el metro
**metro station** la estación de metro
**microphone** micrófono
**microwave oven** el microondas
**midday** las doce del mediodía
**middle** el medio
**middle-aged** de mediana edad
**midge** el mosquito enano
**midnight** la medianoche
  **at midnight** a medianoche
**migraine** la jaqueca ; la migraña
  *I've a migraine* tengo jaqueca
**mile** la milla
**milk** la leche
  *fresh milk* la leche fresca
  *hot milk* la leche caliente
  *long-life milk* la leche de larga
  duración (UHT)
  *powdered milk* la leche en polvo
  *semi-skimmed milk* la leche
  semidesnatada
  *skimmed milk* la leche desnatada
  *soya milk* la leche de soja
  *with milk* con leche
**milkshake** el batido
**millimetre** el milímetro

**mince** *(meat)* la carne picada
**mind: do you mind if...?** ¿le importa
  que...?
  *I don't mind* no me importa
**mineral water** el agua mineral
**minibar** el minibar
**minidisc** el minidisc
**minimum** el mínimo
**minister** *(political)* el/la ministro(a)
  *(church)* el/la pastor(a)
**minor road** la carretera secundaria
**mint** *(herb)* la menta
  *(sweet)* la pastilla de menta
**minute** el minuto
**mirror** el espejo
**miscarriage** el aborto no provocado
**to miss** *(train, etc)* perder
**Miss** la señorita
**missing** *(lost)* perdido(a)
  *my son is missing* se ha perdido
  mi hijo
**mistake** el error
**misty: it's misty** hay neblina
**misunderstanding**
  la equivocación
**to mix** mezclar
**mixer** *(food processor)* el robot
  (de cocina)
  *(hand-held)* la batidora
**mobile** *(phone)* el teléfono móvil
**mobile number** el n úmero de móvil
**modem** el módem
**modern** moderno(a)
**moisturizer** la leche/crema hidratante
**mole** *(on skin)* el lunar
**moment** el momento
  *just a moment* un momento
**monastery** el monasterio
**Monday** el lunes
**money** el dinero
  *I've no money* no tengo dinero
**moneybelt** la riñonera
**money order** el giro postal
**month** el mes
  *this month* este mes
  *last month* el mes pasado
  *next month* el mes que viene
**monthly** mensualmente ; mensual
**monument** el monumento
**moon** la luna
**mooring** el atracadero
**mop** la fregona
**moped** el ciclomotor
**more** más
  *more than* más que
  *more wine* más vino

**morning** la mañana
  *in the morning* por la mañana
  *this morning* esta mañana
  *tomorrow morning* mañana por
  la mañana
**morning-after pill** la píldora
  (anticonceptiva) del día después
**mosque** la mezquita
**mosquito** el mosquito
**mosquito bite** la picadura de mosquito
**mosquito net** la mosquitera
**mosquito repellent** el repelente contra
  mosquitos
**most:** *most of* la mayor parte de ;
  la mayoría de
**MOT** el ITV
**moth** (clothes) la polilla
**mother** la madre
**mother-in-law** la suegra
**motor** el motor
**motorbike** la moto
**motorboat** la lancha motora
**motorway** la autopista
**mountain** la montaña
**mountain bike** la bicicleta de montaña
**mountain rescue** el rescate de montaña
**mountaineering** el montañismo
**mouse** (animal, computer) el ratón
**moustache** el bigote
**mouth** la boca
**mouthwash** el enjuague bucal
**to move** mover
  *it isn't moving* no se mueve
**movie** la película
**MP3 player** el reproductor MP3
**Mr** el señor (Sr.)
**Mrs** la señora (Sra.)
**Ms** la señora (Sra.)
**much** mucho(a)
  *too much* demasiado(a)
**muddy** embarrado(a)
**mugging** el atraco
**mumps** las paperas
**muscle** el músculo
**museum** el museo
**mushrooms** los champiñones
**music** la música
**musical** musical
**must** (to have to) deber
  *I must* debo
  *we must* debemos
  *I musn't* no debo
  *we musn't* no debemos
**mustard** la mostaza
**my** mi

# N

**nail** (fingernail) la uña
  (metal) el clavo
**nailbrush** el cepillo de uñas
**nail clippers** el cortaúñas
**nail file** la lima (de uñas)
**nail polish** el esmalte de uñas
**nail polish remover** el quitaesmalte
**nail scissors** las tijeras de uñas
**name** el nombre
  *my name is...* me llamo...
  *what's your name?* ¿cómo se llama?
**nanny** la niñera
**napkin** la servilleta
**nappies** los pañales
**narrow** estrecho(a)
**national** nacional
**national park** el parque nacional
**nationality** la nacionalidad
**natural** natural
**nature** la naturaleza
**nature reserve** la reserva natural
**navy blue** azul marino
**near to** cerca de
  *near to the bank* cerca del banco
  *is it near?* ¿está cerca?
**necessary** necesario(a)
**neck** el cuello
**necklace** el collar
**nectarine** la nectarina
**to need** necesitar
  *I need...* necesito...
  *we need...* necesitamos...
  *I need to go* tengo que ir
**needle** la aguja
  *a needle and thread* una aguja
  e hilo
**negative** (photo) el negativo
**neighbour** el/la vecino(a)
**nephew** el sobrino
**net** la red
  *the Net* (internet) la Red
**never** nunca
  *I never drink wine* nunca bebo vino
**new** nuevo(a)
**news** (TV, radio, etc) las noticias
**newsagent's** la tienda de prensa
**newspaper** el periódico
**newsstand** el kiosko de prensa
**New Year** el Año Nuevo
  *Happy New Year!* ¡Feliz Año Nuevo!
**New Year's Eve** la Nochevieja
**New Zealand** Nueva Zelanda
**next** próximo(a)
  *next to* al lado de
  *next week* la próxima semana

*the next stop* la próxima parada
*the next train* el próximo tren
**nice** *(person)* simpático(a)
  *(place, holiday)* bonito(a)
**niece** la sobrina
**night** la noche
  *at night* por la noche
  *last night* anoche
  *per night* por noche
  *tomorrow night* mañana por la noche
  *tonight* esta noche
**night club** el club nocturno
**nightdress** el camisón
**night porter** el guarda nocturno
**no** no
  *no entry* prohibida la entrada
  *no smoking* prohibido fumar
  *(without)* sin
  *no sugar* sin azúcar
  *no ice* sin hielo
  *no problem* ¡por supuesto!
**nobody** nadie
**noise** el ruido
  *it's very noisy* hay mucho ruido
**non-alcoholic** sin alcohol
**none** ninguno(a)
**non-smoker** el/la no fumador(a)
**non-smoking** no fumador
**normal** normal
**north** el norte
**Northern Ireland** Irlanda del Norte
**nose** la nariz
**nosebleed** la hemorragia nasal
**not** no
  *I am not...* no estoy... ; no soy...
**note** *(banknote)* el billete
  *(written)* la nota
**note pad** el bloc
**nothing** nada
  *nothing else* nada más
**notice** *(sign)* el anuncio
  *(warning)* el aviso
**notice board** el tablón de anuncios
**novel** la novela
**November** noviembre
**now** ahora
**nowhere** en ninguna parte
**nuclear** nuclear
**nudist beach** la playa nudista
**number** el número
**numberplate** *(car)* la matrícula
**nurse** la/el enfermera(o)
**nursery school** la guardería (infantil)
**nursery slope** la pista para principiantes
**nut** *(for bolt)* la tuerca
**nuts** *(to eat)* los frutos secos

# O

**oar** el remo
**oats** los copos de avena
**to obtain** obtener
**occupation** *(work)* la profesión
**ocean** el océano
**October** octubre
**odd** *(strange)* raro(a)
  *(not even)* impar
**of** de
  *a glass of wine* un vaso de vino
  *made of...* hecho(a) de...
**off** *(light, etc)* apagado(a)
  *(rotten)* pasado(a)
**office** la oficina
**often** a menudo
  *how often?* ¿cada cuánto?
**oil** el aceite
**oil filter** el filtro de aceite
**oil gauge** el indicador del aceite
**ointment** la pomada
**OK** ¡vale!
**old** viejo(a)
  *how old are you?* ¿cuántos años
  tiene?
  *I'm ... years old* tengo ... años
**old age pensioner** el/la pensionista
  (de la tercera edad)
**olive** la aceituna
**olive oil** el aceite de oliva
**olive tree** el olivo
**on** *(light, TV, engine)* encendido(a)
**on** sobre ; encima
  *on the table* sobre la mesa
  *on time* a la hora
**once** una vez
  *at once* en seguida
**one-way** dirección única
**onion** la cebolla
**only** sólo
**open** abierto(a)
**to open** abrir
**opera** la ópera
**operation** la operación
**operator** *(phone)* el/la telefonista
**opposite (to)** enfrente (de)
  *opposite the bank* enfrente del banco
  *quite the opposite!* ¡todo lo contrario!
**optician's** la óptica
**or** o
**orange** *(fruit)* la naranja
  *(colour)* naranja
**orange juice** el zumo de naranja
**orchestra** la orquesta
**order: out of order** averiado(a)

**to order** (in restaurant) pedir
 **can I order?** ¿puedo pedir?
**organic** biológico(a) ; ecológico(a)
**to organize** organizar
**ornament** el adorno
**other: the other one** el/la otro(a)
 **have you any others?** ¿tiene
 otros(as)?
**ounce** = approx. 30 g
**our** nuestro(a)
**out** (light) apagado(a)
 **he's (gone) out** ha salido
**outdoor** (pool, etc) al aire libre
**outside: it's outside** está fuera
**oven** el horno
**ovenproof dish** resistente al horno
**over** (on top of) (por) encima de
**to be overbooked** tener over-booking
**to overcharge** cobrar de más
**overdone** (food) demasiado hecho(a)
**overdose** la sobredosis
**to overheat** recalentar
**to overload** sobrecargar
**to oversleep** quedarse dormido(a)
**to overtake** (in car) adelantar
**to owe** deber
 **I owe you...** le debo...
 **you owe me...** me debe...
**owner** el/la propietario(a)
**oxygen** el oxígeno

# P

**pace** el ritmo
**pacemaker** el marcapasos
**to pack** (luggage) hacer las maletas
**package** el paquete
**package tour** el viaje organizado
**packet** el paquete
**padded envelope** el sobre acolchado
**paddling pool** la piscina hinchable
**padlock** el candado
**page** la página
**paid** pagado(a)
 **I've paid** he pagado
**pain** el dolor
**painful** doloroso(a)
**painkiller** el analgésico ; el calmante
**to paint** pintar
**paintbrush** el pincel
**painting** (picture) el cuadro
**pair** el par
**palace** el palacio
**pale** pálido(a)
**palmtop computer** el ordenador
 de bolsillo

**pan** (saucepan) la cacerola
 (frying) la sartén
**pancake** el crep(e)
**panniers** (for bike) las alforjas
**panties** las bragas
**pants** (men's underwear)
 los calzoncillos
**panty liner** el salvaslip
**paper** el papel
**paper hankies** los pañuelos
 de papel
**paper napkins** las servilletas
 de papel
**papoose** (for carrying baby)
 la mochila portabebés
**paragliding** el parapente
**paralysed** paralizado(a)
**paramedic** el/la paramédico(a)
**parcel** el paquete
**pardon?** ¿cómo?
 **I beg your pardon!** ¿perdón?
**parents** los padres
**park** el parque
**to park** aparcar
**parking disc** el tique de aparcamiento
**parking meter** el parquímetro
**parking ticket** (fine) la multa por
 aparcamiento indebido
**partner** (business) el/la socio(a)
 (boy/girlfriend) el/la compañero(a)
**party** (group) el grupo
 (celebration) la fiesta
 (political) el partido
**pass** (mountain) el puerto
 (train) el abono
 (bus) el bonobús
**passenger** el/la pasajero(a)
**passionfruit** la fruta de la pasión
**passport** el pasaporte
**passport control** el control de
 pasaportes
**password** la contraseña
**pasta** la pasta
**pastry** (dough) la masa
 (cake) el pastel
**path** el camino
**patient** (in hospital) el/la paciente
**pavement** la acera
**to pay** pagar
 **I'd like to pay** quisiera pagar
 **where do I pay** ¿dónde se paga?
**payment** el pago
**payphone** el teléfono público
**PDA** el PDA
**peace** la paz
**peach** el melocotón
**peak rate** la tarifa máxima

pear la pera
pearls las perlas
peas los guisantes
pedal el pedal
pedalo el hidropedal
pedestrian el peatón
pedestrian crossing el paso
   de peatones
to pee hacer pipí
to peel (fruit) pelar
peg (for clothes) la pinza
   (for tent) la estaca
pen el bolígrafo ; el boli
pencil el lápiz
penfriend el/la amigo(a) por
   correspondencia
penicillin la penicilina
penis el pene
penknife la navaja
pensioner el/la jubilado(a) ;
   el/la pensionista
people la gente
pepper (spice) la pimienta
   (vegetable) el pimiento
per por
   per day al día
   per hour por hora
   per week a la semana
   per person por persona
   50 km per hour 50 km por hora
perfect perfecto(a)
performance la función
perfume el perfume
perhaps quizá(s)
period (menstruation) la regla
perm la permanente
permit el permiso
person la persona
personal organizer la agenda
personal stereo el walkman®
pet el animal doméstico
pet food la comida para animales
pet shop la pajarería
petrol la gasolina
   4-star petrol la gasolina súper
   unleaded petrol la gasolina sin plomo
petrol cap el tapón del depósito
petrol pump el surtidor
petrol station la gasolinera
petrol tank el depósito
pharmacy la farmacia
pharmacist farmacéutico(a)
phone el teléfono
   (mobile) el móvil
   (hands free) el teléfono 'manos libres'
   by phone por teléfono
to phone llamar por teléfono

phonebook la guía (telefónica)
phonebox la cabina (telefónica)
phone call la llamada (telefónica)
phonecard la tarjeta telefónica
photocopier la fotocopiadora
photocopy la fotocopia
to photocopy fotocopiar
photograph la fotografía
   to take a photograph hacer una
   fotografía
phrase book la guía de conversación
piano el piano
to pick (choose) elegir
   (pluck) coger
pickled en vinagre
pickpocket el/la carterista
picnic el picnic
   to have a picnic ir de picnic
picnic area el merendero
picnic hamper la cesta de la merienda
picnic rug la mantita
picture (painting) el cuadro
   (photo) la foto
pie (fruit) la tarta
   (meat) el pastel de carne
   (and/or vegetable) la empanada
piece el trozo
pier el embarcadero ; el muelle
pig el cerdo
pill la píldora
   to be on the pill tomar la píldora
pillow la almohada
pillowcase la funda de almohada
pilot el/la piloto
pin el alfiler
pineapple la piña
pink rosa
pint = approx. 0.5 litre
pipe (smoker's) la pipa
   (drain, etc) la tubería
pitch (place for tent/caravan) la parcela
pity: what a pity ¡qué pena!
pizza la pizza
place el lugar
place of birth el lugar de nacimiento
plain (yoghurt) natural
plait la trenza
plan (of town) el plano
plane (airplane) el avión
plant la planta
plaster (sticking) la tirita®
   (for broken limb) la escayola
plastic (made of) de plástico
plastic bag la bolsa de plástico
plate el plato

**platform** el andén
 *which platform?* ¿qué andén?
**play** *(theatre)* la obra
**to play** *(games)* jugar
**play area** la zona recreativa
**play park** el parque infantil
**playroom** el cuarto de juegos
**pleasant** agradable
**please** por favor
**pleased** contento(a)
 *pleased to meet you* encantado(a) de
 conocerle(la)
**pliers** los alicates
**plug** *(electrical)* el enchufe
 *(for sink)* el tapón
**to plug in** enchufar
**plum** la ciruela
**plumber** el/la fontanero(a)
**plumbing** *(pipes)* las cañerías
 *(craft)* la fontanería
**plunger** *(for sink)* el desatascador
**p.m.** de la tarde
**poached** *(egg, fish)* escalfado(a)
**pocket** el bolsillo
**point** el punto
**points** *(in car)* los platinos
**poison** el veneno
**poisonous** venenoso(a)
**police** *(force)* la policía
**policeman/woman** el/la policía
**police station** la comisaría
**polish** *(for shoes)* el betún
 *(for furniture)* el limpiamuebles
**pollen** el polen
**polluted** contaminado(a)
**pony** el poni
**pony-trekking** la excursión a caballo
**pool** la piscina
**pool attendant** el/la encargado(a)
 de la piscina
**poor** pobre
**pop socks** los calcetines cortos
**popular** popular
**pork** el cerdo
**port** *(seaport)* el puerto
 *(wine)* el oporto
**porter** *(hotel)* el portero
 *(at station)* el mozo
**portion** la porción ; la ración
**Portugal** Portugal
**Portuguese** portugués/portuguesa
 *(language)* el portugués
**possible** posible
**post: by post** por correo
**to post** echar al correo
**postbox** el buzón

**postcard** la postal
**postcode** el código postal
**poster** el póster
**postman/woman** el/la cartero(a)
**post office** la oficina de Correos
**to postpone** aplazar
**pot** *(for cooking)* la olla
**potato** la patata
 *baked potato* la patata asada
 *boiled potatoes* las patatas hervidas
 *fried potatoes* las patatas fritas
 *mashed potatoes* el puré de patatas
 *roast potatoes* las patatas asadas
 *sautéed potatoes* las patatas
 salteadas
**potato masher** el pasapurés
**potato peeler** el pelador
**potato salad** la ensalada de patatas
**pothole** el bache
**pottery** la cerámica
**pound** *(weight)* = approx. 0.5 kilo
 *(money)* la libra
**to pour** echar ; servir
**powder** el polvo
 *in powder form* en polvo
**powdered milk** la leche en polvo
**power** *(electicity)* la electricidad
**power cut** el apagón
**pram** el cochecito (de bebé)
**to pray** rezar
**to prefer** preferir
**pregnant** embarazada
 *I'm pregnant* estoy embarazada
**to prepare** preparar
**to prescribe** prescribir
**prescription** la receta médica
**present** *(gift)* el regalo
**preservative** el conservante
**president** el/la presidente(a)
**pressure** la presión
**pretty** bonito(a)
**price** el precio
**price list** la lista de precios
**priest** el sacerdote ; el cura
**prime minister** el/la primer(a)
 ministro(a)
**print** *(photo)* la copia
**to print** imprimir
**printer** la impresora
**printout** el listado
**prison** la cárcel
**private** privado(a)
**prize** el premio
**probably** probablemente
**problem** el problema
**professor** el/la catedrático(a)

**programme** *(TV, radio)* el programa
**prohibited** prohibido(a)
**promise** la promesa
**to promise** prometer
**to pronounce** pronunciar
  *how's it pronounced?* ¿cómo se
  pronuncia?
**Protestant** protestante
**to provide** proporcionar
**public** público(a)
**public holiday** la fiesta (oficial)
**pudding** el postre
**to pull** tirar
  *I've pulled a muscle* me ha dado
  un tirón en el músculo
**to pull over** *(car)* hacerse a un lado
**pullover** el jersey
**pump** *(bike, etc)* la bomba
  *(petrol)* el surtidor
**puncture** el pinchazo
**puncture repair kit** el kit para
  reparar pinchazos
**puppet** la marioneta
**puppet show** el espectáculo
  de marionetas
**purple** morado(a)
**purpose** el propósito
  *on purpose* a propósito
**purse** el monedero
**to push** empujar
**pushchair** la sillita de paseo
**to put** *(place)* poner
**pyjamas** el pijama
**Pyrenees** los Pirineos

## Q

**quality** la calidad
**quantity** la cantidad
**quarantine** la cuarentena
**to quarrel** discutir ; pelearse
**quarter** el cuarto
**quay** el muelle
**queen** la reina
**query** la pregunta
**question** la pregunta
**queue** la cola
**to queue** hacer cola
**quick** rápido(a)
**quickly** de prisa
**quiet** *(place)* tranquilo(a)
**quilt** el edredón (nórdico)
**quite** bastante
  *it's quite good* es bastante bueno
  *quite expensive* bastante caro
**quiz** el concurso

## R

**rabbit** el conejo
**rabies** la rabia
**race** *(sport)* la carrera
**race course** *(horses)* el hipódromo
**racket** *(tennis, etc)* la raqueta
**radiator** *(car, heater)* el radiador
**radio** la radio
  *(digital)* la radio digital
  *(car)* la radio del coche
**railcard** el carné de descuento
  para el tren
**railway** el ferrocarril
**railway station** la estación de tren
**rain** la lluvia
**to rain:** *it's raining* está lloviendo
**raincoat** el impermeable
**rake** el rastrillo
**rape** la violación
**to rape** violar
**rare** *(unique)* excepcional
  *(steak)* poco hecho(a)
**rash** *(skin)* el sarpullido
**raspberry** la frambuesa
**rat** la rata
**rate** *(price)* la tarifa
**rate of exchange** el tipo de cambio
**raw** crudo(a)
**razor** la maquinilla de afeitar
**razor blades** las hojas de afeitar
**to read** leer
**ready** listo(a)
  *to get ready* prepararse
**real** verdadero(a)
**to realize** darse cuenta de
**rearview mirror** el (espejo) retrovisor
**receipt** el recibo
**receiver** *(phone)* el auricular
**reception desk** la recepción
**receptionist** el/la recepcionista
**to recharge** *(battery, etc)* recargar
**recharger** el cargador
**recipe** la receta
**to recognize** reconocer
**to recommend** recomendar
**to record** *(on tape, etc)* grabar
  *(facts)* registrar
**to recover** *(from illness)* recuperarse
**to recycle** reciclar
**red** rojo(a)
**to reduce** reducir
**reduction** el descuento
**to refer to** referirse a
**refill** el recambio
**refund** el reembolso

**to refuse** negarse
**regarding** con respecto a
**region** la región
**register** el registro
**to register** *(at hotel)* registrarse
**registered** *(letter)* certificado(a)
**registration form** la hoja de inscripción
**to reimburse** reembolsar
**relation** *(family)* el/la pariente
**relationship** la relación
**to remain** *(stay)* quedarse
**to remember** acordarse (de)
  *I don't remember* no me acuerdo
**remote control** el mando a distancia
**removal firm** la empresa de mudanzas
**to remove** quitar
**rent** el alquiler
**to rent** alquilar
**rental** el alquiler
**repair** la reparación
**to repair** reparar
**to repeat** repetir
**to reply** contestar
**report** el informe
**to report** informar
**request** la solicitud
**to request** solicitar
**to require** necesitar
**to rescue** rescatar
**reservation** la reserva
**to reserve** reservar
**reserved** reservado(a)
**resident** el/la residente
**resort** el centro turístico
**rest** *(repose)* el descanso
  *(remainder)* el resto
**to rest** descansar
**restaurant** el restaurante
**restaurant car** el coche restaurante
**retired** jubilado(a)
**to return** *(to go back)* volver
  *(to give back something)* devolver
**return** *(ticket)* de ida y vuelta
**to reverse** dar marcha atrás
**to reverse the charges** llamar a cobro revertido
**reverse charge call** la llamada a cobro revertido
**reverse gear** la marcha atrás
**rheumatism** el reumatismo
**rib** la costilla
**rice** el arroz
**rich** *(person)* rico(a)
  *(food)* pesado(a)
**to ride a horse** montar a caballo

**right** *(correct)* correcto(a)
  *to be right* tener razón
**right: on/to the right** a la derecha
**right of way** el derecho de paso
**to ring** *(bell, to phone)* llamar
  *it's ringing* está sonando
**ring** el anillo
**ring road** la carretera de circunvalación
**ripe** maduro(a)
**river** el río
**road** la carretera
**road sign** la señal de tráfico
**roadworks** las obras
**roast** asado(a)
**roll** *(bread)* el panecillo
**rollerblades** los patines en línea
**romantic** romántico(a)
**roof** el tejado
**roof-rack** la baca
**room** *(in house, hotel)* la habitación
  *(space)* sitio
  *double room* la habitación doble
  *single room* la habitación individual
  *family room* la habitación familiar
**room number** el número de habitación
**room service** el servicio de habitaciones
**root** la raíz
**rope** la cuerda
**rose** la rosa
**rosé wine** el (vino) rosado
**rotten** *(fruit, etc)* podrido(a)
**rough** *(sea)* picado(a)
**round** *(shape)* redondo(a)
**roundabout** *(traffic)* la rotonda
**row** *(line, theatre)* la fila
**to row** *(boat)* remar
**rowing** *(sport)* el remo
**rowing boat** el bote de remos
**royal** real
**rubber** *(material)* la goma
  *(eraser)* la goma de borrar
**rubber band** la goma
**rubber gloves** los guantes de goma
**rubbish** la basura
**rubella** la rubeola
**rucksack** la mochila
**rug** la alfombra
**ruins** las ruinas
**ruler** *(for measuring)* la regla
**to run** correr
**rush hour** la hora punta
**rusty** oxidado(a)
**rye** el centeno

# S

sad triste
saddle *(bike)* el sillín
  *(horse)* la silla de montar
safe seguro(a)
  *is it safe?* ¿es seguro(a)?
safe *(for valuables)* la caja fuerte
safety belt el cinturón de seguridad
safety pin el imperdible
to sail *(sport, leisure)* navegar
sailboard la tabla de windsurf
sailing *(sport)* la vela
sailing boat el velero
saint el/la santo(a)
salad la ensalada
  *green salad* la ensalada verde
  *mixed salad* la ensalada mixta
  *potato salad* la ensalada de patatas
  *tomato salad* la ensalada de tomate
salad dressing el aliño
salami el salchichón ; el salami
salary el sueldo
sale(s) las rebajas
salesman/woman el/la vendedor(a)
sales rep el/la representante
salt la sal
salt water el agua salada
salty salado(a)
same mismo(a)
sample la muestra
sand la arena
sandals las sandalias
sandwich el bocadillo ; el sándwich
  *toasted sandwich* el sándwich tostado
sanitary towels las compresas
satellite dish la antena parabólica
satellite TV la televisión por satélite
satnav el sistema de navegación por satélite
Saturday el sábado
sauce la salsa
  *tomato sauce* la salsa de tomate
saucepan la cacerola
saucer el platillo
sauna la sauna
sausage la salchicha
to save *(life)* salvar
  *(money)* ahorrar
savoury salado(a)
saw la sierra
to say decir
scales *(weighing)* el peso
to scan escanear
scan el escáner
scarf *(woollen)* la bufanda
  *(headscarf)* el pañuelo

scenery el paisaje
schedule el programa
school la escuela
  *primary school* la escuela primaria
  *secondary school* el instituto de enseñanza secundaria
scissors las tijeras
score *(of match)* la puntuación
to score a goal marcar un gol
Scot el escocés/la escocesa
Scotland Escocia
Scottish escocés/escocesa
scouring pad el estropajo
screen *(computer, TV)* la pantalla
screenwash el limpiacristales
screw el tornillo
screwdriver el destornillador
  *phillips screwdriver*® el destornillador de estrella
scuba diving el submarinismo
sculpture la escultura
sea el mar
seafood el/los marisco(s)
seam *(of dress)* la costura
to search buscar
search engine el buscador
seasick mareado(a)
seaside la playa
  *at the seaside* en la playa
season *(of year)* la estación
  *(holiday)* la temporada
  *in season* del tiempo
seasonal estacional
season ticket el abono
seasoning el condimento
seat *(chair)* la silla
  *(in bus, train)* el asiento
seatbelt el cinturón de seguridad
seaweed las algas
second segundo(a)
second *(time)* el segundo
second class de segunda clase
second-hand de segunda mano
secretary el/la secretario(a)
security check el control de seguridad
security guard el/la guarda de seguridad
sedative el sedante
to see ver
self-catering sin servicio de comidas
self-employed autónomo(a)
self-service self-service ; el autoservicio
to sell vender
  *do you sell...?* ¿tiene...?

**sell-by date** la fecha de limite de venta
**Sellotape®** el celo
**to send** enviar
**senior citizen** el/la jubilado(a)
**sensible** sensato(a)
**separated** (couple) separado(a)
**separately: to pay separately** pagar por separado
**September** septiembre
**septic tank** el pozo séptico
**serious** (accident, etc) grave
**to serve** servir
**service** (in church) la misa
    (in restaurant) el servicio
    **is service included?** ¿está incluido el servicio?
**service charge** el servicio
**service station** la estación de servicio
**serviette** la servilleta
**set menu** el menú del día
**settee** el sofá
**several** varios(as)
**to sew** coser
**sex** el sexo
**shade** la sombra
    **into the shade** a la sombra
**to shake** (bottle) agitar
**shallow** poco profundo(a)
**shampoo** el champú
**shampoo and set** lavar y marcar
**to share** compartir ; dividir
**sharp** (razor, knife) afilado(a)
**to shave** afeitarse
**shaver** la maquinilla de afeitar
**shaving cream** la crema de afeitar
**shawl** el chal
**she** ella
**sheep** la oveja
**sheet** (bed) la sábana
**shelf** el estante
**shell** (seashell) la concha
    (egg, nut) la cáscara
**sheltered** protegido(a)
**shepherd** el/la pastor(a)
**sherry** el jerez
**to shine** brillar
**shingles** el herpes zóster ; la culebrilla
**ship** el barco
**shirt** la camisa
**shock** el susto
    (electric) la descarga
**shock absorber** el amortiguador
**shoe** el zapato
**shoelaces** los cordones (de los zapatos)

**shoe polish** el betún
**shoe shop** la zapatería
**shop** la tienda
**to shop** hacer las compras ; comprar
**shop assistant** el/la dependiente(a)
**shopping** las compras
    **to go shopping** ir de compras/tiendas
**shopping centre** el centro comercial
**shore** la orilla
**short** corto(a)
**shortage** la escasez
**short circuit** el cortocircuito
**short cut** el atajo
**shorts** los pantalones cortos
**short-sighted** miope
**shoulder** el hombro
**to shout** gritar
**show** (theatrical) el espectáculo
**to show** enseñar
**shower** (bath) la ducha
    (rain) el chubasco
    **to take a shower** ducharse
**shower cap** el gorro de ducha
**shower gel** el gel de ducha
**to shrink** encoger
**shut** (closed) cerrado(a)
**to shut** cerrar
**shutters** (outside) las persianas
**shuttle service** el servicio regular de enlace
**sick** (ill) enfermo(a)
    **I feel sick** tengo ganas de vomitar
**side** el lado
**side dish** la guarnición
**sidelight** la luz de posición
**sidewalk** la acera
**sieve** (for liquids) el colador
    (for flour, etc) el tamiz
**sightseeing: to go sightseeing** hacer turismo
**sightseeing tour** el recorrido turístico
**sign** la señal
**to sign** firmar
**signature** la firma
**signpost** la señal
**silk** la seda
**silver** la plata
**SIM card** la tarjeta SIM
**similar to** parecido(a) a
**since** desde ; puesto que
    **since 1974** desde 1974
    **since you're not Spanish** puesto que no es español(a)
**to sing** cantar
**single** (unmarried) soltero(a)
    (bed, room) individual

single ticket el billete de ida
sink *(in kitchen)* el fregadero
sir señor
sister la hermana
sister-in-law la cuñada
to sit sentarse
  *sit down, please* siéntese, por favor
site *(website)* el sitio
size *(clothes)* la talla
  *(shoes)* el número
to skate patinar
skateboard el monopatín
skates los patines
skating rink la pista de patinaje
ski el esquí
to ski esquiar
ski boots las botas de esquí
skiing el esquí
ski instructor el/la monitor(a)
  de esquí
ski jump el salto de esquí
ski lift el telesquí
ski pants los pantalones de esquí
ski pass el forfait
ski pole/stick el bastón de esquí
ski run/piste la pista de esquí
ski suit el traje de esquí
to skid patinar
skin la piel
skirt la falda
sky el cielo
sledge el trineo
to sleep dormir
  *to sleep in* quedarse dormido(a)
sleeper *(on train)* la litera
sleeping bag el saco de dormir
sleeping car el coche cama
sleeping pill el somnífero
slice *(of bread)* la rebanada
  *(of ham)* la loncha
sliced bread el pan de molde
slide *(photo)* la diapositiva
to slip resbalarse
slippers las zapatillas
slow lento(a)
to slow down reducir la velocidad
slowly despacio
small pequeño(a)
smaller than más pequeño(a) que
smell el olor
  *a bad smell* un mal olor
  *a nice smell* un buen olor
smile la sonrisa
to smile sonreír

to smoke fumar
  *I don't smoke* no fumo
  *can I smoke?* ¿puedo fumar?
smoke el humo
smoke alarm la alarma contra incendios
smoked ahumado(a)
smokers *(sign)* fumadores
smooth liso(a)
SMS message el mensaje SMS
snack el tentempié
  *to have a snack* tomar algo
snack bar la cafetería
snake la serpiente
snake bite la mordedura
  de serpiente
to sneeze estornudar
to snore roncar
snorkel el esnórkel
snow la nieve
to snow nevar
  *it's snowing* está nevando
snow board el snowboard
snowboarding: *to go snowboarding*
  ir a hacer snowboard
snow chains las cadenas (para la nieve)
snow tyres los neumáticos
  antideslizantes
snowed up aislado(a) por la nieve
soap el jabón
soap powder el detergente
sober sobrio(a)
socket *(for plug)* el enchufe
socks los calcetines
soda water la soda
sofa el sofá
sofa bed el sofá-cama
soft blando
soft drink el refresco
software el software
soldier el soldado
sole *(of foot, shoe)* la suela
soluble soluble
some algunos(as)
someone alguien
something algo
sometimes a veces
son el hijo
son-in-law el yerno
song la canción
soon pronto
  *as soon as possible* lo antes posible
sore throat el dolor de garganta
sorry: *sorry!* ¡perdón!
  *I'm sorry!* ¡lo siento!
sort el tipo
  *what sort?* ¿qué tipo?

**soup** la sopa
**sour** amargo(a)
**soured cream** la nata agria
**south** el sur
**souvenir** el souvenir
**spa** el spa ; el balneario
**space** el espacio
**spade** la pala
**Spain** España
**Spaniard** el/la español(a)
**Spanish** español(a)
**spam** (email) el spam ; el correo basura
**spanner** la llave inglesa
**spare parts** los repuestos
**spare room** el cuarto de invitados
**spare tyre** la rueda de repuesto
**spare wheel** la rueda de repuesto
**sparkling** espumoso(a)
  *sparkling water* el agua con gas
  *sparkling wine* el vino espumoso
**spark plug** la bujía
**to speak** hablar
  *do you speak English?* ¿habla inglés?
**speaker** (loudspeaker) el altavoz
**special** especial
**specialist** el/la especialista
**speciality** la especialidad
**speed** la velocidad
**speedboat** la lancha motora
**speeding** el exceso de velocidad
**speeding ticket** la multa por exceso
  de velocidad
**speed limit** la velocidad máxima
  *to exceed the speed limit* exceder
  la velocidad máxima
**speedometer** el velocímetro
**spell: how is it spelt?** ¿cómo se
  escribe?
**to spend** (money) gastar
**spice** la especia
**spicy** picante
**spider** la araña
**SPF** (sun protection factor) el FPS (factor
  de protección solar)
**to spill** derramar
**spinach** las espinacas
**spine** la columna (vertebral)
**spin-dryer** la secadora-centrifugadora
**spirits** el alcohol
**splinter** la astilla
**spoke** (wheel) el radio
**sponge** la esponja
**spoon** la cuchara
**sport** el deporte
**sports centre** el polideportivo
**sports shop** la tienda de deportes

**spot** (pimple) la espinilla
**sprain** el esguince
**spring** (season) la primavera
  (metal) el muelle
**square** (in town) la plaza
**squash** (game) el squash
**to squeeze** apretar
  (lemon) exprimir
**squid** el calamar
**stadium** el estadio
**stage** el escenario
**stain** la mancha
**stained glass** la vidriera
**stairs** las escaleras
**stale** (bread) duro(a)
**stalls** (theatre) las butacas (de patio)
**stamp** (postage) el sello
**to stand** estar de pie
**star** la estrella
**to start** (car) poner en marcha
**starter** (in meal) entrante
  (in car) la puesta en marcha
**station** la estación
**stationer's** la papelería
**statue** la estatua
**stay** la estancia
  *enjoy your stay!* ¡que lo pase bien!
**to stay** (remain) quedarse
  *I'm staying at the hotel...* estoy
  alojado(a) en el hotel...
**steak** el filete
**to steal** robar
**steamed** al vapor
**steel** el acero
**steep: is it steep?** ¿hay mucha subida?
**steeple** la aguja
**steering wheel** el volante
**step** el peldaño
**stepdaughter** la hijastra
**stepfather** el padrastro
**stepmother** la madrastra
**stepson** el hijastro
**stereo** el estéreo
**sterling** (pounds) las libras esterlinas
**steward** (on plane) el auxiliar de vuelo
**stewardess** (on plane) la azafata
**to stick** (with glue) pegar
**sticking plaster** la tirita
**still** (not fizzy) sin gas
**sting** la picadura
**to sting** picar
**stitches** (surgical) los puntos
**stockings** las medias
**stomach** el estómago
**stomach upset** el trastorno estomacal
**stone** la piedra

**to stop** parar
**store** *(shop)* la tienda
**storey** el piso
**storm** la tormenta
  *(at sea)* el temporal
**story** la historia
**straightaway** inmediatamente
**straight on** todo recto
**strange** extraño(a)
**straw** *(for drinking)* la pajita
**strawberry** la fresa
**stream** el arroyo
**street** la calle
**street map** el plano de la ciudad
**strength** la fuerza
**stress** el estrés
**strike** *(of workers)* la huelga
**string** la cuerda
**striped** a rayas
**stroke** *(medical)* la trombosis
**strong** fuerte
**stuck:** *it's stuck* está atascado(a)
**student** el/la estudiante
**student discount** el decuento
  para estudiantes
**stuffed** relleno(a)
**stung** picado(a)
**stupid** tonto(a)
**subscription** la suscripción
**subtitles** los subtítulos
**subway** *(train)* el metro
  *(passage)* el paso subterráneo
**suddenly** de repente
**suede** el ante
**sugar** el azúcar
**sugar-free** sin azúcar
**to suggest** sugerir
**suit** *(men's and women's)* el traje
**suitcase** la maleta
**sum** la suma
**summer** el verano
**summer holidays** las vacaciones
  de verano
**summit** la cumbre
**sun** el sol
**to sunbathe** tomar el sol
**sunblock** la protección solar
**sunburn** la quemadura del sol
**suncream** el protector solar
**Sunday** el domingo
**sunglasses** las gafas de sol
**sunny:** *it's sunny* hace sol
**sunrise** la salida del sol
**sunroof** el techo solar
**sunscreen** el filtro solar
**sunset** la puesta de sol

**sunshade** la sombrilla
**sunstroke** la insolación
**suntan** el bronceado
**suntan lotion** el bronceador
**supermarket** el supermercado
**supper** la cena
**supplement** el suplemento
**to supply** suministrar
**to surf** hacer surf
  *to surf the net* navegar por internet
**surfboard** la tabla de surf
**surgery** *(operation)* la operación
**surname** el apellido
**surprise** la sorpresa
**surrounded by** rodeado(a) de
**to survive** sobrevivir
**to swallow** tragar
**to sweat** sudar
**sweater** el jersey
**sweatshirt** la sudadera
**sweet** *(not savoury)* dulce
**sweet** *(dessert)* el dulce
**sweetener** el edulcorante ; la sacarina®
**sweets** los caramelos
**to swell** *(injury, etc)* hincharse
**to swim** nadar
**swimming pool** la piscina
**swimsuit** el bañador
**swing** *(for children)* el columpio
**swipecard** la tarjeta magnética
**Swiss** suizo(a)
**switch** el interruptor
**to switch off** apagar
**to switch on** encender
**Switzerland** Suiza
**swollen** hinchado(a)
**synagogue** la sinagoga
**syringe** la jeringuilla

# T

**table** la mesa
**tablecloth** el mantel
**tablespoon** la cuchara de servir
**table tennis** el ping-pong
**tablet** *(pill)* la pastilla
**tailor's** la sastrería
**to take** *(medicine, etc)* tomar
  *how long does it take?* ¿cuánto
  tiempo se tarda?
**take-away** *(food)* para llevar
**to take off** despegar
**to take out** *(of bag, etc)* sacar
**talc** los polvos de talco
**to talk to** hablar con
**tall** alto(a)

**tampons** los tampones
**tangerine** la mandarina
**tank** *(petrol)* el depósito
  *(fish)* la pecera
**tap** el grifo
**tap water** el agua corriente
**tape** *(video)* la cinta
**tape measure** el metro
**tape recorder** el casete
**tart** la tarta
**taste** el sabor
**to taste** probar
  *can I taste it?* ¿puedo probarlo?
**tax** el impuesto
**taxi** el taxi
**taxi driver** el/la taxista
**taxi rank** la parada de taxis
**tea** el té
  *herbal tea* la infusión
  *lemon tea* el té con limón
  *strong tea* el té cargado
**teabag** la bolsita de té
**teapot** la tetera
**teaspoon** la cucharilla
**tea towel** el paño de cocina
**to teach** enseñar
**teacher** el/la profesor(a)
**team** el equipo
**tear** *(in material)* el rasgón
**teat** *(on baby's bottle)* la tetina
**teenager** el/la adolescente
**teeth** los dientes
**telegram** el telegrama
**telephone** el teléfono
**to telephone** llamar por teléfono
**telephone box** la cabina (telefónica)
**telephone call** la llamada (telefónica)
**telephone card** la tarjeta telefónica
**telephone directory** la guía (telefónica)
**telephone number** el número de
  teléfono
**television** la televisión
**to tell** decir
**temperature** la temperatura
  *to have a temperature* tener fiebre
**temporary** provisional
**tenant** el/la inquilino(a)
**tendon** el tendón
**tennis** el tenis
**tennis ball** la pelota de tenis
**tennis court** la pista de tenis
**tennis racket** la raqueta de tenis
**tent** la tienda de campaña
**tent peg** la estaca
**terminal** *(airport)* la terminal
**terrace** la terraza

**to test** *(try out)* probar
**testicles** los testículos
**tetanus** el tétanos
**to text** mandar un mensaje de
  texto a
**text message** el mensaje de texto
**to text** mandar un mensaje de texto a
  *I'll text you* te mandaré un mensaje
**than** que
  *more than you* más que tú
  *more than five* más de cinco
**to thank** agradecer
**thank you** gracias
  *thank you very much* muchas gracias
**that** ese/esa
  *(more remote)* aquel/aquella
  *that one* ése/ésa/eso
  *(more remote)* aquél/ aquélla/aquello
**the** el/la/los/las
**theatre** el teatro
**theft** el robo
**their** su/sus
**them** ellos/ellas
  *(direct)* los/las
**there** *(over there)* allí
**there is/there are** hay
**thermometer** el termómetro
**these** estos/estas
  *these ones* éstos/éstas
**they** ellos/ellas
**thick** *(not thin)* grueso(a)
**thief** el ladrón/la ladrona
**thigh** el muslo
**thin** *(person)* delgado(a)
**thing** la cosa
  *my things* mis cosas
**to think** pensar
  *(to be of opinion)* creer
**thirsty: I'm thirsty** tengo sed
**this** este/esta/esto
  *this one* éste/ésta
**thorn** la espina
**those** esos/esas
  *(more remote)* aquellos/aquellas
  *those ones* ésos/ésas
  *(more remote)* aquéllos/aquéllas
**thread** el hilo
**throat** la garganta
**throat lozenges** las pastillas para
  la garganta
**through** por
**thumb** el pulgar
**thunder** el trueno
**thunderstorm** la tormenta
**Thursday** el jueves
**thyme** el tomillo

**ticket** *(bus, train, etc)* el billete
  *(entrance fee)* la entrada
  *a single ticket* un billete de ida
  *a return ticket* un billete de
  ida y vuelta
  *a tourist ticket* un billete turístico
  *a book of tickets* un abono
**ticket collector** el/la revisor(a)
**ticket office** el despacho de billetes
**tide** *(sea)* la marea
  *low tide* la marea baja
  *high tide* la marea alta
**tidy** arreglado(a)
**to tidy up** ordenar
**tie** la corbata
**tight** *(fitting)* ajustado(a)
**tights** las medias
**tile** *(roof)* la teja
  *(floor)* la baldosa
**till** *(cash desk)* la caja
**till** *(until)* hasta
  *till 2 o'clock* hasta las 2
**time** el tiempo
  *(clock)* la hora
  *what time is it?* ¿qué hora es?
**timer** *(on cooker)* el temporizador
**timetable** el horario
**tin** *(can)* la lata
**tinfoil** el papel de estaño
**tin-opener** el abrelatas
**tip** la propina
**to tip** dar propina
**tipped** *(cigarette)* con filtro
**tired** cansado(a)
**tissues** los kleenex®
**to** a
  *to London* a Londres
  *to the airport* al aeropuerto
**toadstool** el hongo venenoso
**toast** *(to eat)* la tostada
  *(raising glass)* el brindis
**tobacco** el tabaco
**tobacconist's** el estanco
**today** hoy
**toddler** el/la niño(a) pequeño(a)
**toe** el dedo del pie
**together** juntos(as)
**toilet** los aseos ; los servicios
  *toilet for disabled* los servicios
  para minusválidos
**toilet brush** la escobilla del wáter
**toilet paper** el papel higiénico
**toiletries** los artículos
  de baño
**token** *(for bus)* el vale
**toll** *(motorway)* el peaje

**tomato** el tomate
  *tinned tomatoes* los tomates en lata
**tomato juice** el zumo de tomate
**tomato soup** la sopa de tomate
**tomorrow** mañana
  *tomorrow morning* mañana por
  la mañana
  *tomorrow afternoon* mañana por
  la tarde
  *tomorrow evening* mañana por
  la tarde/noche
**tongue** la lengua
**tonic water** la tónica
**tonight** esta noche
**tonsillitis** la amigdalitis
**too** *(also)* también
  *too big* demasiado grande
  *too small* demasiado pequeño(a)
  *too hot* *(food)* demasiado caliente
  *too noisy* demasiado ruidoso(a)
**tool** la herramienta
**toolkit** el juego de herramientas
**tooth** el diente
**toothache** el dolor de muelas
**toothbrush** el cepillo de dientes
**toothpaste** la pasta de dientes
**toothpick** el palillo
**top:** *the top floor* el último piso
**top** *(of hill)* la cima
  *(shirt)* el top
  *(t-shirt)* la camiseta
  *on top of...* sobre...
**topless:** *to go topless* hacer topless
**torch** *(flashlight)* la linterna
**torn** rasgado(a)
**total** *(amount)* el total
**to touch** tocar
**tough** *(meat)* duro(a)
**tour** *(trip)* el viaje
  *(of museum, etc)* la visita
  *guided tour* la visita con guía
**tour guide** el/la guía turístico(a)
**tour operator** el/la tour operador(a)
**tourist** el/la turista
**tourist office** la oficina de turismo
**tourist route** la ruta turística
**tourist ticket** el billete turístico
**to tow** remolcar
**towbar** la barra de remolque
**tow rope** el cable de remolque
**towel** la toalla
**tower** la torre
**town** la ciudad
**town centre** el centro de la ciudad
**town hall** el ayuntamiento
**town plan** el plano de la ciudad
**toxic** tóxico(a)

**toy** el juguete
**toy shop** la juguetería
**tracksuit** el chándal
**traditional** tradicional
**traffic** el tráfico
**traffic jam** el atasco
**traffic lights** el semáforo
**traffic warden** el/la guardia de tráfico
**trailer** el remolque
**train** el tren
  *by train* en tren
  *the next train* el próximo tren
  *the first train* el primer tren
  *the last train* el último tren
**trainers** las zapatillas de deporte
**tram** el tranvía
**tranquillizer** el tranquilizante
**to translate** traducir
**translation** la traducción
**to travel** viajar
**travel agent's** la agencia de viajes
**travel guide** la guía de viajes
**travel insurance** el seguro de viaje
**travel sickness** el mareo
**traveller's cheque** el cheque de viaje
**tray** la bandeja
**treatment** el tratamiento
**tree** el árbol
**trip** la excursión
**trolley** *(luggage, shopping)* el carrito
**trouble** el apuro
  *to be in trouble* estar en apuros
**trousers** los pantalones
**truck** el camión
**true** verdadero(a)
**trunk** *(luggage)* el baúl
**trunks** *(swimming)* el bañador
**truth** la verdad
**to try** *(attempt)* probar
**to try on** *(clothes)* probarse
**t-shirt** la camiseta
**Tuesday** el martes
**tumble-dryer** la secadora
**tunnel** el túnel
**to turn** girar
**to turn around** girar
**to turn off** *(light, etc)* apagar
  *(tap)* cerrar
**to turn on** *(light, etc)* encender
  *(tap)* abrir
**turquoise** *(colour)* turquesa
**tweezers** las pinzas
**twice** dos veces
**twin-bedded room** la habitación con dos camas

**twins** los/las mellizos(as)
  *identical twins* los/las gemelos(as)
**twisted** torcido(a)
**to type** escribir a máquina
**typical** típico(a)
**tyre** el neumático
**tyre pressure** la presión de los neumáticos

# U

**ugly** feo(a)
**ulcer** la úlcera
**umbrella** el paraguas
  *(sunshade)* la sombrilla
**uncle** el tío
**uncomfortable** incómodo(a)
**unconscious** inconsciente
**under** debajo de
**undercooked** medio crudo
**underground** *(metro)* el metro
**underpants** los calzoncillos
**underpass** el paso subterráneo
**to understand** entender
  *I don't understand* no entiendo
  *do you understand?* ¿entiende?
**underwear** la ropa interior
**underwater** debajo del agua
**to undress** desvestirse
**unemployed** desempleado(a)
**United Kingdom** el Reino Unido
**United States** Estados Unidos
**university** la universidad
**unleaded petrol** la gasolina sin plomo
**unlikely** poco probable
**to unlock** abrir (con llave)
**to unpack** *(suitcases)* deshacer las maletas
**unpleasant** desagradable
**to unplug** desenchufar
**to unscrew** destornillar
**up: to get up** levantarse
**upstairs** arriba
**urgent** urgente
**urine** la orina
**us** nosotros(as)
**USA** EE.UU.
**to use** usar
**useful** útil
**username** el nombre de usuario
**usual** habitual
**usually** por lo general
**U-turn** el cambio de sentido

## V

**vacancy** *(in hotel)* la habitación libre
**vacant** libre
**vacation** las vacaciones
**vaccination** la vacuna
**vacuum cleaner** la aspiradora
**vagina** la vagina
**valid** válido(a)
**valley** el valle
**valuable** de valor
**valuables** los objetos de valor
**value** el valor
**valve** la válvula
**van** la furgoneta
**vase** el florero
**VAT** el IVA
**vegan** vegetariano(a) estricto(a)
  *I'm vegan* soy vegetariano(a)
  estricto(a)
**vegetables** las verduras
**vegetarian** vegetariano(a)
  *I'm vegetarian* soy vegetariano(a)
**vehicle** el vehículo
**vein** la vena
**velvet** el terciopelo
**vending machine** la máquina
  expendedora
**venereal disease** la enfermedad
  venérea
**ventilator** el ventilador
**very** muy
**vest** la camiseta
**vet** el/la veterinario(a)
**via** por
**to video** *(from TV)* grabar (en vídeo)
**video** el vídeo
**video camera** la videocámara
**video cassette** la cinta de vídeo
**video game** el videojuego
**video recorder** el vídeo
**video tape** la cinta de vídeo
**view** la vista
**village** el pueblo
**vinegar** el vinagre
**vineyard** la viña
**viper** la víbora
**virus** el virus
**visa** el visado
**visit** la visita
**to visit** visitar
**visiting hours** *(hospital)* las horas
  de visita
**visitor** el/la visitante
**vitamin** la vitamina
**voice** la voz

**voicemail** el buzón de voz
**volcano** el volcán
**volleyball** el voleibol
**voltage** el voltaje
**to vomit** vomitar
**voucher** el vale ; el bono

## W

**wage** el sueldo
**waist** la cintura
**waistcoat** el chaleco
**to wait for** esperar
**waiter/waitress** el/la camarero(a)
**waiting room** la sala de espera
**to wake up** despertarse
**Wales** Gales
**walk** un paseo
  *to go for a walk* dar un paseo
**to walk** andar
**walking boots** las botas de montaña
**walking stick** el bastón
**wall** *(inside)* la pared
  *(outside)* el muro
**wallet** la cartera
**to want** querer
  *I want* quiero
  *we want* queremos
**war** la guerra
**ward** *(hospital)* la sala
**wardrobe** el armario
**warehouse** el almacén
**warm** caliente
  *it's warm* *(weather)* hace calor
**to warm up** *(milk, etc)* calentar
**warning triangle** el triángulo
  señalizador
**to wash (oneself)** lavar(se)
**wash and blow dry** lavado y secado a
  mano
**washbasin** el lavabo
**washing machine** la lavadora
**washing powder** el detergente
**washing-up bowl** el barreño
**washing-up liquid** el líquido lavavajillas
**wasp** la avispa
**wasp sting** la picadura de avispa
**waste bin** el cubo de la basura
**to watch** *(look at)* mirar
**watch** el reloj
**watchstrap** la correa de reloj
**water** el agua
  *bottled water* el agua mineral
  *cold water* el agua fría
  *drinking water* el agua potable
  *hot/cold water* el agua caliente/fría

*mineral water* el agua mineral
*sparkling water* el agua con gas
*still water* el agua sin gas
**waterfall** la cascada
**water heater** el calentador de agua
**watermelon** la sandía
**waterproof** impermeable
  *(watch)* sumergible
**to waterski** hacer esquí acuático
**watersports** los deportes acuáticos
**waterwings** los manguitos
**waves** *(on sea)* las olas
**waxing** *(hair removal)* la depilación
  (con cera)
**way** *(manner)* la manera
  *(route)* el camino
**way in** *(entrance)* la entrada
**way out** *(exit)* la salida
**we** nosotros(as)
**weak** *(coffee, tea)* poco cargado(a)
**to wear** llevar
**weather** el tiempo
**weather forecast** el pronóstico
  del tiempo
**web** *(internet)* el/la Internet
**website** la página web
**wedding** la boda
**wedding anniversary**
  el aniversario de boda
**wedding present** el regalo de boda
**wedding ring** la alianza
**Wednesday** el miércoles
**week** la semana
  *last week* la semana pasada
  *next week* la semana que viene
  *per week* por semana
  *this week* esta semana
  *during the week* durante la semana
**weekday** el día laborable
**weekend** el fin de semana
  *next weekend* el próximo fin
  de semana
  *this weekend* este fin de semana
**weekly** semanal
**weekly ticket** el billete semanal
**to weigh** pesar
**weight** el peso
**welcome!** ¡bienvenido(a)!
**well** *(water)* el pozo
**well** bien
  *he's not well* no se encuentra bien
  *well done (steak)* muy hecho(a)
**wellington boots** las botas de agua
**Welsh** galés/galesa
  *(language)* el galés

**west** el oeste
**wet** mojado(a)
  *(weather)* lluvioso(a)
**wetsuit** el traje de bucear
**what?** ¿qué?
**wheel** la rueda
**wheelchair** la silla de ruedas
**wheel clamp** el cepo
**when?** ¿cuándo?
**where?** ¿dónde?
**which?** ¿cuál?
  *which one?* ¿cuál?
  *which ones?* ¿cuáles?
**while:** *in a while* dentro de un rato
**whisky** el whisky
**white** blanco(a)
**who?** ¿quién?
**whole** entero(a)
**wholemeal bread** el pan integral
**whose?** ¿de quién?
**why?** ¿por qué?
**wide** ancho(a)
**widow** la viuda
**widower** el viudo
**width** el ancho
**wife** la mujer
**wig** la peluca
**wild** salvaje
**to win** ganar
**wind** el viento
**windbreak** el cortavientos
**windmill** el molino de viento
**window** la ventana
  *(shop)* el escaparate
  *(in car, train)* la ventanilla
**windscreen** el parabrisas
**windscreen wipers** los limpiaparabrisas
**to windsurf** hacer windsurf
**windy:** *it's windy* hace viento
**wine** el vino
  *red wine* el (vino) tinto
  *white wine* el vino blanco
  *dry wine* el vino seco
  *rosé wine* el (vino) rosado
  *sparkling wine* el (vino) espumoso
  *house wine* el vino de la casa
**wine list** la carta de vinos
**wing** el ala
**wing mirror** el retrovisor exterior
**winter** el invierno
**wire** el alambre
**wireless internet** la internet WiFi
**with** con
  *with ice* con hielo
  *with milk* con leche
  *with sugar* con azúcar

**without** sin
  *without ice* sin hielo
  *without milk* sin leche
  *without sugar* sin azúcar
**woman** la mujer
**wonderful** maravilloso(a)
**wood** *(material)* la madera
  *(forest)* el bosque
**wooden** de madera
**wool** la lana
**word** la palabra
**work** el trabajo
**to work** *(person)* trabajar
  *(machine, car)* funcionar
  *it doesn't work* no funciona
**work permit** el permiso de trabajo
**world** el mundo
**world-wide** mundial
**worried** preocupado(a)
**worse** peor
**worth: it's worth...** vale...
**to wrap** *(parcel)* envolver
**wrapping paper** el papel de envolver
**wrinkles** las arrugas
**wrist** la muñeca
**to write** escribir
  *please write it down* escríbalo,
  por favor
**writing paper** el papel de escribir
**wrong: what's wrong** ¿qué pasa?
**wrought iron** el hierro forjado

# X

**X-ray** la radiografía
**to x-ray** hacer una radiografía

# Y

**yacht** el yate
**year** el año
  *this year* este año
  *next year* el año que viene
  *last year* el año pasado
**yearly** anual ; anualmente
**yellow** amarillo(a)
**Yellow Pages** las páginas amarillas
**yes** sí
**yesterday** ayer
**yet: not yet** todavía no
**yoghurt** el yogur
  *plain yoghurt* el yogur natural
**yolk** la yema
**you** *(polite singular)* usted
  *(polite plural)* ustedes
  *(singular with friends)* tú
  *(plural with friends)* vosotros
**young** joven
**your** *(polite)* su/sus
  *(familiar)* tu/tus
**youth hostel** el albergue juvenil

# Z

**zebra crossing** el paso de peatones
**zero** el cero
**zip** la cremallera
**zone** la zona
**zoo** el zoo
**zoom lens** el zoom
**zucchini** el calabacín

# A

**a** to ; at
  *a la estación* to the station
  *a las 4* at 4 o'clock
  *a 30 kilómetros* 30 km away
**abadejo** m haddock
**abadía** f abbey
**abajo** below ; downstairs
**abanico** m fan (hand-held)
**abeja** f bee
**abierto(a)** open
**abogado(a)** m/f lawyer
**abonado(a)** m/f season-ticket holder
  **abonado a canal/a la televisión digital** subscriber
**abonar** to pay ; to credit
**abono** m season ticket
**aborto** m abortion
  *aborto natural/no provocado* miscarriage
**abrebotellas** m bottle opener
**abrelatas** m tin-opener
**abrigo** m coat
**abril** m April
**abrir** to open ; to turn on (tap)
**abrocharse** to fasten (seatbelt, etc)
**absceso** m abscess
**abuela** f grandmother
**abuelo** m grandfather
**aburrido(a)** boring
**acá** (esp LAm) here
**acabar** to finish
**acampar** to camp
**acceso** m access
  *acceso andenes* to the platforms
  *acceso prohibido* no access
  *acceso vías* to the platforms
  *¿tiene acceso a Internet?* do you have internet access?
**accidente** m accident
**aceite** m oil
  *aceite de girasol* sunflower oil
  *aceite bronceador* suntan oil
  *aceite de oliva* olive oil
**aceituna** f olive
  *aceitunas aliñadas* marinated olives
  *aceitunas rellenas* stuffed olives
**acelerador** m accelerator
**acento** m accent
**aceptar** to accept
**acera** f pavement ; sidewalk
**acero** m steel
**ácido** m acid
**acompañar** to accompany
**aconsejar** to advise
**acto** m act
  *en el acto* while you wait (repairs)
**actor** m actor
**actriz** f actress

**acuerdo** m agreement
  *¡de acuerdo!* OK ; alright
**alojamiento y desayuno** accommodation and breakfast
**adaptador** m adaptor
**adelantar** to overtake (in car)
**adelante** forward
**adicional** extra ; additional
**adiós** goodbye ; bye
**administración** f management
**admitir** to accept ; to permit
  *no se admiten...* ...not permitted
**adolescente** m/f teenager
**aduana** f customs
**adulto(a)** m/f adult
**advertir** to warn
**aerodeslizador** m hovercraft
**aerolínea** f airline
**aeropuerto** m airport
**aerosol** m aerosol
**afeitarse** to shave
**aficionado(a)** m/f fan (cinema, jazz, etc)
**afilado(a)** sharp (razor, knife)
**afiliado(a)** affiliated, member
**afta** f thrush
**agencia** f agency
  *agencia inmobiliaria* state agent's
  *agencia de seguros* insurance company
  *agencia de viajes* travel agency
**agenda** f diary ; personal organizer
  *agenda electrónica* electronic organizer
**agente** m/f agent
  *agente de policía* policeman/woman
**agitar** to shake (bottle)
**agosto** m August
**agotado(a)** sold out ; out of stock
**agradable** pleasant
**agradecer** to thank
**agridulce** sweet and sour
**agua** f water
  *agua caliente/fría* hot/cold water
  *agua destilada* distilled water
  *agua dulce* fresh water
  *agua mineral* mineral water
  *agua potable* drinking water
  *agua salada* salt water
**agudo(a)** sharp ; pointed
**águila** f eagle
**aguja** f needle ; hand (on watch)
  *aguja hipodérmica* hypodermic needle
  *aguja de coser* needle
**agujero** m hole
**ahogarse** to drown
**ahora** now
**ahorrar** to save (money)

**ahumado(a)** smoked
**aire** m air
  *aire acondicionado* air-conditioning
  *al aire libre* open-air ; outdoor
**ajo** m garlic
**ala** f wing
**alargador** m extension lead
**alarma** f alarm
**albahaca** f basil
**albarán** m delivery note
**albaricoque** m apricot
**albergue** m hostel
  *albergue juvenil* youth hostel
**alcanzar** to reach ; to get
**alcohol** m alcohol ; spirits
**alcohólico(a)** alcoholic
**alemán(mana)** German
**Alemania** f Germany
**alergia** f allergy
  *alergia al polen* hay fever
**alérgico(a) a** allergic to
**aletas** fpl flippers
**alfarería** f pottery
**alfiler** m pin
**alfombra** f carpet ; rug
**alforjas** fpl panniers (for bike)
**algas** fpl seaweed
**algo** something
**algodón** m cotton
  *algodón hidrófilo* cotton wool
**alguien** someone
**alguno(a)** some ; any
**algunos(as)** some ; a few
**alicates** mpl pliers
**alimentación** f grocer's ; food
**alimento** m food
**aliño** m dressing (for food)
**allí** there (over there)
**almacén** m store ; warehouse
  *grandes almacenes* department stores
**almendra** f almond
**almohada** f pillow
**almuerzo** m lunch
**alojamiento** m accommodation
**alpargatas** fpl espadrilles
**alquilar** to rent ; to hire
  *se alquila* for hire
**alquiler** m rent ; rental
  *alquiler de coches* car hire
**alrededor** about ; around
**altavoz** m loudspeaker
**alto(a)** high ; tall
  *alta tensión* high voltage
**altura** f altitude ; height
**alubia** f bean
  *alubias blancas* butter beans
  *alubias pintas* red kidney beans

**amable** pleasant ; kind
**amapola** f poppy
**amargo(a)** bitter ; sour
**amarillo(a)** yellow ; amber (traffic light)
**ambientador** m air freshener
**ambos(as)** both
**ambulancia** f ambulance
  *ambulancia aérea* air ambulance
**ambulatorio** m health centre
**América del Norte** f North America
**amigo(a)** m/f friend
  *amigo(a) por correspondencia*
penfriend
**amor** m love
**amortiguador** m shock absorber
**ampolla** f blister
**analgésico** m painkiller
**análisis** m analysis
  *análisis de sangre* blood test
**ananá(s)** m pineapple
**ancho** m width
**ancho(a)** wide
**anchoa** f anchovy (salted)
**anchura** f width
**ancla** f anchor
**Andalucía** f Andalusia
**andaluz(a)** Andalusian
**andar** to walk
**andén** m platform
**añejo(a)** mature ; vintage
**anestesia** f anaesthetic
  *anestesia local* local anaesthetic
  *anestesia general* general anaesthetic
**anfiteatro** m circle (theatre)
**angina (de pecho)** f angina
**anillo** m ring
**animal** m animal
  *animal doméstico* pet
**anís** m aniseed liqueur ; anisette
**aniversario** m anniversary
  *aniversario de boda* wedding
anniversary
**año** m year
  **Año Nuevo** New Year
**ante** m suede
**antena** f aerial
  *antena parabólica* satellite dish
**anteojos** mpl (LAm) binoculars
**antes (de)** before
**antiácido** m antacid
**antibiótico** m antibiotic
**anticonceptivo** m contraceptive
**anticongelante** m antifreeze
**anticuario** m antique shop
  *à anticuario(a)* m/f antique dealer
  **anticuario** adj antiquarian
**antigüedades** fpl antiques
  *tienda de antigüedades* antique shop

**antiguo(a)** old ; ancient
**antihistamínico** m antihistamine
**antiséptico** m antiseptic
**anual** annual
**anular** to cancel
**anunciar** to announce ; to advertise
**anuncio** m advertisement ; notice
**anzuelo** m hook (fishing)
**apagado(a)** off (light, etc)
**apagar** to switch off ; to turn off
**aparato** m appliance
**aparato de aire acondicionado** air-conditioning unit
**aparcamiento** m car park
**aparcar** to park
**apartado de Correos** m PO Box
**apartamento** m flat ; apartment
**apellido** m surname
**apendicitis** f appendicitis
**aperitivo** m aperitif (drink) ; appetizer ; snack (food)
**apertura** f opening
**apio** m celery
**aplazar** to postpone
**apostar por** to bet on
**aprender** to learn
**apretar** to squeeze
**apto(a)** suitable
**aquí** here
  *aquí tiene...* here is...
**araña** f spider
**árbitro** m referee
**árbol** m tree
**arco iris** m rainbow
**ardor de estómago** m heartburn
**arena** f sand
**armario** m wardrobe ; cupboard
**arquitecto(a)** m/f architect
**arquitectura** f architecture
**arrancar** to start
**arreglar** to fix ; to mend
**arriba** upstairs ; above
  *hacia arriba* upward(s)
**arroyo** m stream
**arroz** m rice
**arruga** f wrinkle
**arte** m art
**artesanía** f crafts
**artesano(a)** m/f craftsman/woman
**articulación** f joint (body)
**artículo** m article
  *artículos de ocasión* bargains
  *artículos de regalo* gifts
  *artículos de tocador/baño* toiletries
**artista** m/f artist
**artritis** f arthritis
**asado(a)** roast

**asar a la parrilla/brasa** to barbecue
**ascensor** m lift
**asegurado(a)** insured
**asegurar** to insure
**aseos** mpl toilets
**asiento** m seat
  *asiento de niños* child safety seat
**asistencia** f help ; assistance
  *asistencia técnica* repairs
**asma** m asthma
**aspiradora** f vacuum cleaner
**aspirina** f aspirin
**astilla** f splinter
**atacar** to attack
**atajo** m short cut
**ataque** m fit (seizure)
  *ataque epiléptico* epileptic fit
  *ataque al corazón* heart attack
  *ataque de asma* asthma attack
**atascado(a)** jammed (stuck)
**atasco** m hold-up (traffic jam)
**atención** f attention
  *atención al cliente* customer service
**aterrizar** to land
**ático** m attic ; loft
**atracadero** m mooring
**atraco** m mugging (person)
**atrás** behind
**atropellar** to knock down (car)
**ATS** m/f nurse
**atún** m tuna fish
**audífono** m hearing aid
**aumentar** to increase
**auricular** m receiver (phone)
**auriculares** mpl headphones
**auténtico(a)** genuine ; real
**autostop** m hitch-hiking
**autobús** m bus
**autocar** m coach (bus)
**automático(a)** automatic
**autónomo(a)** self-employed
  *autónomo* freelancer
**autopista** f motorway
**autor(a)** m/f author
**autoservicio** m self-service
**autovía dual** carriageway
**auxiliar de vuelo** m/f air steward/stewardess
**Av./Avda.** abbrev. for **avenida**
**avalancha** f avalanche
**ave** f bird
  *aves de corral* poultry
**avellana** f hazelnut
**avena** f oats
**avenida** f avenue
**avería** f breakdown (car)
**averiado(a)** out of order ; broken down
**avión** m airplane ; aeroplane

**avión sanitario ; ambulancia aérea** air ambulance
**aviso** m notice ; warning
**avispa** f wasp
**ayer** yesterday
**ayudar** to help
**ayuntamiento** m town/city hall
**azafata** f air hostess ; stewardess
**azafrán** m saffron
**azúcar** m sugar
  *azúcar glas(é)* icing sugar
**azul** blue
  *azul claro* light blue
  *azul marino* dark/navy blue
  *día azul* cheap day for train travel
  *zona azul* controlled parking area

# B

**babero** m baby's bib
**baca** f roof rack
**bahía** f bay (along coast)
**bailar** to dance
**baile** m dance
**bajar** to go down(stairs) ; to drop (temperature)
**bajarse (del)** to get off (bus, etc)
**bajo(a)** low ; short ; soft (sound)
  *bajo en calorías* low-fat
  *más bajo* lower
**balcón** m balcony
**balneario** m spa
**balón** m ball
**baloncesto** m basketball
**balsa salvavidas** f life raft
**bañador** m swimming costume/trunks
**banana** f banana
**bañarse** to go swimming ; to bathe ; to have a bath
**banca** f banking ; bank
**banco** m bank ; bench
**banda** f band (musical)
  *banda ancha* broadband
**bandeja** f tray
**bandera** f flag
**bañista** m/f bather
**baño** m bath ; bathroom
  *con baño* with bath
**bar** m bar
  *bar de cóctel* cocktail bar
**barato(a)** cheap
**barba** f beard
**barbacoa** f barbecue
**barbería** f barber's
**barbilla** f chin
**barca** f small boat
**barco** m ship ; boat
  *barco de vela* sailing boat

**barra** f bar ; counter ; bread stick
  *barra de labios* lipstick
  *barra de pan* French bread
**barreño (de plástico)** m washing-up bowl
**barrera** f barrier ; crash barrier
**barrio** m district ; suburb
  *barrio chino* red light district
**barro** m mud
**bastante** enough ; quite
**bastón** m walking stick
  *bastón de esquí* ski pole/stick
**basura** f rubbish ; litter
**bata** f dressing gown
**bate** m bat (baseball, cricket)
**batería** f battery (in car) ; musical instrument (drums)
  *batería de cocina* set of kitchen equipment
**batido** m milkshake
**batidora** f blender (hand-held)
**baúl** m trunk (luggage)
**bautizo** m christening
**to be** ser ; estar
**bebé** m baby
**beber** to drink
**bebida** f drink
  *bebida sin alcohol* soft drink
**beicon** m bacon
**béisbol** m baseball
**berenjena** f aubergine/eggplant
**berro** m watercress
**berza** f cabbage
**besar** to kiss
**beso** m kiss
**betún** m shoe polish
**biberón** m baby's bottle
**biblioteca** f library
**bici** f bicycle
**bicicleta** f bicycle
  *bicicleta de montaña* mountain bike
**bien** well
**bienvenido(a)** welcome
**bifurcación** f fork (in road)
**bigote** m moustache
**billete** m ticket
  *billete de ida* single ticket
  *billete de ida y vuelta* return ticket
**billetera** f wallet
**bistec** m steak
**bisutería** f costume jewellery
**blanco(a)** white
  *dejar en blanco* leave blank (on form)
**blando(a)** soft
**bloc** m note pad
**blusa** f blouse
**boca** f mouth
**bocadillo** m sandwich (made with French bread)

**boda** f wedding
**bodega** f wine cellar ; restaurant
**bolígrafo** m biro ; pen
**bollo** m roll ; bun
**bolsa** f bag ; stock exchange
  **bolsa de plástico** plastic bag
  **bolsa de basura** rubbish/bin bag
  **bolsa de playa** beach bag
**bolsillo** m pocket
**bolsita de té** f teabag
**bolso** m handbag
**bomba** f pump (bike, etc) ; bomb
  **bomba de bicicleta** bicycle pump
**bombero(a)** mf fireman/woman ;
firefighter
**bomberos** mpl fire brigade
**bombilla** f light bulb
**bombona de gas** f gas cylinder
**bombonería** f confectioner's
**bombones** mpl chocolates
**bonito(a)** pretty ; nice-looking
**bono** m voucher
**bonobús** m bus pass
**borracho(a)** drunk
**bosque** m forest ; wood
**bota** f boot
**bote** m boat ; tin ; can
  **bote neumático** rubber dinghy
  **bote salvavidas** lifeboat
**botella** f bottle
**botón** m button
**bragas** fpl knickers
**brazo** m arm
**brécol** m broccoli
**bricolaje** m do-it-yourself ; DIY
**brillar** to shine
**brindis** m toast (raising glass)
**británico(a)** British
**broma** f joke
**bromear** to joke
**bronceado** m suntan
**bronceado(a)** sun-tanned
**bronceador** m suntan lotion
**broncearse** to tan
**bronquitis** f bronchitis
**brújula** f compass
**bucear** to dive
**bueno(a)** good ; fine
  **¡buenos días!** good morning!
  **¡buenas tardes!** good
afternoon/evening!
  **¡buenas noches!** good evening/night!
**bufanda** f scarf (woollen)
**bufé** m buffet
**búho** m owl
**bujía** f spark plug
**bulto** m lump (swelling)
**buñuelo** m fritter ; doughnut

**bunyi** m bungee jumping
**buscador** m search engine
**buscar** to look for
**butacas** fpl stalls (theatre)
**butano** m Calor gas®
**butifarra** f Catalan sausage
**buzón** m postbox ; letterbox
  **buzón de voz** voicemail

## C

**caballeros** mpl gents
**caballo** m horse
  **montar a caballo** to go riding
**cabello** m hair
**cabeza** f head
**cabina** f cabin
  **cabina (telefónica)** phone box
**cable** m wire ; cable
  **cable de cambio** gear cable
  **cable de freno** brake cable
  **cable de remolque** tow rope
  **cables de arranque** jump leads
**cabra** f goat
**cacahuete** m peanut
**cacao** m cocoa
  **cacao para los labios** lip salve
**cacerola** f saucepan
**cachemira** f cashmere
**cada** every ; each
  **cada día** daily (each day)
  **cada uno** each (one)
**cadena** f chain ; channel (TV) ; WC cistern
  **tirar de la cadena/cisterna** pull the
chain (WC)
  **cadena de música** music centre ;
music radio station
**cadera** f hip
**caducado(a)** out-of-date
**caducar** to expire (ticket, passport)
**caer(se)** to fall
**café** m café ; coffee
  **(café) cortado** espresso with a dash of
milk
  **corto de café** milky coffee
  **(café) descafeinado** decaff coffee
  **café en grano** coffee beans
  **(café) exprés/expreso** espresso coffee
  **café con hielo** iced coffee
  **café con leche** white coffee
  **café instantáneo** instant coffee
  **café molido** ground coffee
  **café solo** black coffee
**cafetière** f cafetière
**cafetería** f snack bar ; café
**caja** f cashdesk ; box
  **caja de ahorros** savings bank
  **caja de cambios** gearbox
  **caja de fusibles** fuse box
  **caja fuerte** safe

**cajero(a)** m/f teller ; cashier
  *cajero automático* cash dispenser ;
  auto-teller
**cajón** m drawer
**calabacín** m courgette/zucchini
**calabaza** f pumpkin
**calamares** mpl squid
**calambre** m cramp
**calcetines** mpl socks
**calculadora** f calculator
**caldereta** f stew (fish, lamb)
**caldo** m stock ; consommé
**calefacción** f heating
**calendario** m calendar
**calentador** m heater
  *calentador de agua* water heater
**calentar** to heat up (milk, etc)
**calentura** f cold sore
**calidad** f quality
**caliente** hot
**calle** f street ; fairway (golf)
**callejón sin salida** m cul-de-sac
**calmante** m painkiller
**calvo(a)** bald
**calzada** f roadway
  *calzada deteriorada* uneven road
  surface
**calzado** m footwear
  *calzados* shoe shop
**calzoncillos** mpl underpants
**cama** f bed
  *dos camas* twin beds
  *cama individual* single bed
  *cama de matrimonio* double bed
**cámara** f camera ; inner tube
**camarera** f waitress ; chambermaid
**camarero** m barman ; waiter
**camarote** m cabin
**cambiar** to change ; to exchange
  *cambiarse* to get changed
**cambio** m change ; exchange ; gear
**caminar** to walk
**camino** m path ; road ; route
  *camino particular* private road
**camión** m lorry
**camisa** f shirt
**camisería** f shirt shop
**camiseta** f t-shirt ; vest
**camisón** m nightdress
**campana** f bell
**camping** m campsite
**campo** m countryside ; field ; pitch
  *campo de fútbol* football pitch
  *campo de golf* golf course
**caña** f cane ; rod
  *caña (de cerveza)* glass of beer
  *caña de pescar* fishing rod
**Canadá** m Canada

**canadiense** Canadian
**Canal de la Mancha** m English Channel
**canasto** m large basket
**cancelación** f cancellation
**cancelar** to cancel
**cáncer** m cancer
**cancha** court
  *cancha de tenis* f tennis court
  *cancha de baloncesto* basketball court
**canción** f song
**candado** m padlock
  *candado de bicicleta* bike lock
**candela** f candle ; fire
**canela** f cinnamon
**canguro** m kangaroo
**canguro** m/f babysitter
**canoa** f canoe
**cansado(a)** tired
**cantante** m/f singer
**cantar** to sing
**cantidad** f quantity
**capilla** f chapel
**capital** f capital (city)
**capitán** m captain
**capó** m bonnet ; hood (of car)
**capucha** f hood (jacket)
**cara** f face
**caramelo** m sweet ; caramel
**caravana** f caravan
**carbón** m coal
  *carbón vegetal* charcoal
  *carbón dulce* symbolic sweet
  resembling a piece of charcoal given
  to children for Christmas and for *día
  de Reyes* (6th of January) when they
  haven't behaved well during the year.
**carburador** m carburettor
**carburante** m fuel
**cárcel** f prison
**carga** m charge
  *no tengo batería* I've run out of charge
  *necesito cargar el teléfono* I need to
  charge my phone
**cargador** m recharger
**cargar** to load ; charge
  *cargar en cuenta* to charge to account
**cargo** m charge
  *a cargo del cliente* at the customer's
  expense
**Caribe** m Caribbean
**carnaval** m carnival
**carne** f meat
  *carne asada* roast meat
  *carne picada* mince (meat)
**carné de conducir** m driving licence
**carné de identidad** m identity card (DNI)
**carnicería** f butcher's

**caro(a)** dear ; expensive
**carpintería** f carpenter's shop
**carrera** f career ; race (sport)
**carrete** m film (for camera) ; fishing reel
**carretera** f road
  **carretera comarcal** secondary road, B-road
  **carretera nacional** A-road
  **carretera de circunvalación** ring road
**carril** m lane (on road)
**carrito** m trolley
**carta** f letter ; playing card ; menu
  **carta aérea** air mail letter
  **carta certificada** registered letter
  **carta de vinos** wine list
  **carta verde** green card
**cartel** m poster
**cartelera** f entertainments guide
**cartera** f wallet ; briefcase
**carterista** m/f pickpocket
**cartero(a)** m/f postman/woman
**cartón** m cardboard
**casa** f house ; home ; household
  **casa de socorro** first-aid post
**casado(a)** married
**casarse (con)** to marry
**cascada** f waterfall
**cáscara** f shell (egg, nut)
**casco** m helmet
**casero(a)** home-made
  **comida casera** home cooking
**caseta** f beach hut ; kennel
**casete** m cassette ; tape recorder
**casi** almost
**caso: en caso de** in case of
**caspa** f dandruff
**castaña** f chestnut
**castañuelas** fpl castanets
**castellano(a)** Spanish ; Castilian
**castillo** m castle
**catalán/catalana** Catalonian
**catálogo** m catalogue
**catedral** f cathedral
**católico(a)** Catholic
**causa** f cause
  **a causa de** because of
**causar** to cause
**cava** m cava ; sparkling white wine
**caza** f hunting ; game
**cazar** to hunt
**CD-ROM** m CD ROM
**cebo** m bait (for fishing)
**cebolla** f onion
**ceder** to give way
  **ceda el paso** give way
**celeste** light blue
**celo** m Sellotape®
**celoso(a)** jealous

**cementerio** m cemetery
**cena** f dinner ; supper
**cenar** to have dinner
**cenicero** m ashtray
**centímetro** m centimetre
**céntimo** m euro cent
**centralita** f switchboard
**centro** m centre
  **centro de negocios** business centre
**Centroamérica** f Central America
**cepillo** m brush
  **cepillo de dientes** toothbrush
  **cepillo del pelo** hairbrush
  **cepillo de uñas** nailbrush
  **cepillo de barrer/para el suelo** scrubbing brush
**cera** f wax
  **hacerse la cera** to wax one's legs or arms, etc.
  **cera facial** facial wax
  **cera corporal** body wax
**cerámica** f ceramics ; pottery
**cerca (de)** near ; close to
**cercanías** fpl outskirts
  **tren de cercanías** suburban train
**cerdo** m pig ; pork
**cereza** f cherry
**cerillas** fpl matches
**cero** m zero
**cerrado(a)** closed
  **cerrado por reforma** closed for repairs
**cerradura** f lock
**cerrar con llave** to lock
**cerro** m hill
**certificado** m certificate
**certificado(a)** registered
**certificar** to register
**cervecería** f pub
**cerveza** f beer ; lager
**cesta** f basket
**cestería** f basketwork (shop)
**chalet**(sing) ; **chalets** (pl) m villa
**chaleco** m waistcoat
  **chaleco salvavidas** life jacket
**champán** m champagne
**champiñón** m mushroom
**champú** m shampoo
**chancl(et)as** fpl flip flops
**chaqueta** f jacket
**charcutería** f delicatessen
**chat ; sala de chat** (internet) chatroom
**cheque** m cheque
  **cheque de viaje** traveller's cheque
  **cheque al portador** cheque payable to the bearer
**chica** f girl
**chichón** m lump (on head)

**chico** m boy
**chico(a)** small
**chile** m chilli
**chimenea** f fireplace ; chimney
**chiringuito** m beach bar ; stall
**chocar** to crash *(car)*
**chocolate** m chocolate ; hot chocolate
  **chocolate puro/negro** plain chocolate
  **chocolate blanco** white chocolate
  **chocolate con leche** milk chocolate
**chófer** m chauffeur ; driver
**chorizo** m hard pork sausage
**chubasco** m shower *(rain)*
**chuleta** f cutlet ; chop
**chupete** m dummy *(for baby)*
**churrería** f stand or stall selling churros
  with different shapes and fillings
**churro** m thin/thick fried batter stick
  sprinkled with sugar, usually eaten with
  thick hot chocolate
**ciclista** m/f cyclist
**ciego(a)** blind
**cielo** m sky ; heaven
**cien** hundred
**CIF** m tax number *(for business)*
**cifra** f number ; figure
**cigarra** f cicada
**cigarrillo** m cigarette
**cigarro** m cigar ; cigarette
**cima** f top ; peak
**cine** m cinema
  **cine de verano** open-air cinema
**cinta** f tape ; ribbon
  **cinta de vídeo** video cassette
  **cinta virgen** blank tape
  **cinta métrica** tape measure
  **cinta limpiadora** head-cleaning tape
  **cinta aislante** insulating tape
  **cinta adhesiva** *(also known as **celo**,*
  ***celofán** or **fixo**)* sellotape
**cintura** f waist
**cinturón** m belt
  **cinturón de seguridad** safety belt
**circulación** f traffic
**circular** to drive ; to circulate
  **circule por la derecha** keep right *(road*
  *sign)*
**ciruela** f plum
  **ciruela pasa** prune
**cirujano(a)** m/f surgeon
  **cirujano plástico** plastic surgeon
**cisterna** f cistern ; tank
**cistitis** f cystitis
**cita** f appointment
**ciudad** f city ; town
**ciudadano(a)** m/f citizen
**clarete** m light red wine
**claro(a)** light *(colour)* ; clear

**clase** f class ; type ; lesson
  **clase preferente** club/business class
  **clase turista** economy class
**clavícula** f collar bone
**clavija** f peg
**clavo** m nail *(metal)* ; clove *(spice)*
**cliente** m/f customer ; client
**climatizado(a)** air-conditioned
**clínica** f clinic ; private hospital
**club nocturno** m night club
**cobrador** m conductor *(train, bus)*
**cobrar** to charge ; to cash
  **cobrar demasiado** to overcharge
**cobro** m payment
  **cobro revertido** *(call)* reverse charge
**cocer** to cook ; to boil
**coche** m car ; coach *(on train)*
**coche cama** m sleeping car
**coche comedor** m dining car
**coche restaurante** m restaurant car
**cochecito (de bebé)** m pram
**cocido** m thick stew
**cocido(a)** cooked ; boiled
**cocina** f kitchen ; cooker ; cuisine
**cocinar** to cook
**coco** m coconut
**código** m code
  **código de barras** barcode
  **código postal** postcode
**codo** m elbow
**coger** to catch ; to get ; to pick up
  *(phone)*
**cola** f glue ; queue ; tail
**colador** m strainer ; colander
**colcha** f beadspread
**colchón** m mattress
**colega** m/f colleague
**colegio** m school
**colgante** m pendant
**colgar** to hang up
**coliflor** f cauliflower
**colina** f hill
**colisionar** to crash
**collar** m necklace
**color** m colour
**columna vertebral** f spine
**columpio** m swing *(for children)*
**comedor** m dining room
**comenzar** to begin
**comer** to eat
**comercio** m trade ; business
**comestibles** mpl groceries
**comida** f food ; meal
  **se sirven comidas** meals served
  **comidas caseras** home cooking
**comisaría** f police station
**como** as ; like ; since
**¿cómo?** how? ; pardon?

**cómodo(a)** comfortable
**compañero(a)** m/f colleague ; partner
**compañía** f company
**compartimento** m compartment
**completo(a)** full ; no vacancies
**comportarse** to behave
**compositor(a)** m/f composer
**compra** f purchase
  **compras** shopping
**comprar** to buy
**comprender** to understand
**compresa** f sanitary towel
**comprobar** to check
**con** with
**concha** f sea-shell
**concierto** m concert
**concurrido(a)** busy ; crowded
**concurso** m competition ; quiz
**condón** m condom
**conducir** to drive
**conductor(a)** m/f driver
**conectar** to connect ; to plug in
**conejo** m rabbit
**conferencia** f conference
**confirmación** f confirmation
**confirmar** to confirm
**confitería** f cake shop
**confitura** f jam
**congelado(a)** frozen
**congelador** m freezer
**conjunto** m group (music) ; outfit
**conmoción cerebral** f concussion
**conocer** to know ; to be acquainted
  with
**conseguir** to obtain
**conserje** m caretaker
**conservar** to keep
**conservas** fpl tinned foods
**consigna** f left-luggage office
**construir** to build
**consulado** m consulate
**consultorio** m doctor's surgery
**consumición** f consumption ; drink
**consumir** to eat ; to use
  **consumir (preferentemente) antes de...** best before…
**contacto** m contact ; ignition (car)
**contador** m meter
**contagioso(a)** infectious
**contaminado(a)** polluted
**contener** to hold (to contain)
**contenido** m contents
**contento(a)** pleased
**contestador automático** m
  answerphone

**contestar** to answer ; to reply
**continuación** f sequel
**continuar** to continue
**contra** against
**contrareembolso** cash on delivery
**contrato** m contract
**control** m inspection ; check
  **control de seguridad** security check
**convento** m convent ; monastery
**copa** f glass ; goblet
  **copa de helado** mixed ice cream
  **tomar una copa** to have a drink
**copia** f copy ; print (photo)
**copiar** to copy
**corazón** m heart
**corbata** f tie
**corcho** m cork
**cordero** m lamb ; mutton
**cordillera** f mountain range
**coro** m choir
**corral: de corral** free-range
**correa** f strap ; belt
  **correa de reloj** watchstrap
  **correa del perro** dog's lead
**correcto(a)** right (correct)
**correo** m mail
  **correo basura** spam
  **correo electrónico** e-mail
  **correo certificado** registered post
  **correo urgente** special delivery
**Correos** m post office
**correr** to run
**corrida de toros** f bullfight
**corriente** f power ; current (electric, water) ;
  draught (of air)
**cortacircuito(s)** m circuit breaker
**cortado** m espresso coffee with dash
  of milk
**cortado(a)** blocked (road) ; shy
**cortar** to cut
**cortaúñas** m nail clippers
**corte** m cut
**cortina** f curtain
**corto(a)** short
**cortocircuito(s)** short circuit
**cosa** f thing
**cosecha** f harvest ; vintage (wine)
**coser** to sew
**costa** f coast
**costar** to cost
**costero(a)** coastal
**costumbre** f custom (tradition)
**coto** m reserve
  **coto de caza/pesca** hunting/fishing
  by licence

**crédito** m credit
  *a crédito* on credit
**creer** to think ; to believe
**crema** f cream (lotion)
  *crema bronceadora(s)/solar(es)* suntan lotion
  *crema de afeitar* shaving cream
**cremallera** f zip
**crisis nerviosa** f nervous breakdown
**cruce** m junction ; crossroads
**crucero** m cruise
**crucigrama** m crossword puzzle
**crudo(a)** raw
**cruzar** to cross
**c/u (cada uno)** each (one)
**cuaderno** m exercise book ; notebook
**cuadro** m picture , painting
  *a/de cuadros* checked (pattern)
**cuajada** f curd
**¿cuál?** which?
**¿cuándo?** when?
**¿cuánto?** how much?
**¿cuántos?** how many?
**cuarentena** f quarantine
**Cuaresma** f Lent
**cuarto** m room
  *cuarto de baño* bathroom
  *cuarto de estar* living room
**cubierto** m cover charge (in restaurant) ; menu
**cubierto(a)** covered ; indoor
**cubiertos** mpl cutlery
**cubo** m bucket ; pail ; bin
**cubrir** to cover
**cucaracha** f cockroach
**cuchara** f spoon
  *cuchara de servir* tablespoon
  *chuchara de postre* dessert spoon
**cucharilla** f teaspoon
**cuchillo** m knife
**cuenta** f bill ; account
**cuerda** f string ; rope
**cuero** m leather
**cuerpo** m body
**cuidado** m care
  *¡cuidado!* look out!
  *ten cuidado* be careful!
  *cuidado con el escalón* mind the step!
**cuidadoso(a)** careful
**cultivar** to grow ; to farm
**cumpleaños** m birthday
  *¡feliz cumpleaños!* happy birthday!
**cuna** f cradle ; cot
**cuñado(a)** m/f brother/sister-in-law
**curva** f bend ; curve
  *curvas peligrosas* dangerous bends

# D

**dado** mpl dice
**daltónico(a)** colour-blind
**daños** mpl damage
**dar** to give
  *dar de comer* to feed
  *dar marcha atrás* to reverse
  *dar propina* to tip (waiter, etc)
  *dar un paseo* to go for a walk
**dátil** m date (fruit)
**datos** mpl data ; information
**dcha.** abbrev. for **derecha**
**de** of ; from
**de acuerdo** all right (agreed)
**debajo (de)** under ; underneath
**deber** to owe ; to have to
**debido(a)** a due to
**decir** to tell ; to say
**declarar** to declare
**dedo** m finger
  *dedo anular* ring finger
  *dedo gordo/pulgar* thumb ; big toe
  *dedo índice* index finger
  *dedo meñique* little finger
  *dedo del pie* toe
**defecto** m fault ; defect
**de granja/corral** free-range
**degustación** f tasting (wine, etc)
**dejar** to let ; to leave
  *dejar libre la salida* keep clear
**delante de** in front of
**delegación** f regional office (government)
**delgado(a)** thin ; slim
**delicioso(a)** delicious
**delito** m crime
**demasiado** too much
  *demasiado hecho(a)* overdone
**demora** f delay
**denominación de origen** f guarantee of quality of food products
**dentadura postiza** f dentures
**dentífrico** m toothpaste
**dentista** m/f dentist
**dentro (de)** inside
**departamento** m compartment ; department
**dependiente(a)** m/f sales assistant
**deporte** m sport
**depósito de gasolina** m petrol tank
**derecha** f right(-hand side)
  *a la derecha* on/to the right
**derecho** m right ; law
  *derechos de aduana* customs duty
**derecho(a)** right ; straight
**derramar** to spill
**derrapar** to skid
**derrape** m skid

**derretir** to melt
**desabrochar** to unfasten
**desafilado(a)** blunt *(knife, blade)*
**desaparecer** to disappear
**desarrollar** to develop
**desatascador** m plunger *(for sink)*
**desayuno** m breakfast
**descafeinado(a)** decaffeinated
**descansar** to rest
**descanso** m rest ; interval
**descarga eléctrica** f electric shock
**descargado(a)** flat *(battery)*
**descargar** to download
  **descargarse to** run down ; to go flat *(battery)*
**descongelar** to defrost ; to de-ice
**describir** to describe
**descubrir** to discover
**descuento** m discount ; reduction
**desde** since ; from
**desear** to want ; to wish
**desembarcadero** m quay
**desempleado(a)** unemployed
**desenchufado(a)** off ; disconnected ; unplugged
**deseo** m wish ; desire
**desfile** m parade
**deshacer** to undo ; to unpack
**desinfectante** m disinfectant
**desmaquilladora/desmaquillante** m make-up remover
  **toallitas desmaquilladoras/desmaquillantes** makeup remover towels
**desmayado(a)** fainted
**desnatado(a)** skimmed
**desodorante** m deodorant
**despacho** m office
**despacio** slowly ; quietly
**despegar** to take-off ; to remove ; to peel off
**despertador** m alarm (clock)
**despertarse** to wake up
**después** after ; afterward(s)
**desteñir: no destiñe** colourfast
**destino** m destination
**destornillador** m screwdriver
**destornillar** to unscrew
**desvestirse** to get undressed
**desvío** m detour ; diversion
**detalle** m detail ; nice gesture
  **al detalle** retail *(commercial)*
**detener** to arrest
**detergente** m detergent ; washing powder
**destilería de cerveza artesanal** micro-brewery
**detrás (de)** behind

**deuda** f debt
**devolver** to give/put back
**día** m day
  **día festivo/de fiesta** public holiday ; holiday
  **día laborable/hábil** working day ; weekday
  **día lectivo** school/college day
  **día libre** day off
  **día azul** cheap ticket day
  **todo el día** all day
**diabético(a)** m/f diabetic
**diamante** m diamond
**diario(a)** daily
  **a diario** every day
**diarrea** f diarrhoea
**dibujo** m drawing
**diccionario** m dictionary
**diciembre** m December
**diente** m tooth
**dieta** f diet
**difícil** difficult
**dificultad** f difficulty
**¿diga(me)?** hello *(on phone)*
**dinero** m money
  **dinero (en) efectivo** cash
  **(dinero) suelto** change
**Dios** m God
**diplomático(a)** m/f diplomat
**dirección** f direction ; address ; *(Aut)* steering; steering wheel
  **dirección de correo electrónico** e-mail address
  **dirección particular** home address
  **dirección prohibida** no entry
  **dirección única** one-way
**directo(a)** direct *(train, etc)*
**director(a)** m/f director ; manager
**dirigir** to manage
**disco** m record ; disk
  **disco duro** hard disk
**discoteca** f disco ; nightclub
**discrecional** optional
**discutir** to quarrel ; to argue
**diseño** m design ; drawing
**disponible** available
**disquete** m floppy disk
**distancia** f distance
**distinto(a)** different
**distribuidor automático** m vending machine
**distrito** m district
**DIU** m coil *(IUD)*
**diversión** f fun
**divertido(a)** funny *(amusing)*
**divertirse** to enjoy oneself
**divisa** f foreign currency
**divorciado(a)** divorced
**doblado(a)** folded ; dubbed *(film)*

**doblar** to fold
**doble** double
**docena** f dozen
**documentos** mpl documents
**documentación del vehículo** f log book
  (for car)
**dólar** m dollar
**dolor** m ache ; pain
  *dolor de cabeza* headache
  *dolor de garganta* sore throat
  *dolor de muelas* toothache
  *dolor de oídos* earache
**doloroso(a)** painful
**domicilio** m home address
**domingo** m Sunday
**dominó** m dominoes
**¿dónde?** where?
**dormir** to sleep
**dormitorio** m bedroom
**dorso** m back
  *véase al dorso* please turn over
**dosis** f dose ; dosage
**droga** f drug
**ducha** f shower
**ducharse** to take a shower
**dueño(a)** m/f owner
**dulce** sweet
  *el agua dulce* fresh water
**dulce** m dessert ; sweet
**durante** during
**duro(a)** hard ; tough
**DVD** el DVD

# E

**echar** to pour ; to throw ; to post
**ecológico(a)** organic ; environmentally
  friendly
**ecológico(a)** ecological
**ecoturismo** m eco-tourism
**edad** f age (of person)
  *edad mínima* age limit
**edificio** m building
**edredón (nórdico)** m duvet ; quilt
**edulcorante** m sweetener
**EE.UU.** USA
**efecto** m effect
  *efectos personales* belongings
**eje** m axle (car)
**ejemplar** m copy (of book)
**el** the
**él** he ; him
**electricidad** f electricity
**electricista** m/f electrician
**eléctrico(a)** electric(al)
**electrónico(a)** electronic
**elegir** to choose
**ella** she ; her

**ello** it
**ellos(as)** they ; them
**embajada** f embassy
**embalse** m reservoir
**embarazada** pregnant
**embarcadero** m jetty ; pier
**embarcarse** to board
**embarque** m boarding
**embrague** m clutch (in car)
**emisión** f broadcasting
**emitido por** issued by
**emocionante** exciting
**empachado(a)** upset (stomach)
**empezar** to begin
**empleo** m employment ; use
**empresa** f firm ; company
**empujar** to push
  *empuje* push
**en** in ; into ; on
**encaje** m lace (fabric)
**encantado(a)** pleased to meet you!
**encargado(a)** m/f person in charge
**encargar** to order in advance
**encendedor** m (cigarette) lighter
**encender** to switch on ; to light
  *encender las luces* switch on
  headlights
**encendido(a)** on (light, TV, engine)
**enchufar** to plug in
**enchufe** m plug ; point ; socket
**encima de** onto ; on top of
**encontrar** to find
**encontrarse con** to meet (by chance)
**enero** m January
**enfadado(a)** angry
**enfermedad** f disease
**enfermera(o)** m/f nurse
**enfermería** f infirmary ; first-aid post
**enfermo(a)** ill
**enfrente (de)** opposite
**¡enhorabuena!** congratulations!
**enjuagar** to rinse
**enjuague bucal** m mouthwash
**enlace** m connection (train, etc)
**ensalada** f salad
**enseñar** to show ; to teach
**entender** to understand
**entero(a)** whole
**entierro** m funeral
**entrada** f entrance ; admission ; ticket
  *entrada principal* main entrance
  *entradas limitadas* limited tickets
  *entradas numeradas* numbered
  tickets
  *no hay entradas* sold out
  *entrada de abono* season ticket
  *sacar una entrada* to buy a ticket
  *entrada libre* admission free
  *entrada por delante* enter at the front

**entrar** to go in ; to get in ; to enter
**entre** among ; between
**entreacto** *m* interval
**entregar** to deliver
**entremeses** *mpl* hors d'œuvres
**entrevista** *f* interview
**envase** *m* container ; packaging
**enviar** to send
**envío** *m* shipment
**envolver** to wrap
**epiléptico(a)** epileptic
**equipaje** *m* luggage ; baggage
  *equipaje de mano* hand-luggage
**equipo** *m* team ; equipment
  *equipo manos libres* hands-free kit
  *(for phone)*
**equitación** *f* horseriding
**equivocación** *f* mistake ;
  misunderstanding
**error** *m* mistake
**es** he/she/it is
**escala** *f* stopover
**escalar** to climb *(mountains)*
**escalera** *f* stairs ; ladder
  *escalera de incendios* fire escape
  *escalera (de mano)* ladder
  *escalera mecánica* escalator
**escaleras** *fpl* stairs
**escalón** *m* step *(stair)*
**escanear** to scan
**escáner** *m* scan
**escapar** to escape
**escaparate** *m* shop window
**escenario** *m* stage *(theatre)*
**escoba** *f* broom *(brush)*
**escocés(cesa)** Scottish
**Escocia** *f* Scotland
**escoger** to choose
**esconder** to hide
**escribir** to write
**escrito:** *por escrito* in writing
**escuchar** to listen to
**escuela** *f* school
**escultura** *f* sculpture
**escurrir** to wring
**ese/esa** that
**esguince** *m* sprain
**esmalte** *m* varnish
**esos/esas** those
**espacio** *m* space
**espalda** *f* back *(of body)*
**España** *f* Spain
**español(a)** Spanish
**espantoso(a)** awful
**esparadrapo** *m* sticking plaster
**espárrago** asparagus
**especia** *f* spice

**especialidad** *f* speciality
**especialista** *m/f* specialist
**espectáculo** *m* entertainment ; show
**espejo** *m* mirror
  *espejo retrovisor* rear-view mirror
**esperar** to wait (for) ; to hope
  *espere su turno* please wait your turn
**espina** *f* fish bone ; thorn
  *espina dorsal* spine
**espinacas** *fpl* spinach
**espinilla** *f* spot *(pimple)* ; shin
**esponja** *f* sponge
**esposa** *f* wife
**esposo** *m* husband
**espuma** *f* foam ; mousse *(for hair)*
  *espuma de afeitar* shaving foam
**espumoso(a)** frothy ; sparkling
**esq.** *abbrev. for* **esquina**
**esquí** *m* skiing ; ski
  *esquí acuático* water-skiing
  *esquí de fondo* cross-country skiing
**esquiar** to ski
**esquina** *f* street corner
**está** you *(formal)*/he/she/it is
**estación** *f* railway station ; season
  *estación de autobuses* bus/coach
  station
  *estación de servicio* petrol/service
  station
**estacionamiento** *m* parking space
**estacionar** to park
**estadio** *m* stadium
**Estados Unidos** *mpl* United States
**estanco** *m* tobacconist's
**estante** *m* shelf
  *estantería* bookcase ; shelving
**estar** to be
**estatua** *f* statue
**este** *m* east
**éste/esta** this
**estéreo** *m* stereo
**estómago** *m* stomach
**estornudar** to sneeze
**estos/éstas** these
**estragón** *m* tarragon
**estrecho(a)** narrow
**estrella** *f* star
**estreñimiento** *m* constipation
**estreno** *m* premiere ; new release
**estropeado(a)** out of order ; broken ;
  damaged
**estudiante** *m/f* student
**etiqueta** *f* label ; ticket ; tag
  *de etiqueta* formal dress
**euro** *m* euro
**Europa** *f* Europe
**evidente** obvious
**evitar** to avoid

**examen** m examination
**excelente** excellent
**excepcional** rare *(unique)*
**excepto** except
**exceso** m excess
**excursión** f tour ; excursion
**éxito** m success
**expedido(a)** issued
**experto(a)** expert
**explicar** to explain
**exportación** f export
**exportar** to export
**exposición** f exhibition
**expreso** m express train
**exprimir** to squeeze
**extintor** m fire extinguisher
**extranjero(a)** m/f foreigner
 **en el extranjero** abroad

# F

**FC/f.c.** *abbrev.* for **ferrocarril**
**fabada** f pork and bean stew
**fábrica** f factory
**fácil** easy
**factor** factor
**factura** f receipt ; bill ; account
 **factura detallada** itemized bill
**facturación** f check-in
**falda** f skirt
**falso(a)** fake ; false
**falta** f foul *(football)* ; lack
**familia** f family
**famoso(a)** famous
**farmacia** f chemist's ; pharmacy
 **farmacia de guardia** duty chemist
**farmacéutico(a)** m/f pharmacist
**faro** m headlamp ; lighthouse
 **faro antiniebla** fog-lamp
**farola** f lamppost
**faros** mpl headlights
**favor** m favour
 **por favor** please
**favorito(a)** favourite
**fax** m fax
**febrero** m February
**fecha** f date
 **fecha de adquisición** date of purchase
 **fecha de caducidad/vencimiento**
 expiry date
 **fecha de expedición** date of issue
 **fecha de nacimiento** date of birth
**feliz** happy
 **¡Feliz Año Nuevo!** Happy New Year!
 **¡Feliz navidad!** Merry Christmas!
**femenino(a)** feminine
**feo(a)** ugly

**feria** f trade fair ; funfair
 **feria de artesanía(s)** craft fair
**ferrocarril** m railway
**festivos** mpl public holidays
**fiambre** m cold meat
**fianza** f bail bond ; deposit
**fibra sintética** f man-made fibre
**ficha** f token ; counter *(in games)*
**fichero** m file *(computer)*
**fiebre** f fever
**fiesta** f party ; public holiday
**fila** f row ; line *(row, queue)*
**filete** m fillet ; steak
**filial** f branch
**filtro** m filter
 **filtro de aceite** oil filter
 **filtro solar** sunscreen
**fin** m end
 **fin de semana** weekend
 **fin de curso** end of school year
**finalizar** to end ; to finish
**finca** f farm ; country house
**fino** fine ; thin
**fino** m light, dry, very pale sherry
**firma** f signature
**firmar** to sign
 **firme aquí** sign here
**flojo(a)** weak *(coffee, tea)*
**flor** f flower
**florero** m vase
**floristería** f florist's shop
**foca** f seal
**foco** m spotlight ; headlamp
**folleto** m leaflet ; brochure
**fonda** f inn ; small restaurant
**fondo** m bottom *(of pool, etc)*
**fontanero** m plumber
**forfait** m lift pass *(skiing)*
**formulario** m form
**fósforo** m match
**foto** f picture ; photo
**fotocopia** f photocopy
**fotocopiar** to photocopy
**fotocopiadora** f photocopier
**fotografía** f photograph
**fotógrafo(a)** m/f photographer
**FPS (factor de protección solar)** m SPF
 (sun protection factor)
**fractura** f fracture
**frágil** fragile
**frambuesa** f raspberry
**francés(cesa)** French
**Francia** f France
**frecuente** frequent
**fregadero** m sink *(in kitchen)*
**fregona** f mop *(for floor)*
**freír** to fry

**frenar** to brake
**freno** *m* brake
**frente a** opposite
**frente** *f* forehead
**fresa** *f* strawberry
**fresco(a)** fresh ; crisp ; cool
**frigorífico** *m* fridge
**frío(a)** cold
**frito(a)** fried
**frontera** *f* border ; frontier
**frotar** to rub
**fruta** *f* fruit
  *fruta del tiempo* fruit in season
  *fruta de la pasión* passionfruit
**frutería** *f* fruit shop
**frutos secos** *mpl* nuts *(to eat)*
**fuego** *m* fire
**fuente** *f* fountain
**fuera** outdoors ; out
**fuerte** strong ; loud
**fuga** *f* leak *(of gas, liquid)*
**fumadores** *mpl* smokers
**fumar** to smoke
  *prohibido fumar* no smoking
**función** *f* show
**funcionar** to work ; to function
  *no funciona* out of order
**funcionario(a)** *m/f* civil servant
**funda** *f* case ; cover ; crown *(for tooth)* ;
  pillowcase
  *funda de gafas* glasses case
  *funda nórdica* duvet cover
**fusible** *m* fuse
**fútbol** *m* football
**futbolista** *m/f* football player

# G

**gafas** *fpl* glasses
  *gafas de sol* sunglasses
**galería** *f* gallery
  *galería de arte* art gallery
**galés(lesa)** Welsh
**Gales** *m* Wales
**gallego(a)** Galician
**galleta** *f* biscuit
**ganar** to earn ; to win *(sports, etc)*
**garaje** *m* garage
**garantía** *f* guarantee
**garganta** *f* throat
**gas** *m* gas
  *con gas* fizzy
  *gas butano* Calor gas®
  *gas ciudad* town gas
  *gas natural* natural gas
  *sin gas* non-fizzy ; still
**gasa** *f* gauze ; nappy

**gaseosa** *f* lemonade
**gasoil** *m* diesel fuel
**gasóleo** *m* diesel oil
**gasolina** *f* petrol
  *gasolina sin plomo* unleaded petrol
  *gasolina súper* 4-star petrol
**gasolinera** *f* petrol station
**gastado(a)** worn
**gastar** to spend *(money)*
**gastos** *mpl* expenses
**gastritis** *f* gastritis
**gato** *m* cat ; jack *(for car)*
**gaviota** *f* seagull
**gemelo(a)** *m/f* identical twin
  *gemelos (pl)* cufflink ; binoculars
**gendarme** *m/f* policeman/woman
  *(Lat. Am.)*
**gendarmería** *f* police *(Lat. Am.)*
**género** *m* type ; material
**generoso(a)** *m* generous
**gente** *f* people
**gerente** *m/f* manager/manageress
**ginebra** *f* gin
**ginecólogo(a)** *m/f* gynaecologist
**girar** to turn around
**globo** *m* balloon
**glorieta** *f* roundabout
**gluten** *m* gluten
**golfo de Vizcaya** *m* Bay of Biscay
**goma** *f* rubber ; eraser
**gomita** *f* rubber band
**gordo(a)** fat
**gorra** *f* cap *(hat)*
**gorro** *m* hat
**gotera** *f* leak
**gótico(a)** Gothic
**GPS (sistema global de navegación)**
  GPS (global positioning system)
**grabar en vídeo** to video *(from TV)*
**gracias** thank you
  *muchas gracias* thank you very much
**grada** *f* tier
**gramo** *m* gram(me)
**Gran Bretaña** *f* Great Britain
**grande** large ; big ; tall
**grandes almacenes** *mpl* department
  store
**granja** *f* farm
  *de granja* free-range
**granjero(a)** *m/f* farmer
**grasiento(a)** greasy
**gratinado(a)** au gratin ; grilled
**gratinar** to grill
**gratis** free *(costing nothing)*
**grave** serious *(accident, etc)*
**grifo** *m* tap
**gripe** *f* flu

**gris** grey
**gritar** to shout
**grosella negra** *f* blackcurrant
**grosella roja** *f* redcurrant
**grúa** *f* crane ; breakdown van
**grueso(a)** thick *(not thin)*
**grupo** *m* group ; band *(rock)*
  **grupo sanguíneo** blood group
**guacamole** *m* avocado dip
**guantes** *mpl* gloves
  **guantes de goma** rubber gloves
**guapo(a)** handsome ; attractive
**guardacostas** *m/f* coastguard
**guardar** to put away ; to keep
**guardarropa** *m* cloakroom
**guardería** *f* nursery
  **guardia infantil** nursery school
**guardia** *f* guard
  **de guardia** on duty
  **Guardia Civil** Civil Guard
**guarnición** *f* garnish
**guerra** *f* war
**guía** *m/f* courier ; guide
**Guía del ocio** *f* What's on
**guía (telefónica)** *f* phone directory
**guiar** to guide
**guindilla** *f* chilli pepper
**guiso** *m* stew ; casserole
**guitarra** *f* guitar
**gusano** *m* maggot ; worm
**gustar** to like ; to enjoy
**guayaba** *f* guava

# H

**haba** *f* broad bean
**habano** *m* Havana cigar
**habitación** *f* room
  **habitación doble** double room
  **habitación familiar** family room
  **habitación individual** single room
  **habitación triple** triple room
**hablar (con)** to speak/talk to
  **se habla inglés** English spoken
**hacer** to do ; to make
  **hacer autostop** to hitchhike
  **hacer cola** to queue
  **hacer daño** to hurt ; to damage
  **hacer footing** to jog
  **hacer las maletas** to pack *(case)*
  **hacer punto** to knit
  **hacer surf** to surf
  **hacer topless** to go topless
  **hacer transbordo de** to change *(bus/train)*
  **hacer transbordo en** to change at
  **hacer turismo** to sightsee

**hacia** toward(s)
  **hacia arriba** upwards, up
  **hacia abajo** downwards, down
  **hacia adelante** forwards
  **hacia atrás** backwards
**hamburguesa** *f* hamburger
**harina** *f* flour
  **harina con levadura** self-raising flour
  **harina de pescado** fish-meal
  **harina de repostería** pastry flour
  **harina de trigo** wheat flour
**hasta** until ; till
**hay** there is/there are
**hecho(a)** finished ; done
  **hecho a (la) medida** made-to-measure
  **hecho a mano** handmade
  **hecho(a) de...** made of...
**helada** *f* frost
**heladería** *f* ice-cream parlour
**helado** *m* ice cream
**helicóptero** *m* helicopter
**hemorragia** *f* haemorrhage
**hemorroides** *fpl* haemorrhoids
**hepatitis** *f* hepatitis
**herida** *f* wound ; injury
**herido(a)** injured
**herir** to hurt
**hermano(a)** *m/f* brother/sister
**hermoso(a)** beautiful
**hernia** *f* hernia
**herramienta** *f* tool
**hervido(a)** boiled
**hervidor de agua** *m* kettle
**hervir** to boil
**hidrofoil** *m* hydrofoil
**hidropedal** *m* pedal boat/pedalo
**hielo** *m* ice
  **con/sin hielo** with/without ice
**hierba** *f* grass ; herb
**hierbabuena** *f* mint
**hierro** *m* iron
  **hierro forjado** wrought iron
**hígado** *m* liver
**higo** *m* fig
  **higos chumbos** prickly pears
**hijo(a)** *m/f* son/daughter
**hilo** *m* thread ; linen
**hincha** *m/f* fan *(football, etc)*
**hinchado(a)** swollen
**hipermercado** *m* hypermarket
**hípica** *f* showjumping
**hipódromo** *m* racecourse *(horses)*
**histórico(a)** historic
**hogar** *m* home ; household
**hoja** *f* sheet ; leaf
  **hoja de registro** registration form
  **hoja de afeitar** razor blade
**hola** hello ; hi!

**hombre** *m* man
**hombro** *m* shoulder
**homeopatía** homeopathy
**homeopático(a)** homeopathic
**hora** *f* hour ; appointment
  **hora punta** rush hour
  **horas de visita** visiting hours
**horario** *m* timetable
  **horario de apertura** opening hours
  **horario de cierre** closing time
  **horario de visitas** visiting hours
**horchata de chufa** *f* refreshing tiger
  nut drink
**hormiga** *f* ant
**horno** *m* oven
  **al horno** baked ; roasted
  **(horno) microondas** microwave
**horquilla** *f* hairgrip
**hospital** *m* hospital
**hostal** *m* small hotel ; hostel
**hotel** *m* hotel
**hoy** today
**huelga** *f* strike *(of workers)*
**hueso** *m* bone
**huésped** *m/f* guest
**huevo** *m* egg
  **huevo de Pascua** Easter egg
  **huevos de corral** free-range eggs
  **huevos duros** hard-boiled eggs
  **huevos escalfados** poached eggs
  **huevos revueltos** scrambled eggs
**humo** *m* smoke

# I

**ida** *f* outward journey
  **de ida y vuelta** return *(ticket)*
**idioma** *m* language
**iglesia** *f* church
**igual** equal
**imán** *m* magnet
**impar** odd *(number)*
**imperdible** *m* safety pin
**impermeable** *m* raincoat ; waterproof
**importante** important
**importar** to matter ; to import
**importe total** *m* total *(amount)*
**imprescindible** essential
**impreso** *m* form
  **impreso de solicitud** application form
  **impresos** printed matter
**impuesto** *m* tax
**incendio** *m* fire
**incluido(a)** included
**incómodo(a)** uncomfortable
**inconsciente** unconscious
**indicaciones** *fpl* directions
**índice** *m* index

**indigestión** *f* indigestion
**individual** individual ; single
**infarto** *m* heart attack
**infección** *f* infection
**inferior** inferior ; lower
**inflamación** *f* inflammation
**información** *f* information
**informe** *m* report *(medical, police)*
**infracción** *f* offence
  **infracción de tráfico** traffic offence
**ingeniero(a)** *m/f* engineer
**Inglaterra** *f* England
**inglés(lesa)** English
**ingredientes** *mpl* ingredients
**inhalador** *m* inhaler *(for medication)*
**inmediatamente** immediately
**inmobilizador** immobilizer
**inmunización** *f* immunisation
**inquilino(a)** *m/f* tenant
**insecto** *m* insect
**insolación** *f* sunstroke
**instituto** *m* institute ; secondary school
**instrucciones** *fpl* directions ; instructions
**instructor(a)** *m/f* instructor
**instrumento** *m* tool
**insulina** *f* insulin
**interesante** interesting
**interior** inside
**intermitente** *m* indicator *(in car)*
**internacional** international
**Internet** *m or f* internet
  **Internet sin cables ; Internet WiFi**
  wireless internet
**intérprete** *m/f* interpreter
**interruptor** *m* switch
**intoxicación por alimentos** *f* food
  poisoning
**introducir** to introduce ; to insert
  **introduzca monedas** insert coins
**inundación** *f* flood
**invierno** *m* winter
**invitación** *f* invitation
**invitado(a)** *m/f* guest
**invitar** to invite
**inyección** *f* injection
**iPod®** iPod®
**ir** to go
  **ir a buscar** to fetch
  **ir de compras/tiendas** to go shopping
  **ir en bicicleta** to cycle
  **irse a casa** to go home
  **irse de** to leave *(a place)*
**Irlanda** *f* Ireland
**Irlanda del Norte** *f* Northern Ireland
**irlandés(desa)** Irish
**isla** *f* island
**Italia** *f* Italy
**italiano(a)** Italian

**itinerario** *m* route ; schedule
**ITV** *m* MOT
**IVA** *m* VAT
**izq./izqda.** *abbrev. for* **izquierda**
**izquierda** *f* left
**izquierdo(a)** left

# J

**jabón** *m* soap
**jamás** never
**jamón** *m* ham
  **jamón serrano** cured ham
  **jamón (de) York** cooked ham
**Japón** *m* .Japan
**japonés(nesa)** *m/f* Japanese
**jaqueca** *f* bad headache
**jardín** *m* garden
**jarra** *f* jug ; mug
**jefe(a)** *m/f* chief ; head ; boss
**jerez** *m* sherry
**jerga** *f* slang
**jeringuilla** *f* syringe
**joven** young
**joya** *f* jewel
  **joyas** jewellery
**joyería** *f* jeweller's
**jubilado(a)** *m/f* retired person
**jubilarse** to retire
**judías** *fpl* beans
  **judías verdes** green beans
**judío(a)** Jew
**juego** *m* game
**jueves** *m* Thursday
**juez(a)** *m/f* judge
**jugador(a)** *m/f* player
**jugar** to play ; to gamble
**julio** *m* July
**jugo** *m* juice
**juguete** *m* toy
**juguetería** *f* toy shop
**junio** *m* June
**junto(a)** together
  **junto a** next to
**juventud** *f* youth

# K

**kikos** *(snack)* salted, toasted maize,
  very popular in Spain.
**kilo** *m* kilo(gram)
**kilometraje** *m* mileage
  **kilometraje (i)limitado** (un)limited
  mileage
**kilómetro** *m* kilometre
**kiosko (de prensa)** *m* newsstand
**kiwi** *m* kiwi fruit
**kleenex**® *m* tissue

# L

**la** the ; her ; it ; you *(formal)*
**labio** *m* lip
**laborable** working *(day)*
  **laborables** weekdays
**laca** *f* hair spray
**lado** *m* side
  **al lado de** beside
**ladrar** to bark
**ladrillo** *m* brick
**ladrón(ona)** *m/f* thief
**lago** *m* lake
**lámpara** *f* lamp
**lana** *f* wool
**lancha** *f* launch
  **lancha motora** motor launch
**lápiz** *m* pencil
  **lápiz de ojos** eyeliner ; eye pencil
  **lápiz de labios** lipstick
**largo(a)** long
  **largo recorrido** long-distance *(train, etc)*
**lata** *f* can *(container)* ; tin
**latón** *m* brass
**lavable** washable
**lavabo** *m* lavatory ; washbasin
**lavado de coches** *m* car wash
**lavado(a)** washed
  **lavado en seco** dry-cleaning
  **lavado y marcado** shampoo and set
**lavadora** *f* washing machine
**lavanda** *f* lavender
**lavandería** *f* laundry ; launderette
**lavavajillas** *m* dishwasher
**lavar** to wash
  **lavarse** to wash oneself
**laxante** *m* laxative
**leche** *f* milk
  **leche desnatada** skimmed milk
  **leche de soja** soya milk
  **leche de vaca** cow's milk
  **leche entera** wholemilk
  **leche hidratante** moisturizer
  **leche semidesnatada** semi-skimmed
  milk
**lechuga** *f* lettuce
**lectura de labios** *f* lip-reading
**leer** to read
**legumbres** *fpl* pulses
**lejía** *f* bleach
**lejos** far
**lencería** *f* lingerie
**lengua** *f* language ; tongue
**lente** *f* lens
  **lentes de contacto** contact lenses
**lentejas** *fpl* lentils
**lentillas** *fpl* contact lenses
**lento(a)** slow
**león** *m* lion

**lesbiana** f lesbian
**letra** f letter (of alphabet)
**levantar** to lift
**levantarse** to get up ; to rise
**ley** f law
**libra** f pound (currency, weight)
  **libra esterlina** pound sterling
**libre** free/vacant
  **dejen el paso libre** keep clear
  **libre de impuestos** tax-free
**librería** f bookshop
**libro** m book
**licencia** f permit ; licence
**licenciarse** to graduate
**licor** m liqueur
  **licores** spirits
**lidia** f bullfight
**ligero(a)** light (not heavy)
**lima** f file (for nails) ; lime
**límite** m limit ; boundary
  **límite de velocidad** speed limit
**limón** m lemon
**limonada** f lemonade
**limonaria** f lemongrass
**limpiar** to clean
**limpieza en seco** f dry-cleaning
**limpio(a)** clean
**línea** f line
**lino** m linen
**linterna** f torch ; flashlight
**liquidación** f sales
  **liquidación por cierre** closing-down
  sale
  **liquidación de existencias** stock
  clearance
**líquido** m liquid
  **líquido de frenos** brake fluid
**liso(a)** plain ; smooth
**lista** f list
  **lista de correos** poste restante
  **lista de espera** waiting list
  **lista de precios** price list
**listo(a)** ready
  **listo(a) para comer** ready-cooked
**listado** m printout
**litera** f berth ; couchette ; sleeper
**litoral** m coast
**litro** m litre
**llaga** f ulcer (mouth)
**llamada** f call
  **llamada a cobro revertido** reverse
  charge call
**llamar** to call ; to ring ; to knock
  (on door)
**llano(a)** flat
**llanta** f tyre

**llave** f key ; tap ; spanner
  **llave de contacto** ignition key
  **llaves del coche** car keys
  **llave inglesa** spanner
  **llave tarjeta** card key
**llavero** m keyring
**Lleg.** abbrev. for **llegadas**
**llegada** f arrival
  **llegadas (Lleg.)** arrivals
**llegar** to arrive ; to come
**llenar** to fill ; to fill in
**lleno(a)** full (up)
  **lleno, por favor** fill it up, please
**llevar** to bring ; to wear ; to carry
  **para llevar** to take away
**llorar** to cry (weep)
**lluvia** f rain
**lobo** m wolf
**local** m premises ; bar
**localidad** f place
  **localidades** tickets (theatre)
**loción** f lotion
**loncha** f slice (ham, etc)
**Londres** m London
**longitud** f length
**lotería** f lottery
**luces** fpl lights
**luchar** to fight
**lugar** m place
  **lugar de expedición** issued in
  **lugar fresco/seco** cool/dry place
  **lugar de nacimiento** place of birth
**lujo** m luxury
**luna** f moon
  **luna de miel** honeymoon
**lunes** m Monday
**lupa** f magnifying glass
**luz** f light
  **luz de carretera/larga** full-beam
  headlights
  **luz corta/de cruce** dipped headlights
  **luz de freno** brake light
  **luz de posición** sidelight

## M

**macedonia** f fruit salad
**madera** f wood
**madrastra** f stepmother
**madre** f mother
**maduro(a)** ripe ; mature
**maíz** m maize ; corn
**mal/malo(a)** bad (weather, news)
**maleta** f case ; suitcase
**maletero** m boot (car)
**maletín de ordenador portátil** m
  laptop bag
**Mallorca** f Majorca

**malo(a)** bad
**mañana** tomorrow
**mañana** f morning
**mancha** f stain ; mark
**mandar** to send
 *mandar un mensaje de texto* to text
 *te mandaré un mensaje de texto*
 *I'll text you*
**mandíbula** f jaw
**mando a distancia** m remote control
**manera** f way ; manner
**manga** f sleeve
**mango** m mango
**manguera** f hosepipe
**manillar** m handlebars
**manicura** f manicure
**mano** f hand
 *de segunda mano* secondhand
**manopla** f mitten
 *manopla de horno* oven glove
**maquinilla de afeitar** shaver
**manso(a)** tame *(animal)*
**manta** f blanket
**mantel** m tablecloth
**mantener** to maintain ; to keep
**mantequería** f dairy products
 *(Lat. Am.)*
**mantequilla** f butter
 *mantequilla de cacahuete* peanut
 butter
**mantita** f picnic rug
**manzana** f apple ; block *(of houses)*
**manzanilla** f camomile tea ; dry sherry
**mapa** m map
 *mapa de carreteras* road map
**maquillaje** m make-up
**máquina** f machine
 *máquina de afeitar* razor
 *máquina de fotos* camera
**mar** m sea
**marca** f brand ; make
**marcapasos** m pacemaker
**marcar** to dial
 *marcar un gol* to score a goal
**marcha** f gear
 *marcha atrás* reverse gear
**marco** m picture frame
**marea** f tide
 *marea alta/baja* high/low tide
**mareado(a)** sick *(car, sea)* ; dizzy
**margarina** f margarine
**marido** m husband
**marioneta** f puppet
**mariposa** f butterfly
**marisco** m seafood ; shellfish
**marisquería** f seafood restaurant
**mármol** m marble
**marrón** brown

**marroquí** Moroccan
**marroquinería** f leather goods
**martes** m Tuesday
**martillo** m hammer
**marzo** m March
**más** more ; plus
 *más que* more than
 *más tarde* later
**masa** f pastry *(dough)*
**masaje** m massage
**masculino(a)** male
**matar** to kill
**matrícula** f number plate
**matrimonio** m marriage
**máximo** m maximum
**mayo** m May
**mayonesa** f mayonnaise
**mayor** bigger ; biggest
 *la mayor parte de* most of
 *mayor de edad* adult
 *mayor que* bigger than
 *mayores de 18 años* over-18s
**mayúscula** f capital letter
**mazapán** m marzipan
**mazo** m mallet
**mecánico** m mechanic
**mechero** m lighter
**medianoche** f midnight
**medias** fpl tights ; stockings
**medicina** f medicine ; drug
**médico(a)** m/f doctor
**medida** f measurement ; size
**medio** m the middle
**medio(a)** half
 *media hora* half an hour
 *media pensión* half board
 *medio hecho(a)* medium rare
**mediodía: las doce del**
 **mediodía** midday ; noon
**medir** to measure
**Mediterráneo** m Mediterranean
**medusa** f jellyfish
**megabyte** m megabyte
**mejicano(a)** m/f Mexican
**Méjico** m Mexico
**mejilla** f cheek
**mejor** best ; better
 *mejor que* better than
**mejorana** f marjoram
**melocotón** m peach
**melón** m melon
**menaje** m kitchen utensils
 *menaje de hogar* household goods
**mendigo(a)** m/f beggar
**menestra** f vegetable stew
**meningitis** f meningitis
**menor** smaller/smallest ; least
**Menorca** f Minorca

**menos** minus ; less ; except
  **menos que** less than
**mensaje** *m* message
  **mensaje de texto** text message
**mensual** monthly
**menta** *f* mint ; peppermint
**mentira** *f* lie *(untruth)*
**menú** *m* menu
  **menú del día** set menu
**mercado** *m* market
  **mercado agrícola** farmers' market
**mercadillo** flea market
**mercancías** *fpl* goods
**mercería** *f* haberdasher's
**merendero** *m* open-air snack bar ; picnic area
**merienda** *f* afternoon snack ; picnic
**mermelada** *f* jam
  **mermelada de naranja** orange marmalade
**mes** *m* month
**mesa** *f* table
**mesón** *m* traditional restaurant
**metal** *m* metal
**metro** *m* metre ; underground ; tape measure
**México** *m* Mexico
**mezclar** to mix
**mi** my
**mí** me
**micrófono** *m* microphone
**miel** *f* honey
**mientras** while
**miércoles** *m* Wednesday
**miga** *f* crumb
**migraña** *f* migraine
**mil** thousand
**mil millones** billion
**milímetro** *m* millimetre
**millón** *m* million
**minidisc** *m* minidisk
**mínimo** *m* minimum
**minusválido(a)** *m/f* disabled person
**minuto** *m* minute
**miope** short-sighted
**mirar** to look at ; to watch
**misa** *f* mass *(in church)*
**mismo(a)** same
**mitad** *f* half
**mixto(a)** mixed
**mochila** *f* backpack ; rucksack
  **mochila portabebés** baby sling
**moda** *f* fashion
**moderno(a)** modern
**modo** *m* way ; manner
  **modo de empleo** instructions for use
**mojado(a)** wet
**mole** *m* black chilli sauce

**molestar** to disturb
**molestia** *f* nuisance ; discomfort
**molido(a)** ground *(coffee beans, etc)*
**molino** *m* mill
  **molino de viento** windmill
**monasterio** *m* monastery
**moneda** *f* currency ; coin
  **introduzca monedas** insert coins
**monedero** *m* purse
**monitor(a) de esquí** *m/f* ski instructor
**montaña** *f* mountain
**montañismo** *m* mountaineering
**montar** to ride
  **montar a caballo** to horse ride
**montilla** *f* a sherry-type wine
**monumento** *m* monument
**moqueta** *f* fitted carpet
**mora** *f* mulberry ; blackberry
**morado(a)** purple
**mordedura** *f* bite
**morder** to bite
**moratón** *m* bruise
**morir** to die
**mosca** *f* fly
**mosquitera** *f* mosquito net
**mostrador** *m* counter ; desk
**mostrar** to show
**moto** *f* (motor)bike ; moped
  **moto acuática** jet ski
**motocicleta** *f* motorbike
**motor** *m* engine ; motor
**móvil** *m* mobile phone
**mozo** *m* luggage porter
**media pensión (MP)** half board
**mucho** a lot ; much
**mucho(a)** a lot (of) ; much
**muchos(as)** many
**muela** *f* tooth
**muelle** *m* quay ; pier
**muerto(a)** dead
**muestra** *f* exhibition ; sample
**mujer** *f* woman ; wife
**multa** *f* fine *(to be paid)*
**mundo** *m* world
**muñeca** *f* wrist ; doll
**muro** *m* wall
**músculo** *m* muscle
**museo** *m* museum ; art gallery
**música** *f* music
**muy** very
  **muy hecho(a)** well done *(steak)*

# N

**nacer** to be born
**nacimiento** *m* birth
**nación** *f* nation

**nacional** national ; domestic *(flight)*
**nacionalidad** f nationality
**nada** nothing
  *de nada* don't mention it
  *nada más* nothing else
**nadador(a)** m/f swimmer
**nadar** to swim
**nadie** nobody
**naipes** mpl playing cards
**naranja** f orange
**naranjada** f orangeade
**nariz** f nose
**nata** f cream
  *nata agria* soured cream
  *nata montada* whipped cream
**natación** f swimming
**natural** natural ; fresh ; plain
**naturista** m/f naturist
**navaja** f pocketknife ; penknife
**Navidad** f Christmas
**neblina** f mist
**necesario(a)** necessary
**necesidades especiales** :
  *personas con necesidades especiales*
  people with special needs
**necesitar** to need ; to require
**nectarina** f nectarine
**negarse** to refuse
**negativo** m negative *(photo)*
**negocios** mpl business
**negro(a)** black
**neumático** m tyre
  *neumáticos antideslizantes* snow
  tyres
**nevar** to snow
**nevera** f refrigerator
  *nevera portátil* cool-box
**nido** m nest
**niebla** f fog
**nieto(a)** m/f grandson/daughter
**nieve** f snow
**niña** f girl ; baby girl
**niñera** f nanny
**ningún/ninguno(a)** none
**niño** m boy ; baby ; child
  *niños* children *(infants)*
**nivel** m level ; standard
**Nº** abbrev. for **número**
**noche** f night
  *esta noche* tonight
**Nochebuena** f Christmas Eve
**Nochevieja** f New Year's Eve
**nocivo(a)** harmful
**nombre** m name
  *nombre de pila* first name
  *nombre de usuario* username
**norte** m north
**Norteamérica** f America ; USA

**norteamericano(a)** American
**nosotros(as)** we
**notaría** f solicitor's office
**notario(a)** m/f notary ; solicitor
**noticias** fpl news
**novela** f novel
**novia** f girlfriend ; fiancée ; bride
**noviembre** m November
**novio** m boyfriend ; fiancé ; bridegroom
**nube** f cloud
**nublado(a)** cloudy
**nudo** m knot
**nuestro(a)** our ; ours
**Nueva Zelanda** f New Zealand
**nuevo(a)** new
**nuez** f walnut
**número** m number ; size ; issue
  *número par/impar* even/odd *(number)*
  *número de móvil* mobile mumber
**nunca** never

## O

**o** or
  *o... o...* either... or...
**obispo** m bishop
**objetivo** m lens *(on camera)*
**objeto** m object
  *objetos de valor* valuables
**obligatorio(a)** compulsory
**obra** f work ; play *(theatre)*
  *obra maestra* masterpiece
  *obras* road works
**observar** to watch
**obstruido(a)** blocked *(pipe)*
**obtener** to get *(to obtain)*
**océano** m ocean
**ocio** m spare time
**octubre** m October
**ocupado** engaged
**oeste** m west
**oferta** f special offer
**oficina** f office
  *oficina de Correos* Post Office
**oficio** m church service ; profession
**ofrecer** to offer
**oído** m ear
**oír** to hear
**ojo** m eye
  *¡ojo!* look out!
**ola** f wave *(on sea)*
**olivo** m olive tree
**olor** m smell
**oloroso** m cream sherry
**olvidar** to forget
**onda** f wave
**ópera** f opera

**operación** *f* operation
**operador(a)** *m/f* operator
**oportunidades** *fpl* bargains
**orden** *f* command
**orden** *m* order
**ordenador** *m* computer
  *ordenador portátil* laptop
  *ordenador de bolsillo* palmtop
**oreja** *f* ear
**organizar** to arrange ; to organize
**orilla** *f* shore
**orina** *f* urine
**oro** *m* gold
**oscuro(a)** dark ; dim
**oso** *m* bear *(animal)*
**ostra** *f* oyster
**otoño** *m* autumn ; fall
**otro(a)** other ; another
  *otra vez* again
**oxígeno** *m* oxygen

## P

**paciente** *m/f* patient *(in hospital)*
**padrastro** *m* stepfather
**padre** *m* father
  *padres* parents
**paella** *f* paella *(rice dish)*
**pagado(a)** paid
**pagar** to pay for ; to pay
  *pagar al contado* to pay cash
  *pagar a plazos* to pay for something
  in instalments
  *pagar por separado* to pay separately
**pagaré** *m* IOU
**página** *f* page
  *página web* website
  *Páginas Amarillas* *fpl* Yellow Pages
**pago** *m* payment
  *pago por adelantado* payment in
  advance
  *pago al contado* cash payment
  *pague en caja* please pay at cash desk
**país** *m* country
**paisaje** *m* landscape ; countryside
**pájaro** *m* bird
**pajita** *f* straw *(for drinking)*
**palabra** *f* word
**palacio** *m* palace
**palco** *m* box *(in theatre)*
**pálido(a)** pale
**palillo** *m* toothpick
**palo** *m* stick ; mast
  *palo de golf* golf club
**paloma** *f* pigeon ; dove
**pan** *m* bread ; loaf of bread
  *pan de centeno* rye bread
  *pan de molde* sliced bread

  *pan integral* wholemeal bread
  *pan tostado* toast
**panadería** *f* bakery
**pañal** *m* nappy
**panecillo** *m* bread roll
**paño** *m* flannel ; cloth
**pantalla** *f* screen
**pantalones** *mpl* trousers
  *pantalones cortos* shorts
  *pantalones de montar* riding
  breeches
  *pantalones pirata* pirate trousers
**pantys** *mpl* tights
**pañuelo** *m* handkerchief ; scarf
  *pañuelo de papel* tissue
**papa** *m* pope
**papel** *m* paper
  *papel de cocina/absorbente* kitchen
  roll
  *papeles del coche* log book *(car)*
  *papel higiénico* toilet paper
**papelería** *f* stationer's
**paquete** *m* packet ; parcel
**par** even *(number)*
**par** *m* pair
**para** for ; towards
**parabrisas** *m* windscreen
**parachoques** *m* bumper *(car)*
**parada** *f* stop
**parado(a)** unemployed
**parador** *m* state-run hotel
**parafarmacia** shop selling
  pharmaceutical supplies, such as baby
  foods, suntan lotions, etc., but not
  prescriptions
**parafina** *f* paraffin
**paraguas** *m* umbrella
  *paraguas plegable* small foldable
  umbrella
**paramédico(a)** *f* paramedic
**parar** to stop
**parcela** *f* pitch *(for tent/caravan)*
**parecido(a)** a similar to
**pared** *f* wall *(inside)*
**pareja** *f* couple *(2 people)*
**parque** *m* park
  *parque de atracciones* funfair
  *parque nacional* national park
**parquímetro** *m* parking meter
**parrilla** *f* grill ; barbecue
  *a la parrilla* grilled
**particular** private
**partida** *f* game ; departure
  *partida de nacimiento* birth certificate
**partido** *m* match *(sport)* ; party *(political)*
**partir** to depart
**pasa** *f* raisin ; currant
**pasado(a)** stale *(bread)* ; rotten

**pasaje** *m* ticket ; fare ; alleyway
**pasajero(a)** *m/f* passenger
**pasaporte** *m* passport
**pasar** to happen
**pasatiempo** *m* hobby ; pastime
**Pascua** *f* Easter
  **¡Felices Pascuas!** Happy Easter!
**paseo** *m* walk ; avenue ; promenade
**pasillo** *m* corridor ; aisle
**paso** *m* step ; pace
  **paso a nivel** level crossing
  **paso de ganado** cattle crossing
  **paso de peatones** pedestrian crossing
  **paso inferior** subway
  **paso subterráneo** subway
**pasta** *f* pastry ; pasta
  **pasta de dientes** toothpaste
**pastel** *m* cake ; pie
  **pasteles** pastries
**pastelería** *f* cakes and pastries ;
  cake shop
**pastilla** *f* tablet ; pill
  **pastilla de jabón** bar of soap
**pastor(a)** *m/f* shepherd ; minister
**patata** *f* potato
  **patatas fritas** french fries ; crisps
**patinaje** *m* skating
**patinar** to skate ; skid
**patinazo** *m* skid
**patines** *mpl* skates
  **patines en línea** rollerblades
**pato** *m* duck
**pavo** *m* turkey
**paz** *f* peace
**PDA** PDA
**pensión completa (PC)** full board
**p. ej.** *abbrev. for* por ejemplo
**peaje** *m* toll
**peatón(ona)** *m/f* pedestrian
**peces** *mpl* fish
**pecho** *m* chest ; breast
**pechuga** *f* breast *(poultry)*
**pedir** to ask for ; to order
  **pedir prestado** to borrow
**podólogo(a) ; callista** chiropodist
**pegamento** *m* gum ; glue
**pegar** to stick (on) ; to hit
**peine** *m* comb
**pelar** to peel *(fruit)*
**película** *f* film
**peligro** *m* danger
  **peligro de incendio** fire hazard
**peligroso(a)** dangerous
**pelo** *m* hair
**pelota** *f* ball
  **pelota vasca** Basque ball game
  **pelota de golf** golf ball
  **pelota de tenis** tennis ball

**peluca** *f* wig
**peluquería** *f* hairdresser's
**pendientes** *mpl* earrings
**pene** *m* penis
**penicilina** *f* penicillin
**pensar** to think
**pensión** *f* guesthouse
  **media pensión** half board
  **pensión completa** full board
**pensionista** *m/f* senior citizen
**peor** worse ; worst
**pequeño(a)** little ; small ; tiny
**pera** *f* pear
**percha** *f* coat hanger
**perder** to lose ; to miss (train, etc)
**perdido(a)** missing *(lost)*
**perdiz** *f* partridge
**perdón** *m* pardon ; sorry
**perdonar** to forgive
**perejil** *m* parsley
**perezoso(a)** lazy
**perfecto(a)** perfect
**perforar: no perforar** do not pierce
**perfumería** *f* perfume shop
**periódico** *m* newspaper
**periodista** *m/f* journalist
**perla** *f* pearl
**permiso** *m* permission ; pass ; permit ;
  licence
  **permiso de caza** hunting permit
  **permiso de residencia** residence
  permit
  **permiso de trabajo** work permit
**permitido(a)** permitted ; allowed
**permitir** to allow ; to let
**pero** but
**perro** *m* dog
**persiana** *f* blind *(for window)*
**persona** *f* person
**personal** *m* staff
**pesado(a)** heavy ; boring
**pesar** to weigh
**pesca** *f* fishing
**pescadería** *f* fishmonger's
**pescado** *m* fish
**pescador(a)** *m/f* fisherman/woman
**pescar** to fish
**peso** *m* weight ; scales
**petirrojo** *m* robin
**pez** *m* fish
**picado(a)** chopped ; minced ; rough
  *(sea)* ; stung *(by insect)*
**picadura** *f* insect bite ; sting
**picante** peppery ; hot ; spicy
**picar** to itch ; to sting
**pie** *m* foot
**piedra** *f* stone

**piel** f fur ; skin ; leather
**pierna** f leg
**pieza** f part ; room
  *piezas del coche* car parts
**pijama** m pyjamas
**pila** f battery *(radio, etc)*
**píldora** f pill
**pileta** f sink ; *(LAm)* washbasin
**pimienta** f pepper *(spice)*
  *a la pimienta* au poivre
**pimiento** m pepper *(vegetable)*
**piña** f pineapple
**pinacoteca** f art gallery
**pinchar** to have a puncture
**pinchazo** m puncture
**pinchitos** kebabs
**pinchos** mpl savoury titbits
  *pinchos morunos* kebabs
**pintar** to paint
**pintura** f paint ; painting
**pinza** f clothes peg
  *pinzas* tweezers
**pipa** f pipe *(smoker's)*
**pipas** sunflower seeds
**pipirrana** f salad with tomato, pepper,
  onion, egg and fish
**Pirineos** mpl Pyrenees
**piruleta** f lollipop
**pisar** to step on ; to tread on
  *no pisar el césped* keep off grass
**piscina** f swimming pool
**piso** m floor ; storey ; flat
  *piso deslizante* slippery road
**pista** f track ; court
**pistacho** m pistachio
**pisto** m sautéed vegetables
**pistola** f gun
**placa** f licence plate
**plancha** f iron *(for clothes)*
  *a la plancha* grilled
**planchar** to iron
**plano** m plan ; town map
**planta** f plant ; floor ; sole *(of foot)*
  *planta baja/alta* ground/top floor
**plata** f silver ; *(LAm)* money
  *plata de ley* sterling silver
**plátano** m banana ; plane tree
**platea** f stalls *(theatre)*
**platería** f jeweller's
**platillo** m saucer
**platinos** mpl points *(in car)*
**plato** m plate ; dish *(food)* ; course
  *plato del día* dish of the day
  *plato principal* main course
**playa** f beach ; seaside
**plaza** f square *(in town)*
  *plaza de toros* bull ring
  *plazas libres* vacancies

**plazo** m period ; expiry date
**plomo** m lead *(metal)*
**pluma** f feather
**pobre** poor
**poco(a)** little
  *poco hecho(a)* rare *(steak)*
  *pocos(as)* (a) few
  *un poco de* a bit of
**poder** to be able
**podólogo(a)** m/f chiropodist
**podrido(a)** rotten *(fruit, etc)*
**policía** f police
  *Policía Municipal/Local* local police
  *Policía Nacional* national police
**policía** m/f policeman/woman
**polideportivo** m leisure centre
**póliza** f policy ; certificate
  *póliza de seguros* insurance policy
**pollería** f poultry shop
**pollo** m chicken
**polo** m ice lolly
**poltrona** f armchair
**polvo** m powder ; dust
  *polvos de talco* talcum powder
**pomada** f ointment
**pomelo** m grapefruit
**ponche** m punch
**poner** to put
  *poner en marcha* to start *(car)*
  *ponerse en contacto* to contact
**por** by ; per ; through ; about
  *por adelantado* in advance
  *por correo* by mail
  *por ejemplo* for example
  *por favor* please
**porción** f portion
**porque** because
**portaequipajes** m luggage rack
**portero** m caretaker ; doorman
**portugués/portuguesa** Portuguese
**posible** possible
**posología** f dosage
**postal** f postcard
**postigos** mpl shutters
**postre** m dessert ; pudding
**potable** drinkable
**potaje** m stew ; thick soup
**pote** m stew
**potito** m baby food
**pozo** m well *(water)*
  *pozo séptico* septic tank
**prado** m meadow
**precio** m price ; cost
**precioso(a)** lovely
**precipicio** m cliff ; precipice
**preciso(a)** precise ; necessary
**preferir** to prefer
**prefijo** m dialling code

**pregunta** *f* question
**preguntar** to ask
**premio** *m* prize
**prensa** *f* press
**preocupado(a)** worried
**preparado(a)** cooked
**preparar** to prepare ; to cook
**presa** *f* dam
**prescribir** to prescribe
**presentar** to introduce
**preservativo** *m* condom
**presión** *f* pressure
  **presión arterial** blood pressure
**prestar** to lend
**primavera** *f* spring *(season)*
**primer/o(a)** first
  **primeros auxilios** *mpl* first aid
**primo(a)** *m/f* cousin
**princesa** *f* princess
**principal** main
**príncipe** *m* prince
**principiante** *m/f* beginner
**prioridad (de paso)** *f* right of way
**prismáticos** *mpl* binoculars
**privado(a)** private
**probador** *m* changing room
**probar** to try ; to taste
**probarse** to try on *(clothes)*
**problema** *m* problem
**problemas de aprendizaje:**
  **tiene dificultades/problemas de aprendizaje** he/she has a learning disability
**procedente de…** coming from…
**productos** *mpl* produce ; products
  **productos lácteos** dairy products
**profesión** *f* profession ; job
**profesor(a)** *m/f* teacher
**profundo(a)** deep
**programa** *m* programme
  **programa de ordenador** computer program
**prohibido(a)** prohibited/no…
  **prohibido aparcar/estacionar** no parking
  **prohibido bañarse** no bathing
  **prohibido el paso** no entry
**prometer** to promise
**prometido(a)** engaged *(to be married)*
**pronóstico** *m* forecast
  **pronóstico del tiempo** weather forecast
**pronto** soon
**pronunciar** to pronounce
**propiedad** *f* property
**propietario(a)** *m/f* owner
**propina** *f* tip

**propio(a)** own
**protector solar** *m* suncream
**protegido(a)** sheltered
**provisional** temporary
**próximo(a)** next
**público** *m* audience
**público(a)** public
**puchero** *m* cooking pot ; stew
**pueblo** *m* village ; country
**puente** *m* bridge
**puerro** *m* leek
**puerta** *f* door ; gate
  **cierren la puerta** close the door
  **puerta de embarque** boarding gate
  **puerta principal** front door
**puerto** *m* port
  **puerto de montaña** moutain pass
**puerto del coche** car port
**puesta de sol** *f* sunset
**puesta en marcha** *f* starter *(of car)*
**puesto de socorro** first-aid post
**puesto que** since
**pulgar** *m* thumb
**pulgas** *fpl* fleas
**pulmón** *m* lung
**pulpo** *m* octopus
**pulsera** *f* bracelet
**punto** *m* stitch
  **punto muerto** neutral *(car)*
**puntuación** *f* score *(of match)*
**puré** *m* purée
**puro** *m* cigar
**puro(a)** pure

## Q

**que** than ; that ; which
**¿qué?** what? ; which?
  **¿qué tal?** how are you?
**quedar** to remain ; to be left
  **quedar bien** to fit *(clothes)*
**queja** *f* complaint
**quemado(a)** burnt
**quemadura** *f* burn
  **quemadura del sol/solar** sunburn
**quemar** to burn
**querer** to want ; to love
  **querer decir** to mean
**querido(a)** dear *(on letter)*
**queroseno** *m* paraffin
**queso** *m* cheese
  **queso curado** cured cheese
  **queso fresco** green cheese
**¿quién?** who?
**quincena** *f* fortnight
**quinientos(as)** five hundred
**quiosco** *m* kiosk

**quiste** *m* cyst
**quitaesmalte** *m* nail polish remover
**quitamanchas** *m* stain remover
**quitar** to remove
**quizá(s)** perhaps

# R

**rabia** *f* rabies
**ración** *f* portion
  *raciones* snacks ; tapas
**radiador** *m* radiator
**radio** *f* radio
**radio** *m* spoke *(wheel)*
**radiocasete** *m* cassette player
**radiografía** *f* X-ray
**rallador** *m* grater
**rama** *f* branch *(of tree)*
**ramo** *m* bunch *(of flowers)*
**rápido** *m* express train
**rápido(a)** quick ; fast
**raqueta** *f* racket
**rasgar** to tear ; to rip
**rastrillo** *m* rake
**rastro** *m* flea market
**rata** *f* rat
**ratero** *m* pickpocket
**rato** *m* a while
**ratón** *m* mouse
**razón** *f* reason
**real** royal
**rebajas** *fpl* sale(s)
**recalentar** to overheat ; to reheat
**recambio** *m* spare ; refill
**recargar** to recharge *(battery, etc)*
**recepción** *f* reception
**recepcionista** *m/f* receptionist
**receta** *f* prescription ; recipe
**recibir** to receive
**recibo** *m* receipt
**recientemente** recently
**reclamación** *f* claim ; complaint
**reclamar** to claim
**recoger** to collect
**recogida** *f* collection
  *recogida de billetes* ticket collection
  point *(at the airport, railway station...)*
  *recogida de equipajes* baggage
  reclaim
**recomendar** to recommend
**reconocer** to recognize
**recordar** to remember
**recorrido** *m* journey ; route
  *de largo recorrido* long-distance
**recuerdo** *m* souvenir
**recuperarse** to recover *(from illness)*

**red** *f* net
**redondo(a)** round *(shape)*
**reducción** *f* reduction
**reducir** to reduce
**reembolsar** to reimburse ; to refund
**reembolso** *m* refund
**refresco** *m* refreshment ; drink
**refugio** *m* shelter ; moutain hut
**regadera** *f* watering can
**regalo** *m* gift ; present
**régimen** *m* diet
**región** *f* district ; area ; region
**registrarse** to register *(at hotel)*
**regla** *f* period *(menstruation)* ; ruler
  *(for measuring)*
**reina** *f* queen
**Reino Unido** *m* United Kingdom
**reintegro** *m* withdrawal *(from bank
  account)*
**reírse** to laugh
**rejilla** *f* rack *(luggage)*
**relámpago** *m* lightning
**rellenar** to fill in
**reloj** *m* clock ; watch
**remar** to row *(boat)*
**remitente** *m/f* sender
**remolcar** to tow
**remolque** *m* tow rope ; trailer
**RENFE** *f* Spanish National Railways
**reparación** *f* repair
**reparar** to repair
**repetir** to repeat
**repollo** *m* cabbage
**representante** *m/f* sales rep
**reproductor de CD** *m* CD player
**reproductor de DVD** *m* DVD player
**reproductor MP3** *m* MP3 player
**repuestos** *mpl* spare parts
**resaca** *f* hangover
**resbaladizo(a)** slippery
**resbalarse** to slip
**rescatar** to rescue
**reserva** *f* booking(s) ; reservation
**reservado(a)** reserved
**reservar** to reserve ; to book
**resfriado** *m* cold *(illness)*
**residente** *m/f* resident
**resistente a** resistant to
  *resistente al agua* waterproof
  *resistente al calor* resistant to heat
**respirar** to breathe
**responder** to answer ; to reply
**responsabilidad** *f* responsibility
**respuesta** *f* answer
**restaurante** *m* restaurant
**resto** *m* the rest

retrasado(a) delayed
retraso m delay
  sin retraso on schedule
retrato m portrait
retrovisor exterior m wing mirror
reumatismo m rheumatism
reunión f meeting
revelar to develop (photos)
reventón m blowout (of tyre)
revisar to check
revisión f car service ; inspection
revisor(a) m/f ticket collector
revista f magazine
rey m king
rezar to pray
riada f flash flood
rico(a) rich (person)
rincón m corner
riñón m kidney
riñonera f bumbag
río m river
robar to steal
robo m robbery ; theft
robot (de concina) m food processor
rodaballo m turbot
rodeado(a) de surrounded by
rodilla f knee
rodillo m rolling pin
rojo(a) red
románico(a) Romanesque
romántico(a) romantic
romería f procession
romper to break ; to tear
ron m rum
roncar to snore
ropa f clothes
  ropa de cama bedclothes
  ropa interior underwear
ropero m wardrobe
rosa f rose
rosa pink
rosado m rosé
roto(a) broken
rotonda f roundabout (traffic)
rotulador m felt-tip pen
rubeola f rubella ; German measles
rubio(a) blond ; fair haired
rueda f wheel
  rueda de repuesto spare tyre
  rueda pinchada flat tyre
ruido m noise
ruinas fpl ruins
ruta f route
  ruta turística tourist route

# S

S.A. abbrev. for Sociedad Anónima
sábado m Saturday
sábana f sheet (bed)
saber to know (facts) ; to know how
sabor m taste ; flavour
sacacorchos m corkscrew
sacar to take out (of bag, etc)
sacarina f saccharin
saco m sack
  saco de dormir sleeping bag
sagrado(a) holy
sal f salt
  sin sal unsalted
sala f hall ; hospital ward
  sala de chat chatroom
  sala de conciertos concert hall
  sala de embarque departure lounge
  sala de espera waiting room
salado(a) savoury ; salty
salario m wage
salchicha f sausage
saldo m balance (of account) ; credit
  (on mobile phone)
saldos mpl sales
salida f exit/departure
  salida de incendios fire exit
  salida del sol sunrise
salir to go out ; to come out
salmón m salmon
  salmón ahumado smoked salmon
salsa f gravy ; sauce ; dressing
saltar to jump
salteado(a) sauté ; sautéed
salud f health
  ¡salud! cheers!
salvar to save (life)
salvaslip m panty liner
salvavidas m lifebelt
salvia f sage (herb)
sandalias fpl sandals
sandía f watermelon
sangrar to bleed
sangría f sangria (red wine and fruit
  punch)
santo(a) saint ; holy ; saint's day
sarampión m measles
sarpullido m skin rash
sartén f frying pan
sastrería f tailor's
secado a mano m blow-dry
secador (de pelo) m hairdryer
secadora f dryer (spin, tumble)
secar to dry
seco(a) dry ; dried (fruit, beans)
secretario(a) m/f secretary
seda f silk
  seda dental dental floss

**seguida:** *en seguida* straight away
**seguido(a)** continuous
  *todo seguido* straight on
**seguir** to continue ; to follow
**según** according to
**segundo** m second *(time)*
**segundo(a)** second
  *de segunda mano* secondhand
**seguramente** probably
**seguridad** f reliability ; safety ; security
**seguro** m insurance
  *seguro del coche* car insurance
  *seguro de vida* life insurance
  *seguro médico* medical insurance
**seguro(a)** safe ; certain
**sello** m stamp *(postage)*
**semáforo** m traffic lights
**semana** f week
  *Semana Santa* Holy Week ; Easter
**semanal** weekly
**semilla** f seed ; pip
**señal** f sign ; signal ; road sign
**sencillo(a)** simple ; single *(ticket)*
**señor** m gentleman
  *Señor (Sr.)* Mr ; Sir
**señora** f lady
  *Señora (Sra.)* Mrs ; Ms ; Madam
**señoras** ladies
**señorita** f Miss
  *Señorita (Srta.)...* Miss...
**sentarse** to sit
**sentir** to feel
**separado(a)** separated
**septentrional** northern
**septiembre** m September
**sequía** f drought
**ser** to be
**seropositivo(a)** HIV positive
**serpiente** f snake
**servicio** m service ; service charge
  *área de servicios* service area
  *servicio incluido* service included
  *servicios* toilets
  *servicios de urgencia* emergency
  services
**servilleta** f serviette ; napkin
**servir** to serve
**sesión** f performance ; screening
  *sesión de noche* late night
  performance
  *sesión de tarde* eve performance
  *sesión numerada* seats bookable in
  advance
**sesos** mpl brains
**seta** f mushroom
**sexo** m sex ; gender
**si** if
**sí** yes

**sida** m AIDS
**sidra** f cider
**siempre** always
**siento:** *lo siento* I'm sorry
**sierra** f mountain range ; saw
**siga** follow
  *siga adelante* carry on
  *siga recto* keep straight on
**siglo** m century
**siguiente** following ; next
**silencio** m silence
**silla** f chair ; seat
  *silla de paseo* pushchair
  *silla de ruedas* wheelchair
**sillón** m armchair
**simpático(a)** nice ; kind
**sin** without
  *sin plomo* unleaded
**síndrome (de) Down** m Down's
  syndrome
**síntoma** m symptom
**sírvase vd./ud. mismo** serve/help
  yourself
**sistema** m system
  *sistema de navegación por satélite*
  satellite navigation system
**sitio** m place ; space ; position ; site
**slip** m pants ; briefs
**SMS** m SMS message
**sobre** on ; upon ; about ; on top of
**sobre** m envelope
  *sobre acolchado* padded envelope
**sobrecarga** f surcharge
**sobrecargar** to overload
**sobredosis** f overdose
**sobrino(a)** m/f nephew/niece
**sobrio(a)** sober
**sociedad** f society
  *Sociedad Anónima* Ltd ; plc
**socio(a)** m/f member ; partner
**socorrista** m/f lifeguard
**¡socorro!** help!
**soja** f soya
**sol** m sun ; sunshine
**solamente** only
**soldado** m/f soldier
**solicitar** to request
**solitario** m patience *(cardgame)*
**solo(a)** alone ; lonely
**sólo** only
**solomillo** m sirloin
**soltero(a)** m/f bachelor/spinster
**soltero(a)** single *(unmarried)*
**sombra** f shade ; shadow
  *sombra de ojos* eye shadow
**sombrero** m hat
**sombrilla** f sunshade ; parasol
**somnífero** m sleeping pill

**sonido** m sound
**sonreír** to smile
**sonrisa** f smile
**sopa** f soup
**sordo(a)** deaf
**sorpresa** f surprise
**sótano** m basement
**soya** f soya
**spam** m spam (email)
**Sr.** abbrev. for **señor**
**Sra.** abbrev. for **señora**
**Srta.** abbrev. for **señorita**
**stop** m stop (sign)
**su** his/her/its/their/your
**suavizante** m hair conditioner ; fabric softener
**submarinismo** m scuba diving
**subterráneo(a)** underground
**subtítulo** m subtitle
**sucio(a)** dirty
**sucursal** f branch (of bank, etc)
**sudadera** f sweatshirt
**sudar** to sweat
**suegro(a)** m/f father/mother-in-law
**suela** f sole (of foot, shoe)
**sueldo** m wage
**suelo** m soil ; ground ; floor
**suelto** m loose change (money)
**sueño** m dream
**suerte** f luck
  **¡(buena) suerte!** good luck!
**Suiza** f Switzerland
**suizo(a)** Swiss
**sujetador** m bra
**superior** higher
**supermercado** m supermarket
**supositorio** m suppository
**sur** m south
**surfing** m surfing
**surtidor** m petrol pump
**sus** his/her/their/your

# T

**tabaco** m tobacco ; cigarettes
**tabla** f board
  **tabla de cortar** chopping board
  **tabla de planchar** ironing board
  **tabla de surf** surf board
**tablao (flamenco)** m Flamenco show
**tableta** f tablet ; bar (chocolate)
**taco** m stuffed tortilla
**tacón** m heel (shoe)
**taladradora** f drill (tool)
**talco** m talc
**TALGO** m Intercity express train
**talla** f size

**tallarines** mpl noodles ; tagliatelle
**taller** m garage (for repairs)
**talón** m heel ; counterfoil ; stub
  **talón bancario** cheque
**talonario** m cheque book
**también** as well ; also ; too
**tampoco** neither
**tampones** mpl tampons
**tapa** f lid
**tapas** fpl appetizers ; snacks
**tapón** m cap (of bottle etc)
**taquilla** f ticket office
**tarde** f evening ; afternoon
  **de la tarde** pm
**tarde** late
**tarifa** f price ; rate
  **tarifa baja** cheap rate
  **tarifa máxima** peak rate
**tarjeta** f card
  **tarjeta de crédito** credit card
  **tarjeta de embarque** boarding pass
  **tarjeta de visita** business card
  **tarjeta telefónica** phonecard
**tarjeta llave** keycard
  **tarjéta de débito** debit card
  **tarjeta magnética** swipecard
  **tarjeta de memoria** memory stick
  **tarjeta SIM** SIM card
**tarro** m jar ; pot
**tarta** f cake ; tart
**tasca** f bar ; cheap restaurant
**taxista** m/f taxi driver
**taza** f cup
**tazón** m bowl (for soup, etc)
**té** m tea
**teatro** m theatre
**techo** m ceiling
  **techo solar** sunroof
**tejado** m roof
**tela** f material ; fabric
  **tela impermeable** groundsheet
**telaraña** f web (spider)
**teleférico** m cablecar
**telefonear** to phone
**telefonista** m/f telephonist
**teléfono** m phone
  **teléfono 'manos libres'** hands free phone
  **teléfono móvil** mobile phone
  **teléfono público** payphone
**teléfono inalámbrico** cordless phone
**telegrama** m telegram
**telesilla** m ski lift ; chairlift
**telesquí** m ski lift
**televisión** f television
**televisor** m television set
**télex** m telex

**temperatura** f temperature
**templo** m temple
**temporada** f season
  **temporada alta/baja** high/low season
**temporal** m storm
**temporizador** m timer (on cooker)
**temprano(a)** early
**tendedero** m clothes line
**tenedor** m fork (for eating)
**tener** to have
  **tener fiebre** to have a temperature
  **tener miedo de** to be afraid of
  **tener morriña** to be homesick
  **tener 'overbooking'** to be
  overbooked
  **tener que** to have to
  **tener razón** to be right
  **tener suerte** to be lucky
**tentempié** m snack
**tequila** m tequila
**tercero(a)** third
**terciopelo** m velvet
**termo** m flask (thermos)
**termómetro** m thermometer
**ternera** f veal
**terraza** f terrace ; balcony
**terremoto** m earthquake
**terreno** m land
**terrorista** m/f terrorist
**testículos** mpl testicles
**tetera** f teapot
**tetina** f teat (on baby's bottle)
**ti** you (sing. with friends)
**tía** f aunt
**tiempo** m time ; weather
**tienda** f store ; shop ; tent
  **tienda de ropa** clothes shop
**tierra** f earth
**tijeras** fpl scissors
**timbre** m doorbell ; official stamp
**tímido(a)** shy
**timón** m rudder
**tinta** f ink
**tinte** m dye
  **tinte de pelo** hair dye
**tinto** m red wine
**tintorería** f dry-cleaner's
**tío** m uncle
**típico(a)** typical
**tipo** m sort
  **tipo de cambio** exchange rate
**tique** m ticket
**tirador** m handle
**tirar** to throw (away) ; to pull
  **para tirar** disposable
**tire** pull
**tirita** f (sticking) plaster

**toalla** f towel
**tobillo** m ankle
**tocar** to touch ; to play (instrument)
  **no tocar** do not touch
**tocino** m bacon ; fat
**todo(a)** all
  **todo** everything
  **todo el mundo** everyone
  **todo incluido (TI)** all inclusive
**toldo** awning
**tomar** to take ; to have (food/drink)
  **tomar el aire/fresco** to get some
  fresh air
  **tomar el sol** to sunbathe
**tomate** m tomato
**tomillo** m thyme
**tónica** f tonic water
**tono** m tone
  **tono de llamada** ringing tone
  **tono de marcado/marcar** dialling
  tone
**tonto(a)** stupid
**toquen: no toquen/tocar** do not touch
**torcedura** f sprain
**torero** m bullfighter
**tormenta** f thunderstorm
**tornillo** m screw
**toro** m bull
**torre** f tower
**torta** f cake
**tortilla** f omelette
**tos** f cough
**toser** to cough
**tostada** f toast
**trabajar** to work (person)
**trabajo** m work
**tradicional** traditional
**traducción** f translation
**traducir** to translate
**traer** to fetch ; to bring
**tráfico** m traffic
**tragar** to swallow
**traje** m suit ; outfit
  **traje de baño** swimsuit
  **traje de bucear** wetsuit
  **traje de etiqueta** evening dress (man's)
  **traje de noche** evening dress (woman's)
**trampolín** m diving board
**tranquilo(a)** calm ; quiet
**tranquilizante** m tranquilliser
**transbordador** m car ferry
**transbordo** m transfer
**transgénico(a)** genetically modified
**tranvía** m tram ; short-distance train
**trapo** m cloth (for cleaning, etc)
**tras** after ; behind
**trastorno estomacal** m stomach upset
**tratar con cuidado** handle with care

travesía f crossing
tren m train
triángulo señalizador m warning triangle
triste sad
trozo m piece
trucha f trout
trueno m thunder
trufa f truffle
tú you (singular with friends)
tu your (singular with friends)
tubería f pipe (drain, etc)
tubo de escape m exhaust pipe
tumbarse to lie down
tumbona f deckchair
túnel m tunnel
turista m/f tourist
turístico(a) tourist
turno m turn
  espere su turno wait your turn
turrón m nougat
TVE abbrev. for Televisión Española

# U

Ud(s). abbrev. for usted(es)
úlcera f ulcer (stomach)
últimamente lately
último(a) last
ultracongelador m deep freeze
  ultracongelado deep-frozen
ultramarinos m grocery shop
un(a) a/an
uña f nail (finger, toe)
ungüento m ointment
únicamente only
unidad f unit
Unión Europea f European Union
universidad f university
unos(as) some
urgencias fpl casualty department
urgente urgent ; express
usar to use
uso m use ; custom
  uso externo/tópico for external use only
usted you (polite singular)
ustedes you (polite plural)
usuario (nombre de) username
útil useful
utilizar to use
uva f grape
  uvas verdes/negras green/black grapes
UVI/UCI f intensive care unit

# V

vaca f cow
vacaciones fpl holiday
  vacaciones de verano summer holidays
vacío(a) empty
vacuna f vaccination
vagina f vagina
vagón m railway carriage
vale OK
vale... it's worth...
vale m token ; voucher
válido(a) valid (ticket, licence, etc)
valle m valley
valor m value
válvula f valve
vapor m steam
  al vapor steamed
vaqueros mpl jeans
variado(a) assorted ; mixed
varios(as) several
vasco(a) Basque
vaso m glass (for drinking)
Vd(s). abbrev. for usted(es) (less common)
veces fpl times
vecino(a) m/f neighbour
vegetariano(a) m/f vegetarian
vehículo m vehicle
vela f candle ; sail ; sailing
velocidad f speed
  límite de velocidad speed limit
  velocidad máxima speed limit
velocímetro m speedometer
vena f vein
venda f bandage
vendedor(a) m/f salesman/woman
vender to sell
  se vende for sale
veneno m poison
venenoso(a) poisonous
venir to come
venta f sale ; country inn
ventana f window
ventanilla f window (in car, train)
ventilador m fan (electric)
ver to see ; to watch
verano m summer
verdad f truth
  ¿de verdad? really?
verdadero(a) true ; genuine
verde green
verdulería f greengrocer's
verduras fpl vegetables
vereda f footpath (in the country)
verificar to check
versión f version
  versión original original version

**vespa**® f motor scooter
**vestido** m dress
**vestir de etiqueta** formal dress
**vestirse** to get dressed
**veterinario(a)** m/f vet
**vez** f time
**VI derrape ; patinazo ; derrapar ; patinar** n skid
**vía** f track ; rails ; platform
  *por vía oral/bucal* orally
**viajar** to travel
**viaje** m journey ; trip
  *viaje de negocios* business trip
  *viaje organizado* package tour
**viajero** m traveller
**víbora** f adder ; viper
**vida** f life
**vídeo** m video ; video recorder
**videocámara** f camcorder
**videojuego** m video game
**vidriera** f stained-glass window
**vidrio** m glass (substance)
**vieira** f scallop
**viejo(a)** old
**viento** m wind
**viernes** m Friday
  *Viernes Santo* Good Friday
**viña** f vineyard
**vinagre** m vinegar
**vinagreta** f vinaigrette (dressing)
**vino** m wine
  *vino blanco* white wine
  *vino rosado* rosé wine
  *vino seco* dry wine
  *vino tinto* red wine
**violación** f rape
**violar** to rape
**violeta** f violet (flower)
**virgen** blank
**virus** m virus
  *virus del sida, VIH* HIV
**visa** f visa
**visita** f visit
**visitar** to visit
**víspera** f eve
**vista** f view
**viudo(a)** m/f widow/widower
**vivir** to live
**V.O. (versión original)** undubbed version (of film)

**volante** m steering wheel
**volar** to fly
**volcán** m volcano
**voleibol** m volleyball
**voltaje** m voltage
**volumen** m volume
**volver** to come/go back ; to return
**vomitar** to vomit
**vosotros** you (plural with friends)
**voz** f voice
**vuelo** m flight
**vuelta** f turn ; return ; change (money)
**vuestro(a)** your (plural with friends)

# W

**Walkman**® m Walkman®
**wáter** m lavatory ; toilet
**whisky** m whisky
**windsurf** m windsurfing

# Y

**y** and
**yate** m yacht
**yerno** m son-in-law
**yo** I ; me
**yogur** m yoghurt
  *yogur azucarado* sweet yogurt
  *yogur desnatado* low-fat yogurt
  *yogur natural* plain yoghurt

# Z

**zanahoria** f carrot
**zapatería** f shoe shop
**zapatillas** fpl slippers
  *zapatillas de deporte* trainers
**zapato** m shoe
**zarzuela** f Spanish light opera ; casserole
**zona** f zone
  *zona azul* controlled parking area
  *zona de descanso* layby
  *zona restringida* restricted area
**zorro** m fox
**zumo** m juice
  *zumo de arándanos* cranberry juice

# How Spanish Works

## Nouns

> A **noun** is a word such as **car**, **horse** or **Mary** which is used to refer to a person or thing.

Unlike English, Spanish nouns have a gender: they are either *masculine* (**el**) or *feminine* (**la**). Therefore words for *the* and *a(n)* must agree with the noun they accompany – whether *masculine*, *feminine* or *plural*:

|        | *masc.*     | *fem.*       | *plural*                  |
|--------|-------------|--------------|---------------------------|
| the    | **el gato** | **la plaza** | **los gatos, las plazas** |
| a, an  | **un gato** | **una plaza**| **unos gatos, unas plazas** |

The ending of the noun will usually indicate whether it is *masculine* or *feminine*:

-**o** or -**or** are generally *masculine*
-**a**, -**dad**, -**ión**, -**tud**, -**umbre** are generally *feminine*

NOTE: *Feminine* nouns beginning with a stressed **a**- or **ha**- take the *masculine* article **el**, though the noun is still *feminine*.

## Formation of Plurals
The articles **el** and **la** become **los** and **las** in the plural. Nouns ending with a vowel become plural by adding -**s**:

> el gato > los gatos
> la plaza > las plazas
> la calle > las calles

Where the noun ends in a consonant, -**es** is added:

> el color > los colores
> la ciudad > las ciudades

Nouns ending in -**z** change their ending to -**ces** in the plural:

> el lápiz > los lápices
> la voz > las voces

### Adjectives

> An **adjective** is a word such as **small**, **pretty** or **practical** that describes a person or thing, or gives extra information about them.

Adjectives normally follow the nouns they describe in Spanish, e.g. **la manzana roja** (the red apple). Some exceptions which go before the noun are:

| | |
|---|---|
| **buen** good | **gran** great |
| **ningún** no, not any | **mucho** much, many |
| **poco** little, few | **primer/primero** first |
| **tanto** so much, so many | **último** last |
| e.g. **el último tren** (the last train) | |

Spanish adjectives also reflect the gender of the noun they describe. To make an adjective *feminine*, the *masculine* **-o** ending is changed to **-a** ; and the endings **-án**, **-ón**, **-or**, **-és** change to **-ana**, **-ona**, **-ora**, **-esa**:

| | |
|---|---|
| *masc.* **el libro rojo** | *fem.* **la manzana roja** |
| (the red book) | (the red apple) |
| *masc.* **el hombre hablador** | *fem.* **la mujer habladora** |
| (the talkative man) | (the talkative woman) |

To make an adjective plural an **-s** is added to the singular form if it ends in a vowel. If the adjective ends in a consonant, **-es** is added:

| | |
|---|---|
| *masc.* **los libros rojos** | *fem.* **las manzanas rojas** |
| (the red books) | (the red apples) |
| *masc.* **los hombres habladores** | *fem.* **las mujeres habladoras** |
| (the talkative men) | (the talkative women) |

### My, your, his, her...

These words also depend on the gender and number of the noun they accompany and not on the sex of the 'owner'.

| | with masc. sing. noun | with fem. sing. noun | with plural nouns |
|---|---|---|---|
| **my** | mi | mi | mis |
| **your** (familiar sing.) | tu | tu | tus |
| **your** (polite sing.) | su | su | sus |
| **his/her/its** | su | su | sus |
| **our** | nuestro | nuestra | nuestros/nuestras |
| **your** (familiar pl.) | vuestro | vuestra | vuestros/vuestras |
| **their** | su | su | sus |
| **your** (polite pl.) | su | su | sus |

There is no distinction between **his** and **her** in Spanish: **su billete** can mean either **his** or **her** ticket.

### Pronouns

> A **pronoun** is a word that you use to refer to someone or something when you do not need to use a noun, often because the person or thing has been mentioned earlier. Examples are *it*, *she*, ***something*** and ***myself***.

| subject | | object | |
|---|---|---|---|
| I | **yo** | me | **me** |
| you *(familiar sing.)* | **tú** | you | **te** |
| you *(polite sing.)* | **usted (Ud.)** | you | **le** |
| he/it | **él** | him/it | **le, lo** |
| she/it | **ella** | her/it | **le, la** |
| we | **nosotros** | us | **nos** |
| you *(familiar pl.)* | **vosotros** | you | **os** |
| you *(polite pl.)* | **ustedes (Uds.)** | you | **les** |
| they *(masc.)* | **ellos** | them | **les, los** |
| they *(fem.)* | **ellas** | them | **les, las** |

Subject pronouns (**I**, **you**, **he**, etc.) are generally omitted in Spanish, since the verb ending distinguishes the subject:

>**habl<u>o</u>**      <u>I</u> speak
>**habl<u>amos</u>**      <u>we</u> speak

However, they are used for emphasis or to avoid confusion:

>**<u>yo</u> voy a Mallorca y <u>él</u> va a Alicante**
><u>I</u> am going to Mallorca and <u>he</u> is going to Alicante

Object pronouns are placed before the verb in Spanish:

>**<u>la</u> veo**      I see <u>her</u>
>**<u>los</u> conocemos**      we know <u>them</u>

However, in commands or requests they follow the verb:

>**¡ayúda<u>me</u>!**      help <u>me</u>!
>**¡escúcha<u>le</u>!**      listen to <u>him</u>

Except when they are expressed in the negative:

>**¡no <u>me</u> ayudes!**      don't help <u>me</u>
>**¡no <u>le</u> escuches!**      don't listen to <u>him</u>

The object pronouns shown above can be used to mean *to me*, *to us*, etc., but *to him/to her* is **le** and *to them* is **les**. If **le** and **les** occur in combinations with **lo/la/las/los** then **le/les** change to **se**, e.g. **se lo doy** (I give it to him).

## Verbs

> A **verb** is a word such as **sing**, **walk** or **cry** which is used with a subject to say what someone or something does or what happens to them. **Regular verbs** follow the same pattern of endings. **Irregular verbs** do not follow a regular pattern so you need to learn the different endings.

There are three main patterns of endings for Spanish verbs – those ending -**ar**, -**er** and -**ir** in the dictionary.

|            | CANT**AR**    | TO SING               |
|------------|---------------|-----------------------|
|            | **canto**     | I sing                |
|            | **cantas**    | you sing              |
| (usted)    | **canta**     | (s)he sings/you sing  |
|            | **cantamos**  | we sing               |
|            | **cantáis**   | you sing              |
| (ustedes)  | **cantan**    | they sing/you sing    |

|            | VIV**IR**     | TO LIVE               |
|------------|---------------|-----------------------|
|            | **vivo**      | I live                |
|            | **vives**     | you live              |
| (usted)    | **vive**      | (s)he lives/you live  |
|            | **vivimos**   | we live               |
|            | **vivís**     | you live              |
| (ustedes)  | **viven**     | they live/you live    |

|            | COM**ER**     | TO EAT                |
|------------|---------------|-----------------------|
|            | **como**      | I eat                 |
|            | **comes**     | you eat               |
| (usted)    | **come**      | (s)he eats/you eat    |
|            | **comemos**   | we eat                |
|            | **coméis**    | you eat               |
| (ustedes)  | **comen**     | they eat/you eat      |

Like French, in Spanish there are two ways of addressing people: the polite form (for people you don't know well or who are older) and the familiar form (for friends, family and children). The polite you is **usted** in the singular, and **ustedes** in the plural. You can see from above that **usted** uses the same verb ending as for he and she; **ustedes** the same ending as for they. Often the words **usted** and **ustedes** are omitted, but the verb ending itself indicates that you are using the polite form. The informal words for you are **tú** (singular) and **vosotros** (plural).

### The Verb 'to be'

There are two different Spanish verbs for **to be** – **ser** and **estar**.
**Ser** is used to describe a permanent state:

|                   |                 |
|-------------------|-----------------|
| **soy inglés**    | I am English    |
| **es una playa**  | it is a beach   |

**Estar** is used to describe a temporary state or where something is located:

| | |
|---|---|
| **¿cómo está?** | how are you? |
| **¿dónde está la playa?** | where is the beach? |

| | SER | TO BE |
|---|---|---|
| | **soy** | I am |
| | **eres** | you are |
| (usted) | **es** | (s)he is/you are |
| | **somos** | we are |
| | **sois** | you are |
| (ustedes) | **son** | they are/you are |

| | ESTAR | TO BE |
|---|---|---|
| | **estoy** | I am |
| | **estás** | you are |
| (usted) | **está** | (s)he is/you are |
| | **estamos** | we are |
| | **estáis** | you are |
| (ustedes) | **están** | they are/you are |

Other common irregular verbs include:

| | TENER | TO HAVE |
|---|---|---|
| | **tengo** | I have |
| | **tienes** | you have |
| (usted) | **tiene** | (s)he has/you have |
| | **tenemos** | we have |
| | **tenéis** | you have |
| (ustedes) | **tienen** | they have/you have |

| | IR | TO GO |
|---|---|---|
| | **voy** | I go |
| | **vas** | you go |
| (usted) | **va** | (s)he goes/you go |
| | **vamos** | we go |
| | **vais** | you go |
| (ustedes) | **van** | they go/you go |

| | PODER | TO BE ABLE |
|---|---|---|
| | **puedo** | I can |
| | **puedes** | you can |
| (usted) | **puede** | (s)he can/you can |
| | **podemos** | we can |
| | **podéis** | you can |
| (ustedes) | **pueden** | they can/you can |

| | QUERER | TO WANT |
|---|---|---|
| | **quiero** | I want |
| | **quieres** | you want |
| (usted) | **quiere** | (s)he wants/you want |

| | queremos | we want |
|---|---|---|
| | queréis | you want |
| (ustedes) | quieren | they want/you want |

| | HACER | TO DO |
|---|---|---|
| | hago | I do |
| | haces | you do |
| (usted) | hace | (s)he does/you do |
| | hacemos | we do |
| | hacéis | you do |
| (ustedes) | hacen | they do/you do |

| | VENIR | TO COME |
|---|---|---|
| | vengo | I come |
| | vienes | you come |
| (usted) | viene | (s)he comes/you come |
| | venimos | we come |
| | venís | you come |
| (ustedes) | vienen | they come/you come |

## Past Tense

To form the past tense, for example: I gave/I have given, I finished/I have finished, combine the present tense of the verb **haber** – to have with the past participle of the verb (**cantado, comido, vivido**):

| | HABER | TO HAVE |
|---|---|---|
| | he | I have |
| | has | you have |
| (usted) | ha | (s)he has/you have |
| | hemos | we have |
| | habéis | you have |
| (ustedes) | han | they have/you have |
| e.g. | he cantado | I sang/I have sung |
| | ha comido | he ate/he has eaten |
| | hemos vivido | we lived/we have lived |

To form a negative **no** is placed before all of the verb:

| e.g. | no he cantado | I haven't sung |
|---|---|---|
| | no ha comido | he hasn't eaten |
| | no hemos vivido | we haven't lived |